THE GIFT OF SAINT JOHN PAUL II

A CELEBRATION OF HIS
ENDURING LEGACY

THE GIFT OF SAINT JOHN PAUL II

A CELEBRATION OF HIS ENDURING LEGACY

Cardinal Donald Wuerl
Archbishop of Washington

Published by The Word Among Us Press
7115 Guilford Drive
Frederick, MD 21704

17 16 15 14 13   1 2 3 4 5

ISBN: 978-1-59325-249-6
eISBN: 978-1-59325-462-9

Cover design by David Crosson
Front Cover Photo Credit: Pope John Paul II, during his visit to Nigeria, February 1982,
© Vittoriano Rastelli/CORBIS

Made and printed in the United States of America

Library of Congress Control Number: 2013948979

Contents

PREFACE

The Petrine ministry of Pope John Paul II was expressed in so many ways during his nearly twenty-seven-year pontificate. His pastoral visits took him around the world to more than one hundred nations, where he was embraced with both reverence and affection. He used his Wednesday audiences at the Vatican and his numerous talks, discourses, and addresses to proclaim the gospel message. In hundreds of parish visits in Rome, he demonstrated the spiritual care of a pastor of souls. Everywhere he exercised his ministry to teach, to lead, to sanctify on a global and local scale.

One vivid expression of the teaching ministry of Pope John Paul II is found in his many encyclical letters and post-synodal apostolic exhortations. Here we find a profoundly spiritual, deeply theological, and engagingly pastoral presentation of the faith of the Church, the gospel imperative, and its implications and application to the circumstances of our day.

Cardinal Donald Wuerl of Washington has, over a number of years, written reflections on each of the Holy Father's encyclicals and those apostolic exhortations that followed one of the Ordinary Assemblies of the Synod of Bishops presided over by Pope John Paul II. It is my pleasure, as one who served our Holy Father as his personal secretary throughout his pontificate, to express appreciation for these reflections on his writings, presented in a volume fittingly entitled *The Gift of Saint John Paul II*.

May the canonization of Pope John Paul II, which this volume celebrates, be a time for all of us to renew our appreciation for him as we thank God for the gift that this extraordinary priest, bishop, and pope has been and continues to be for the Church.

Stanislaus Cardinal Dziwisz
Archbishop of Krakow, Poland
Personal Secretary to Pope John Paul II

Pope John Paul II ordained Cardinal Donald Wuerl a bishop on Epiphany, January 6, 1986, in St. Peter's Basilica, Rome.

THE GIFT OF SAINT JOHN PAUL II

A MINISTRY OF GRACE AND WISDOM

The world watched on Sunday, October 22, 1978, as Pope John Paul II, the 264th bishop of Rome and vicar of Christ, stepped out of St. Peter's Basilica to celebrate the Eucharistic liturgy before tens of thousands of people filling St. Peter's Square.

The first ever Polish pope and first non-Italian elected by the College of Cardinals since the sixteenth century had caught the imagination and hearts of people from the moment he appeared at the basilica's balcony on the evening of his election six days earlier. What John Paul was to say during his homily would mark the solemn beginning of his ministry as universal pastor of the Church and set the focus of his entire pontificate.

It was an exciting day—one that I will always remember—as I sat there with so many others awaiting what the new pope would have to say in his first *Urbi et Orbi* (his homily to the city of Rome and to the world).

"Open wide the doors for Christ," he announced. The image was a dramatic one—the doors being broken off their hinges to make way for Christ into our hearts and into our world.

I would return to Rome and to that same *sagrato*, the platform in front of St. Peter's Basilica, as Pope John Paul II celebrated the twenty-fifth anniversary of his pontificate on October 16, 2003. His health was already failing, and I went precisely because I felt in my heart that this might be the last time I would ever have an opportunity to concelebrate Mass with this holy man whom so much of the world had come to love.

This was not my first visit with Pope John Paul II. In January 1980, as I was completing my service in Rome, he graciously received me in audience, wished me well as I returned to my new ministry in the Diocese of Pittsburgh, and gave me his apostolic blessing. Six years later he would call me back to Rome for ordination as a bishop at his hands and my first episcopal assignment as auxiliary bishop in the Archdiocese of Seattle, Washington. In the years to come, there would be multiple opportunities to visit with the pope, concelebrate Mass with him in his private chapel, and grow more profoundly aware that he was truly a holy man.

Wherever we were on Easter Saturday, April 2, 2005, when we heard the news of the death of Pope John Paul II, we will, I believe, remember the moment. Even though it was apparent for some days that our Holy Father was dying, the finality of the announcement of his death hit us hard.

With the passage of time, however, that initial sorrow has been transformed into deepening amazement at his accomplishments, as well as gratitude to God for the gift of St. John Paul II to the Church. His canonization provides us with an opportunity to express once again our appreciation for the ministry, care, love, guidance, and leadership of Pope John Paul II.

What a fitting conclusion to a pontificate that began with his installation Mass on the *sagrato* of St. Peter's Basilica, the same place where his body rested for his funeral Mass. People came from around the world by the hundreds of thousands—even millions—to pay homage to an extraordinary life and a ministry that John Paul II exercised for more than twenty-six years as successor to St. Peter, bishop of Rome, and chief shepherd of the universal Church.

Called to the Service of Christ

The life of Karol Wojtyla was marked by profound faith, rooted in his consciousness of a vocation from God. He felt called to enter the seminary and undertake priestly formation studies that eventually brought him to ordination and the service of the Church. In 1958 he was consecrated a bishop, and in 1964 he became the archbishop of Krakow, which was then, like so much of Eastern Europe, groaning under the weight of Communist oppression and Soviet domination. In June 1967 he was created a cardinal by Pope Paul VI. Throughout his life there was a profound sense of being called to the service of Christ and his people, his Church.

When the cardinals went into conclave in mid-October 1978 following the death of Albino Luciani, John Paul I, who could have imagined that as they concluded their work, the newly elected pope who would step out onto the balcony of St. Peter's Basilica would be a fifty-eight-year-old Polish survivor of both Nazi and Communist totalitarian oppression and the first non-Italian in over four centuries to assume the responsibilities of Peter?

The senior cardinal deacon, Cardinal Pericle Felici, intoned the traditional and ancient proclamation: "I announce to you with great joy: We have a pope, Cardinal Karol Wojtyla, who has taken the name John Paul II."

In the square below, already crowded with tens of thousands of people, this question was heard amidst the applause: "*Who?*" "*Who?*" It was clear that this was not an Italian name. Who was Karol Wojtyla, the man who had just been elected Pope John Paul II?

The answer is foremost a theological one. It is the same response given to each and every successor to Peter. John Paul II was the vicar of Christ, the 264th in a line of apostolic succession that brings us from today back to the apostles and Peter. He was, as is Pope Francis today, the touchstone for the unity of the Church spread throughout the world. The very purpose of the Apostolic See is to be that rock on which the Church is founded and that visible living sign and source of the unity of the Church.

In September 2004, when I joined the bishops of Pennsylvania for our *ad limina* visit that occurs every five years to make our report on the stewardship of our dioceses, the unique role of the pope became all the more manifest—at least for me. As we gathered in the room to greet him, the pontiff who had walked out onto the *sagrato* of St. Peter's in 1978 with such vim, vigor, energy, and stamina was now wheeled into the room. He could no longer walk on his own and had some difficulty when he addressed us. The one thing that remained totally unchanged was the answer to the question "Who is this?" This is Peter. He is the visible sign of the unity of the Church. He is the touchstone of our communion.

All the crowds in St. Peter's Square in 1978 knew this. They were looking for the second part of the answer. Who is this individual who is now Peter? Who is—and was—Karol Wojtyla? Much of what we would learn about him would unfold in the next twenty-six years. We would learn about his childhood, the loss of his parents early in his life, and the occupation of his native land, first by the Nazi powers and then by the Communists.

But we would also come to learn of his disarming charm and ease with people, his mastery of languages, his brilliant intellect, his ability to articulate profound philosophical and theological concepts in pastoral language, and his gift of winning over people everywhere in the world so that everyone had a sense of a one-on-one relationship with him.

All you had to do was stand in St. Peter's Square on any Sunday at noon. Many of you have been there and have witnessed this. At a certain point, just as the clock struck twelve, the window opened, and out stepped this figure dressed in white. From the square he looked miniscule. But if you looked around, you recognized that everyone had a one-on-one personal relationship with that figure on the balcony.

He could speak to crowds of tens of thousands—even millions—and leave everyone there with the sense that he had spoken just to him or her. How many young people at World Youth Day in Denver, or later in Manila, or still later in Rome or elsewhere have said to me, "He looked straight at me and said . . . "

At the same time, he never lost the ability to stop in the middle of everything else that was going on and speak directly to an individual. I can still feel his hand on my shoulder today as clearly as I felt it more than thirty-three years ago. He was visiting Cardinal John Wright in his apartment a month after being elected pope. Cardinal Wright was not well, and his old friend had come to spend some time with him. As he left, the pope put his hand on my shoulder and said to me, "You must always love and serve Christ and Peter."

For over twenty-six years, Pope John Paul II exercised a worldwide ministry that was rooted in the understanding that his task was to be supreme pastor of the Church, to feed his sheep, to be the rock upon which the Church rests, and to sustain and strengthen the faith of us all.

This message he carried to the ends of the earth in visits to every continent and to nearly every nation, speaking a multiplicity of languages in an unending sequence of events. He used his office to proclaim the Church's teaching on social justice, religious freedom, personal dignity, and the value of life. At the same time, he built bridges of understanding with people of all faiths. His interfaith and ecumenical outreach rested on his call that we come to understand one another and treat each other with mutual respect.

In January 2004 the Pittsburgh Symphony Orchestra presented a special concert in the Vatican to commemorate the pope's interfaith and ecumenical outreach. Surrounded by Jewish, Christian, and Muslim leaders from around the world, the pope once again challenged all of us to build a world of justice, mutual respect, peace, and love. On that evening in the great Vatican audience hall, I felt a special awareness that this was the legacy of this extraordinary man, priest, bishop, and pope.

Given his accomplishments on the world stage as well as in the Church, it will not be surprising if history accords him that accolade so rarely bestowed but in this case so rightly deserved: John Paul the Great.

In the following chapters, I have tried to reflect briefly but faithfully on one aspect of the gift of St. John Paul II: his beautifully presented encyclical letters and apostolic exhortations. This small effort on my part is intended to be, to the best of my ability, an affectionate salute to a holy and inspiring man, and one small contribution in celebration of his enduring legacy.

A Rich Treasure of Reflection and Guidance

John Paul II's papacy was the third longest pontificate in the history of the papacy. The longest was that of St. Peter, for which precise dates remain unknown, followed by Pope Pius IX (1846–1878), which was thirty-one years and seven months.

In the years of his pontificate, Pope John Paul II wrote fourteen encyclicals and many apostolic exhortations and letters, addressing just about every aspect of the life and mission of the Church. Besides taking part in Vatican Council II when he was a bishop (with an important contribution to the elaboration of the constitution *Gaudium et Spes*), he participated in every assembly of the Synod of Bishops as a cardinal and pope since it was created by Pope Paul VI in 1965. The post-synodal apostolic exhortations in this book are the fruit of the general synods over which he presided as pope.

During one of the synods in which I participated, he asked how many members were attending for the first time. A large number of hands went up. He asked how many had attended as many as five synods. A smaller number of hands went up. He asked if there were any who had participated in more than ten. I believe a few hands went up. He then asked if there was anyone who had participated in all of them. No hands were raised. Then he lifted his hand, much to the amusement and applause of the synodal fathers.

All of his writings, whether encyclicals or exhortations, reflect those first words addressed to the whole Church during his inaugural Mass as successor to Peter: "Brothers and sisters, do not be afraid to welcome Christ and accept his power. . . . Do not be afraid. . . . Let Christ speak. . . . He alone has words of life, yes, of eternal life."

In this homily, televised to nearly fifty nations, including the first Vatican religious ceremony to be transmitted (and this one in its entirety) to Poland, the pope set before the Church the figure of Christ and the importance of faith:

> "You are the Christ, the Son of the living God." These words were spoken by Simon, son of Jonah, in the district of Caesarea Philippi. . . . These words mark the beginning of Peter's mission in the history of salvation, in the history of the people of God. From that moment, from that confession of faith, the sacred history of salvation and of the people of God was bound to take on a new dimension: to express itself in the historical dimension of the church.

Not long after he had begun his papal ministry, the Holy Father wrote his first encyclical letter, *Redemptor Hominis* (The Redeemer of Man). That letter, addressed to his "venerable brothers in the episcopate, the priests, the religious families, the sons and daughters of the Church and to all men and women of good will," was to set the point of reference for his entire pontificate, whose fruits we are experiencing in such great abundance today.

In this book, I will attempt to unfold some of the teaching of this extraordinary shepherd of a flock of more than one billion followers as it is found in both his encyclical letters and post-synodal apostolic exhortations. I have also included an apostolic exhortation on St. Joseph (*Redemptoris Custos*) that was not preceded by a synod, as well as an apostolic letter on the Rosary (*Rosarium Virginis Mariae*). I have taken each document and explored its spiritual and pastoral wealth and how we can apply it to our lives today. Thus these chapters will not be just a report on the content of the letters and exhortations, but rather an overview of the text with an effort to apply its message to our particular moment in history.

Most of the encyclical letters and apostolic exhortations are available in a convenient softcover format through the publishing division of the United States Conference of Catholic Bishops in Washington, D.C. They can also be readily accessed at the Vatican Web site, www.vatican.va. I highlight these resources to remind the readers of this book that there is no substitute for the actual words of the Holy Father, which are expressed so beautifully and clearly in his encyclical letters and apostolic exhortations. The most that I can hope to accomplish in the ensuing chapters, based in great part on work I was privileged to do over a number of years for *Columbia* magazine, is a reflection on some of the points that St. John Paul II raised and an application of them to the circumstances of our day.

As we begin our journey through this rich field of papal reflection and pastoral guidance, I would like to describe exactly what an encyclical letter and an apostolic exhortation are. The pope, as successor to Peter and vicar of Christ, has a unique teaching role. At a pivotal moment in St. Matthew's gospel, we read the account of Simon, the disciple of Jesus, making a profoundly moving profession of faith in Jesus as the Messiah. This episode, as we noted, formed part of the Holy Father's first homily as the supreme pastor of the universal Church.

The "Rock" of St. Peter

When Simon had come to place his faith in Jesus, the Lord conferred on him a new sacred role and identity, giving him a new name, Peter, which means "rock." Jesus promised Peter that he would be the rock, or foundation, on which he (Jesus) would build his Church, and neither the debilitating force of time, nor even death itself, would extend its power over the Church. To Peter, the "rock," Jesus would give the keys to the kingdom—the authority to bind and to loose, the authorization to lead his flock, and to do so in the name and by the power of Christ (Matthew 16:17-19).

Around the magnificent and imposing Michelangelo dome of St. Peter's Basilica, hundreds of feet in the air above the place where tradition and excavation tell us Peter was buried, is the Latin inscription in letters six feet high proclaiming this citation from the Gospel of St. Matthew. The pope—every pope—succeeds to the role of Peter and the awesome responsibility of teaching the faith and providing pastoral leadership for the Church universal.

The fulfillment of the Petrine promises is recorded as well in the gospels. John tells us how after the resurrection, Jesus confirmed Peter in the role of shepherd and leader of his flock: "'Simon, son of John, do you love me more than these?' He said to him, 'Yes, Lord, you know that I love you.' Jesus said to him, . . . 'Feed my sheep'" (John 21:15, 17).

Peter's role was to continue in the Church. Distinguished ecclesiastical writers of the early centuries, including Origen and Eusebius, have reported the list of ancient popes compiled by St. Irenaeus. St. Clement, the third successor to Peter as bishop of Rome, followed St. Peter, Linus, and Cletus. St. Clement's own service as the servant of the servants of God lasted nine years until he was martyred under the emperor Trajan in A.D. 99. His writings tell us a great deal about the structure of the early Church and the unique role of the Petrine office.

St. Clement is noted among other things for his letter to the Corinthians, in which he intervenes in the affairs of the church at Corinth. Clement is writing as bishop of Rome. Under that title he does not hesitate to correct, rebuke, and order other churches. He makes no justification for his intervention in the internal affairs of Corinth other than that he is bishop of Rome. As such, he is the voice of Peter, competent to speak with the authority of Christ.

His letter and its instruction show us another fact about the makeup of the Church in its earliest days: It was a hierarchical Church. St. Clement speaks very clearly of the role of clergy (bishops and deacons) within the Church. He points out that all authority within the Church is channeled through apostolic succession. He is also quite explicit in noting that bishops were appointed by the apostles when the apostles knew that they were to die and that others would need to carry on their work. All of this takes place before the end of the first century of the Christian era.

The reverence paid to the voice of Pope John Paul II is a respect that grows out of the understanding that Christ sent the apostles, and the apostles through their successors, to continue Christ's ministry with Peter as their head.

The shepherding role conferred on Peter is that of leading and guiding the Church. To the apostles as a group, in conjunction with Peter, Christ gave the commission to exercise authority in his Church. Yet it is always to Peter as head of the College of Apostles, and to his successor as head of the College of Bishops, that the Church looks for guidance, instruction, teaching, and leadership.

For the Whole Church

An encyclical is a letter through which the pope exercises his teaching responsibility. Essentially, an encyclical letter is a pastoral letter written by the pope, addressed to the whole Church, as distinct from a pastoral letter that a bishop would prepare just for his diocese. Usage has created a noun out of the adjective "encyclical," or "circular," so that we now speak of the letter as the pope's "encyclical."

There is a long history of formal papal letters written for a specific local or diocesan church yet applicable to the Church universal. The Letter of Clement to the Corinthians is an example. The modern usage of the encyclical as we know it is dated by most historians to Benedict XIV and his December 3, 1740, encyclical letter, *Ubi Primum,* which dealt with the responsibilities of bishops.

Ever since then, whenever a pope determines that it is time to offer some guidance, teaching, or instruction to the whole Church—to all the faithful—he expresses himself in the form of a letter sent to all of the bishops so that they can circulate or share it with all of the faithful; thus the name "encyclical."

Over the decades, through the pontificates of many popes, the teaching function of encyclicals is apparent. To cite but a few, these encyclicals include Pope Leo XIII's *Rerum Novarum* (On Labor), 1891; Pope Pius XI's *Casti Connubii* (On Christian Marriage), 1930; Pope Pius XII's *Mystici Corporis* (On the Mystical Body of Christ), 1943; Pope John XXIII's *Pacem in Terris* (Peace on Earth), 1963; Pope Paul VI's *Humanae Vitae* (On Human Life), 1968; the many encyclicals of Pope John Paul II; Pope Benedict XVI's encyclicals, beginning with his first, *Deus Caritas Est* (God Is Love), 2005; and now Pope Francis' first encyclical, *Lumen Fidei* (The Light of Faith), 2013.

Synod of Bishops

With the conclusion in 1965 of the Second Vatican Council, there arose a new institution in the Church called the "Synod of Bishops." So enriching for the Church was the Council that many of the Council fathers, including Pope Paul VI, felt that there should be some mechanism or instrumentality to bring together the bishops from time to time. This would not involve all the bishops of the world at once. Instead, a number of bishops representative of the Church in different parts of the world would convene periodically to offer advice to the pope on issues he would select. Thus came into existence the modern-day ecclesiastical institution, the Synod of Bishops.

On September 15, 1965, Pope Paul VI with the document *Apostolica Sollicitudo* brought into being this gathering of bishops and provided its constitution. The document notes that the aims of the synod are (1) to encourage close union and valued assistance between the sovereign pontiff and the bishops of the entire world; (2) to ensure that direct and real information is provided on the questions involving the internal action of the Church and its necessary action in the world today; and (3) to facilitate agreement on essential points of doctrine and on methods of procedure in the life of the Church.

In practice, what developed was that an ordinary general assembly of the synod was convoked every three or four years and an extraordinary meeting when one was warranted. The first synod met in 1967 and was followed by one in 1969 and another in 1971. The 1969 meeting was an extraordinary meeting and is not numbered in the sequence of general assemblies. Thus the 1974 synod, though the fourth in number, is designated the "Third General Assembly of the Synod of Bishops."

Pope Paul VI issued the first post-synodal apostolic exhortation, *Evangelii Nuntiandi* (On Evangelization of the Modern World), on December 8, 1975. This began the tradition of the pope summing up the work of the synod and presenting it in the form of an instruction or exhortation to the faithful—but in his own name and on his own authority. The content of such an exhortation is found in the synodal experience, which allows the bishops an opportunity to express their beliefs on the subject and then over a period of several weeks reach a consensus on which points should receive attention and be incorporated into the final document. At the end of a synod, the reflections of the bishops are presented to the Holy Father, who uses them to express his own thoughts in what becomes his exhortation to the Catholic faithful on the theme of the synod.

Pope John Paul II often expressed his support for the Synod of Bishops, which he indicated was established by "a truly providential act" of Pope Paul VI. In an address to the Council of the General Secretariat of the Synod of Bishops in 1983, John Paul praised the synod: "The experience of the post-councilor period shows clearly in what noteworthy measure the synodal activity can set the pace for the pastoral life of the universal Church" (April 30, 1983).

In his first encyclical letter, Pope John Paul II spoke of the relationship between the Synod of Bishops and episcopal collegiality and referred to the synod as "a permanent organ of collegiality" (*Redemptor Hominis*, 5). In a later talk, he went on to say: "The synod constitutes a realization and an illustration of the collegial nature of the order of bishops, of which the Second Vatican Council has, so to speak, come to a renewed awareness" (Address at the Conclusion of the Eighth Ordinary General Assembly of the Synod of Bishops, October 27, 1990).

On October 16, 1979, the first anniversary of his election to the See of Peter, Pope John Paul II published *Catechesi Tradendae* (On Catechesis in our Time). His inaugural apostolic exhortation was issued, he said, "in response to the request which was expressly formulated by the bishops at the end of the fourth general assembly of the synod," which met in the fall of 1977. In this way Pope John Paul II continued the initial practice of Pope Paul VI and published seven such exhortations meant for the entire Church, all of which form a part of this book.

The encyclicals and exhortations are presented here in chronological order. Now let us begin with Pope John Paul II's first encyclical, *Redemptor Hominis*, which in many ways sets the tone for the rest of his pontificate.

Chapter 1

FOCUS ON THE FUTURE

Redemptor Hominis

ENGLISH TITLE: **The Redeemer of Man**
DATE ISSUED: **March 4, 1979**
TYPE OF DOCUMENT: **Encyclical Letter**

A t the very beginning of his ministry as universal shepherd of the Church, Pope John Paul II turned his attention to the perennial proclamation of the gospel and the advent of a new millennium. Looking back from our current vantage point, it appears that the pope, from the very initiation of his ministry, was calling the Church to focus on the future.

He challenged us to bring Christ to the third millennium and the new generations still in need of Jesus' redemption. Another way of understanding the Holy Father's first encyclical is to see it as the answer to a set of ever-arising questions: Who is Christ? What is Jesus' meaning for people today? What is the role of his Church in the contemporary world?

Even though this first encyclical letter, *Redemptor Hominis,* came two decades before the beginning of the third millennium, it is clear that the pope was already calling our attention to the great changes taking place around us, to the challenges facing our modern world, and to the fact that Christ continues to be the answer to the most pressing questions of the human heart and mind.

He begins the encyclical with this clear statement: "The redeemer of man, Jesus Christ, is the center of the universe and of history."

Not only do we place our faith in Jesus as our Lord and Savior, but we are called to recognize him as the central figure of all human history. As we date our history from his birth, so should we recall each day that it is Jesus who gives meaning to our lives, our culture, and our society. Only in him can we be truly reflective of God's plan for us from the very beginning.

Perhaps nowhere did what the pope have to say to us become more apparent than in our struggle to understand the implications of the attack on our country on September 11, 2001, and how such evil could be directed at us. The basic questions still remained: How shall I live? What is the purpose of life? What values should I accept? But after the attack, we faced additional questions: How could something like this happen? How can terrible things happen to good people? How can such evil come into our world? How should we respond in the face of evil and violence?"

Though he could not have foreseen the events of September 11, 2001, more than two decades earlier, John Paul was already reinforcing in this encyclical the ancient teaching of the Church: that it is only in Christ that we can find the true meaning of life and the answer to life's demanding and sometimes overwhelming questions.

Most of us will long remember where we were when we received word of the terrible acts that brought so much death to New York City, Washington, D.C., and Somerset County in Pennsylvania. Some actions are so horrendous that they outstrip our vocabulary's ability to express them. Yet our memory holds the moment forever in high profile.

I was in our nation's capital with fifty other bishops from around the United States as the administrative committee of our Conference of Bishops met in preparation for our annual November general assembly. At a certain point, the meeting was interrupted as we were informed of the first plane crash into the World Trade Center. In succession came the news of the other tower and then the Pentagon as targets of terrorist action. Finally came the word of the plane crash and loss of life in Somerset County.

We adjourned and did what the Church does in moments such as these—the only thing the Church can do: We prayed. We walked from our conference building to the National Shrine of the Immaculate Conception where the archbishop of Washington led us in the celebration of the Eucharist.

All over the country, there was a spontaneous outpouring of prayer as people turned to God in this time of darkness. In churches and places of prayer of every faith tradition, crowds of people were gathered in prayer.

We prayed, and we asked God for courage, enlightenment, and guidance as we were reminded of the enormous conflict that goes on every day in every hearts. It is the conflict between good and evil, the conflict between light and darkness, the conflict between hatred and love.

Whatever the geographical and material origin of the attack on our country, the true origin is to be found in the human heart. It is difficult—if not impossible—to imagine a heart so laden in hatred and so encrusted in evil that it would drive a plane full of innocent people into a building full of innocent people.

The Struggle within Our Hearts

All violent acts of injustice and destruction and the taking of innocent human life find their origin in the attitudes of the human heart. Evil comes from within. The great cosmic struggle between good and evil, between light and darkness, between war and peace, between violence and harmony, or between hatred and love begins first in each human heart and is waged there. It is on the outcome of that struggle that true peace depends.

The beatitudes draw the demanding picture that Jesus sets before us of a world of peacemakers and those who hunger and thirst for holiness, justice, mercy, compassion, and consolation. To the extent that each one of us participates in that effort, there is just a little bit more light, peace, harmony, and love in the world.

One of the popular hymns of our day has the compelling and haunting refrain "Let there be peace on earth, and let it begin with me." The great battle between good and evil is won in every single human heart. It is for this reason that the pope addresses his encyclical letter *Redemptor Hominis* to each and every member of the Church. The responsibility of accepting Christ in our lives and transforming not only ourselves but the world we encounter and eventually the whole world rests personally with each one of us.

In reading the Holy Father's first encyclical, it is apparent immediately that he is speaking as a pastor—a shepherd of souls—to individuals, even though collectively those individuals are the whole Church. He is writing to you and me. His message is that we need to open our hearts to Christ who is our redeemer. As we face the struggles of our own moment in history, we need to do our best to be faithful to Christ and to his gospel of love.

What is needed is the commitment of all of us to a basic human solidarity that banishes all those things that are the source of division: ethnic and racial bias, religious bigotry, political opportunism, and media manipulation. Around us in this community are people of many national heritages, ethnic traditions, and religious convictions. Jewish, Muslim, and Christian religious traditions call us to peace, harmony, unity, and solidarity. It is an abuse and betrayal of those religious principles to kill innocent human life.

Good trees must bear good fruit. Those who are fed from the fruit of religious proclamation should grow in respect for and toleration of all peoples as children of the one loving and compassionate God. Light can win out over darkness. Truth will triumph over falsehood. Love does conquer hatred.

No pulpit in a church, synagogue, mosque, or other place of prayer used by any religious leader should be an instrument to ferment hatred and its fruit. Whether we are speaking about the Sudan, Bosnia, the Middle East, Nigeria, Afghanistan, or parts of our own United States, hatred should have no place.

Shortly after the September 11 attacks, as I was leaving an interfaith prayer service, I was asked what good might come out of this attack on America. I responded that we could renew our resolve to be guided by God's word and our own religious convictions and thus not allow ourselves to be overcome by evil or hatred. September 11 also gave us an opportunity for a moral reawakening, as does each day we live, to look into our hearts to see how well we have allowed the goodness of God to dwell there. We must recognize our common humanity, our solidarity as children of the same God and as members of the same human race.

With the prophetic insight that so marks his writings, the pope in the first paragraph of *Redemptor Hominis* reminded us that the Great Jubilee—the marking of the new millennium—would "recall and reawaken in us in a special way our awareness of the key truth of faith which St. John expressed at the beginning of his Gospel: 'the Word became flesh and made his dwelling among us' (John 1:14), and elsewhere: God so loved the world that he gave his only Son, that whoever believes in him should not perish but have eternal life' (John 3:16)."

God Speaks to Us

With clarity and directness, this encyclical sets before us the two elements of the great dynamic of revelation, of God speaking to us. First is the proclamation that Jesus is God who has come among us to be one of us. Second is our response in faith. God speaks. We hear and respond. God calls. We open our hearts to his word in acceptance and belief.

Life brings with it so many challenges. On the one hand, it sets before us great hope. On the other, it bears within itself profound tragedies. *Gaudium et Spes* (The Pastoral Constitution on the Church in the Modern World) of the Second Vatican Council speaks of the hope and joy, the grief and anxiety that are somehow intermingled in our world. This theme is developed by St. John Paul over and over again in his writings, not just in his first encyclical.

We all recognize that hope and joy in life are very real. Even though there is a sense of failure and sin around us and even within us, there is also the intuitive recognition that what God has made is very good. The beautiful things that are a part of God's creation mirror God in countless ways and continue to delight the human heart. In the arts and sciences, in the things we learn and in the work of our hands, we can find enjoyment. Great gladness wells up within us, especially when we give and receive friendship and experience the reality of unselfish love.

At the same time, grief and anxiety are also real. Human history is in large part a record of wars, personal failures, and tragedies. Our bewilderment over pain is also recognized in the pages of Scripture. The apostles themselves asked Christ why a person had been born blind (John 9:2).

At the core of human experience is the recognition that life promises much and yet so frequently disappoints. Why is this so? How are we to respond to the goodness that we recognize and to the failure that is all too often equally apparent?

God Enters Our History

Redemptor Hominis holds out for us the vision of Christ, the Son of God, who was born of the Virgin Mary and became man. "This act of redemption marked the high point of the history of man within God's loving plan. God entered the history of humanity and, as a man, became an actor in that history, one of the thousands of millions of human beings but at the same time Unique!" (1.2).

The gospels speak with a sublime simplicity of the events surrounding the conception and birth of Jesus. The coming of Jesus, which we celebrate every year at Christmas, was quiet and gentle. The One who came to restore our communion with God arrived among the poor and the little. In view of the greatness of the divine promise, the circumstances of his coming seemed most unlikely. His mother was, in earthly estimation, an unimportant figure, as was also her husband Joseph, a carpenter.

Only great faith could have accepted the announcement made to Mary. She was to conceive in her womb and bear a son who would be called the "Son of the Most High." He would reign over the house of Jacob forever. His kingdom would be without end. The great divine-human dynamic was at work and most wonderfully modeled in the annunciation to Mary that she was to become the Mother of God. The word of God was spoken. Mary heard, accepted, believed, and acted accordingly.

Pope John Paul II's first encyclical letter begins with the repetition of this most ancient of Christian messages: It is God who has come among us in Christ, and this divine intervention took place in order to restore whatever was destroyed or wounded in our relationship with God.

The Pope's Personal Reflections

Setting the stage for his teaching, John Paul turns to some personal reflections as if to give us an example of how we are to deal with the profound challenge of faith. Offering us a glimpse of his own reaction to being elected pope, he tells us that when asked whether he would accept the election, he replied, "With obedience in faith to Christ, my Lord, and with trust in the Mother of God and of the Church, in spite of the great difficulties, I accept."

Encyclicals are rarely autobiographical. Usually, they are quite formal and solemn. They represent a teaching instrument by which the head of the Church instructs the faithful. Yet in his first message to the Church universal, Pope John Paul II chose to speak of his own trust in God as a model of how every believer is to respond to the call of God as it is articulated in his own life experience. "Today I wish to make that reply known publicly to all without exception, thus showing that there is a link between the first fundamental truth of the Incarnation, already mentioned, and the ministry that, with my acceptance of my election as Bishop of Rome and Successor of the Apostle Peter, has become my specific duty in his See" (2.1).

As I reflect over and over again on these words, it seems to me that the pope is reinforcing what will be more theologically expressed as the encyclical unfolds. Yet he now shares with us on the level of his personal experience. Christ is the center of all history—personal and institutional. We are called by God. In faith we are to be open to his word and thus respond and direct our lives.

A Spirit of Collaboration

The task of the pope is to speak the truth in love. Conscious of his role as head of the Church, St. John Paul announces in *Redemptor Hominis* that he will carry out his responsibility as shepherd of the flock. He will do so in communion with the College of Bishops, all the bishops spread throughout the whole Church. In highlighting this spirit of collaboration and shared responsibility, the pope calls bishops to experience the same with their co-workers, the priests. Laypeople, "conscious of their responsibility for the Church," must commit themselves as well to collaborating with their pastors for the good of the gospel and its dissemination.

At the Mass that the newly elected Pope John Paul II celebrated with the cardinals of the conclave, he pointed out that his agenda would be that of the Second Vatican Council. The renewal of and direction for the Church given by that Council would be his mission. As a bishop who had participated in both the Second Vatican Council and the synods of the Church prior to his election to the See of Peter, the pope brought with him a rich understanding of collegiality—that unity and pastoral ministry of the successors to the apostles together with the pope, the successor to Peter. In a later post-synodal exhortation on the subject of the laity, the Holy Father pointed out that the document is meant to be a faithful and coherent expression of the work of the synod—"a fruit of collegiality" (*Christifideles Laici*, 2.12).

It was primarily to Peter and the other apostles that Christ entrusted the preaching of the gospel. The Catholic Church teaches that just as the Holy Father and the other bishops are the successors of the apostles in ruling his flock, so also are they the apostles' successors as the authentic teachers and witnesses of the faith. They are the witnesses that Christ has established to teach the Church. To the work of the Holy Father and the College of Bishops as teachers, God has given the charism of truth that does not fail. In them especially he causes the word that he had sent the apostles to speak to be faithfully spoken. In them he guards the word with divine care, not to glorify them, but to make them centers of unity and truth for those he calls to faith. Clearly, the Catholic bishops have a duty to teach collegially in unity of faith with the Holy Father and his brother bishops.

Pope John Paul II in this first encyclical highlights the importance of the communion of bishops with Peter at the service of the Church:

In spite of all appearances, the Church is now more united in the fellowship of service and in the awareness of apostolate. This unity springs from the principle of collegiality, mentioned by the Second Vatican Council. Christ himself made this principle a living part of the apostolic College of the Twelve with

Peter at their head, and he is continuously renewing it in the College of the Bishops, which is growing more and more over all the earth, remaining united with and under the guidance of the Successor of St. Peter. (5.1)

Ecumenical Emphasis

Before moving on to the doctrinal content of this encyclical, the pope completes his vision of how we are to carry out our responsibilities to Christ as members of the Church by challenging us to recognize the need to walk the road to Christian unity. It was never Christ's intention that the Church be fragmented or divided. "True ecumenical activity means openness, drawing closer, availability for dialogue, and a shared investigation of the truth in the full evangelical and Christian sense; but in no way does it or can it mean giving up or in any way diminishing the treasures of divine truth that the Church has constantly confessed and taught" (6.2).

Examples abound of the Holy Father's ecumenical outreach near and far. The Joint Declaration on Justification issued by the Lutheran World Federation and the Vatican's Secretariat for Christian Unity (1998) is just one example. A more personal effort was seen in the pope's many journeys. Perhaps one of the most dramatic was his visit to Athens in 2001 in his long-articulated quest for unity between the Catholic and Orthodox Churches. Even in the face of a less than enthusiastic welcome, the pope courageously, gently, and lovingly called his hearers to the goal of Christian unity.

The pope's call and challenge to Christian unity is deeply rooted in the Second Vatican Council. In its documents *Lumen Gentium* (The Dogmatic Constitution on the Church) and *Unitatis Redintegratio* (The Decree on Ecumenism), we read that "many elements of sanctification and of truth" are found outside the visible confines of the Catholic Church: "the written word of God; the life of grace; faith, hope and charity, with the other interior gifts of the Holy Spirit, as well as visible elements" (LG, 8; UR, 3; cf. LG, 15).

Separated churches and ecclesial communities remain close to us. They "are bound to the Catholic Church by a specially close relationship as a result of the long span of earlier centuries when the Christian people had lived in ecclesiastical communion" (UR, 19). Their Christian way of life is nourished by faith in the one Christ and is strengthened by the grace of baptism and the hearing of God's word, and the faith by which they believe in Christ does bear fruit in a number of ways (cf. UR, 23).

In the first part of this encyclical, we see the Holy Father's profound conviction—a conviction shared by the Catholic faithful—that the central point of all human experience is the birth of Christ, who is "God with us." We have been called to respond to the generous word of God spoken to us in Jesus Christ. The reply to revelation is the act of faith. The Church as Christ's body, guided by its apostolic leadership and vivified in the Spirit, is the living continuation of the dynamic of divine intervention in our lives. What Christ did, the Church continues to do.

Redemptor Hominis goes on in doctrinal terms to speak of the mystery of redemption, redeemed man and his situation in the modern world, the Church's mission, and man's destiny. John Paul concludes with a call to all of us to live out the fullness of who we have become in grace for the glory of God and our salvation.

Redemption and the New Creation

The encyclical is divided into four chapters. The first chapter, "Inheritance," focuses on the pope's understanding of his pontificate within the perspective of the Second Vatican Council and the coming of the new millennium. In chapter two, "The Mystery of Redemption," the pope provides us with a reflection on Christ the

Redeemer. Chapter three, "Redeemed Man and His Situation in the Modern World," reminds us that Christ is the source of our redemption and therefore our hope. Finally, in chapter four, "The Church's Mission and Man's Destiny," the pope explains how the Church carries out its vocation to be priest, prophet, and king in the modern world.

Often we think of redemption as our personal relationship with God. There is a sense in which that is very true. But there is also a far wider vision of Christ's work among us. St. Paul speaks of a whole new creation. The Book of Revelation describes a cosmic struggle going on between the worlds of light and darkness. St. John's gospel particularly develops the theological implications of Jesus' coming among us and his death for us.

The pope begins his reflection on redemption as a new creation by going back to the Book of Genesis:

> The Redeemer of the world! In him has been revealed in a new and more wonderful way the fundamental truth concerning creation to which the Book of Genesis gives witness when it repeats several times: "God saw that it was good." The good has its source in Wisdom and Love. In Jesus Christ the visible world which God created for man—the world that, when sin entered, "was subjected to futility"—recovers again its original link with the divine source of Wisdom and Love. (8.1)

At the very beginning, everything was good. There was an order and a harmony to all of creation, and human beings enjoyed a relationship with God. Human persons at peace and in friendship with God have both a grandeur and an awareness of their own status as creatures. The first pages of Genesis speak of the nearness of man and woman to God, of God's care for them, and of the obedience God demanded of them.

Nothing could be more noble and empowering for a person than to recognize the reality of God and the truth of the relationship he has to God, for God is the source of all that an individual is and possesses. All the possibilities of life and friendship, all the limitless scope of what one can become, depend utterly upon God. But God is generous. He invites us to the greatness of hope. We are called to share the divine life, to inherit the fullness of everything that is.

In the Garden of Eden, the goodness God intended for us was evident and accessible. In Christ we have not only the restoration of the initial goodness that God intended for us but a whole new level of relationship. Church tradition speaks of the *felix culpa*, the "happy fault." Because of our fall from the order of the first creation, God sent his only begotten Son to redeem and restore us. But he chose to go much, much further. In a gratuitous act of divine love, God elevated us in grace to adopted sonship.

The Grace of God at Work

When *Redemptor Hominis* speaks of the divine dimension of the mystery of redemption, it talks about the power of God at work. When it speaks of the "human dimension of the mystery of redemption," it speaks of the transformation taking place in us as a result of what Jesus has accomplished.

Christ is the life of the world in many ways. "For in him all the fullness was pleased to dwell, and through him to reconcile all things for him" (Colossians 1:19-20). God has graced the humanity of Jesus with the fullness of all divine gifts. The goodness and loving kindness of God were made visible in Jesus.

Christ is the Fountain and Source of life. We are not merely to imitate him but to live in him and from him. "Remain in me, as I remain in you. Just as a branch cannot bear fruit on its own unless it remains on the vine, so neither can you unless you remain in me. I am the vine, you are the branches" (John 15:4-5).

The newness of life that Christ brings through his redemptive action involves both the healing of our wounds and the elevation of our lives to a sharing in divine life. Human integrity has been wounded by sin, and so it is in our very humanity that we are healed by the new life Jesus brings. Grace does not make us less human, any less concerned with the personal and social good of mankind and true temporal values. It makes us more human, more concerned. "Nothing that is genuinely human fails to find an echo in their hearts" (Vatican II, *Gaudium et Spes*, 1).

The gift of Christ's life does far more than restore mankind's full humanity. Through Christ we are called to a true friendship with the Trinity, with the God who chooses to dwell with those who love Christ. We are called to share in the very nature of God (2 Peter 1:4). Thus we are now called God's children and challenged to live already on earth in a divine way, sharing God's knowledge in unshakeable faith and sharing in God's innermost life by the gift of his love. Because the new creation is already unfolding in Christ, the Church is the beginning and the manifestation of the fullness of the kingdom of God.

This brings us to the final two chapters of *Redemptor Hominis*. "Redeemed Man and His Situation in the Modern World" challenges us to take our place in the community in which we live. We are to be a leaven capable of renewing the temporal order, bringing not only to each of us individually but to humanity as a whole a realization of the new creation. In "The Church's Mission and Man's Destiny," John Paul outlines how the Church is the means by which the new creation comes to be. In fact, the Church as the great sacrament of God's presence is the beginning of the new creation. The sacraments and especially the Eucharist place us in direct contact with the glorified Christ at work within the heart of every believer to bring to fulfillment the new creation.

Echoes of the encyclical were heard clearly at the Mass closing the Jubilee Year World Youth Day held August 15–20, 2000, in Rome. With more than two million people gathered at Tor Vergata, a university campus on Rome's periphery, for the August 20 Mass, the pope said: "[We] must be fervent witnesses to Christ's presence on the altar. [Let] the Eucharist mold your life and the life of the families you will form. Let it guide all life's choices. May the Eucharist, the true and living presence of the love of the Trinity, inspire in you ideals of solidarity, and may it lead you to live in communion with your brothers and sisters in every part of the world" (6.3).

As he did at the Mass opening his ministry as pope, so again at the World Youth Day vigil service on August 14, the Holy Father challenged his hearers: "Have no fear of entrusting yourself to [Christ]! He will guide you, he will grant you the strength to follow him every day and in every situation."

Some years earlier in our country at World Youth Day in Denver, the pope called us "never to be ashamed" but to always "be proud" of our faith. God's great gift of faith is a precious one. This heritage is passed on in the Church. We should be proud of our faith and never hesitate to let it lead us, mold us, and form us in all the decisions we make.

In concluding his first encyclical letter, the pope ends with what was to become a trademark of his pontificate: a plea to Mary as Mother of the Church. He asks that she intercede to help achieve the vision of God's plan for us, which is set forth in Christ who is God's Son—one of us and the redeemer of mankind.

Chapter 2

HANDING ON THE FAITH

Catechesi Tradendae

ENGLISH TITLE: **On Catechesis in Our Time**
DATE ISSUED: **October 16, 1979**
TYPE OF DOCUMENT: **Post-Synodal Apostolic Exhortation**

In October 1977 bishops from around the world discussed the catechetical work of the Church—the passing on and proclamation of the faith. Catechesis is *"education in the faith* of children, young people, and adults which includes especially the teaching of Christian doctrine . . . with a view to initiating the hearers into the fullness of Christian life" (*Catechism of the Catholic Church*, 5). It is an ongoing and never-ending work of the Church. Jesus sent out the apostles with a commission to teach all that he had revealed and to baptize in the name of the Triune God, thus building up and perfecting the body of Christ. On October 16, 1979, on the first anniversary of his election as pope, John Paul II issued his first post-synodal apostolic exhortation, *Catechesi Tradendae* (On Catechesis in Our Time).

When Jesus taught here on earth, men and women flocked to him. Indeed, the world has always been drawn to Christ. Over the centuries he has been loved by countless millions who have known him only through faith. He has come into the lives of so many because so many others have borne witness to Jesus in both word and deed. *Catechesi Tradendae* offers an inspiriting vision of how the Church must carry out her catechetical mission, constantly alert to the need to pass on all that Christ teaches and to do so in a way that engages and invites the hearer to become more deeply united to Jesus and his Church.

This apostolic exhortation contains nine chapters in addition to a brief introduction and conclusion. In the first chapter, entitled "We Have But One Teacher, Jesus Christ," the pope points out that all catechetical efforts must focus on Christ. Christ is our teacher. "You call me 'teacher' and 'master,' and rightly so, for indeed I am" (John 13:13). All that the Catholic Church teaches is Christ's answer to us in our search for the true meaning of life and our desire to understand the longings of the human heart. The gospel of Christ is a message of joy to a world in need of guidance, direction, and hope. As John Paul points out:

> The primary and essential object of catechesis is, to use an expression dear to St. Paul and also to contemporary theology, "the mystery of Christ." Catechizing is in a way to lead a person to study this mystery in all its dimensions: "to make all men see what is the plan of the mystery . . . comprehend with all the saints what is the breadth and length and height and depth . . . know the love of Christ which surpasses knowledge . . . (and be filled) with all the fullness of God (Ephesians 3:9, 18-19)." (5.3)

In chapter two, entitled "An Experience as Old as the Church," the pope offers examples of how catechesis has been carried on in the Church from the apostolic age until our own day. Citing the Fathers of the Church, ecclesiastical councils, and the witness of saints and missionaries, the pope reminds us that there is never a time in the life of the Church when catechetical activity is not an ongoing manifestation of the Church.

In the third chapter, "Catechesis in the Church's Pastoral and Missionary Activity," the pope highlights again that "Catechesis cannot be disassociated from the Church's pastoral and missionary activity as a whole" (18.1). Describing what he means by catechesis, John Paul says it is "an education of children, young people, and adults in the faith, which includes especially the teaching of Christian doctrine imparted, generally speaking, in an organic and systematic way, with a view to initiating the hearers into the fullness of Christian life" (18.4).

It is in this section that John Paul reminds us that catechesis is a stage in evangelization. Already he is underscoring a theme that he will return to over and over again in documents, teachings, homilies, and public discourses. The overarching concept under which the Church's ongoing daily activity takes place is that of evangelization. Catechesis "is one of these moments—a very remarkable one—in the whole process of evangelization" (18.6).

Chapter four, "The Whole of the Good News Drawn from Its Source," deals with the content of catechesis. Leading up to the synod that produced the reflections in *Catechesi Tradendae*, there was great emphasis on the methodology used to pass on the faith. Unfortunately, a false dichotomy arose between method and content, which leads in too many cases to the devaluing of content and the overemphasis on creative methodology. The wisdom of the Church in her catechetical effort is reflected in this document, which balances both solid content and engaging methodology.

In chapter five, "Everybody Needs to Be Catechized," the exhortation describes those to whom catechesis is directed. Chapters six and seven deal with the ways and means of catechesis and how to impart it. Chapter eight, "The Joy of Faith in a Troubled World," considers the difficulties in teaching the faith today. The final chapter, "The Task Concerns All of Us," is an appeal to all members of the Church to undertake responsibility for fostering proper catechetical renewal.

New Catechetical Tools

The pope's reflections on the difficulties we face in teaching the faith are every bit as applicable today as they were in 1979, but there is one significant difference. Since the publication of *Catechesi Tradendae*, we have witnessed the publication of the *Catechism of the Catholic Church* and the *General Directory for Catechesis*. Both of these catechetical tools focus our attention on the need for ongoing catechesis at every stage in our lives, and both confront the difficulties the Holy Father spoke about in *Catechesi Tradendae*.

In response to the Holy See's request that the *General Directory* be adapted for each nation, a national directory of catechesis was published by the United States Conference of Catholic Bishops. And in 2006, the USCCB published the *United States Catholic Catechism for Adults* in response to Pope John Paul's call that local catechisms be prepared based on the *Catechism of the Catholic Church*.

Today's challenges continue to loom large, but they are not insurmountable. Our culture is aggressively secular to such an extent that the environment can actually be hostile to the Christian faith. In examining our societal context, we recognize that the social mores have so changed in the past years as to produce a climate that is not only secular but is also almost entirely focused on the material world. Ours is a generation that, to some significant extent, has lost its moral compass.

Concomitant with this situation is the disintegration of the community and social structures that once supported religious faith and encouraged family life. The heavy emphasis on the individual and his or her rights has greatly eroded the concept of the common good and its ability to call people to something beyond themselves. This condition strongly impacts the capacity of some people to accept revealed teaching that cannot be changed by democratic process and to follow an absolute moral imperative that is not the result of prior popular approbation.

The context of our proclamation of the good news of Jesus Christ is what is increasingly described as "the American mind-set." It is more individual than communal, more competitive than cooperative, and generally more self-serving than self-giving. Given this mind-set, many of our faithful find it difficult to feel comfortable in a Church that existed prior to the decision of individual members to bring it into being, that claims to bind conscience, and that expects more from Sunday worship than warm feelings.

A Second Chance

There is today, as there has always been to some extent, a temptation by some of the faithful to treat the Church as if it were incidental to salvation. The *Catechism of the Catholic Church* has, perhaps, devoted such a large section to the teaching role of the Church and the function of bishops and priests precisely because the acceptance of the teaching authority of Christ exercised by bishops and priests in union with the bishops throughout the world is a "hard saying" today.

In our pastoral experience, we often encounter young parents—those who are called to be the first teachers of their children in the ways of the faith—who face their first serious personal catechesis when they themselves are invited to share in the catechetical programs for their children. As lamentable as this situation may be, it is also an extraordinary one. This is a second chance both for them and for those who teach the faith.

Many pastors have noted that the new evangelization is unfolding on two levels simultaneously: the introduction into the faith of very young children and the instruction of their parents. For many catechists and those catechized, this is a particularly enriching moment because this time around, the young adults approach the faith with a great deal more openness out of their own felt need to know more.

As he concludes the apostolic exhortation *On Catechesis in Our Time*, the pope reminds us that catechesis, "which is growth in faith and the maturing of Christian life toward its fullness, is consequently a work of the Holy Spirit, a work that he alone can initiate and sustain in the Church" (72.6). It is for that reason that prayer must form both the context and animating force of true catechesis. The first and most powerful teacher of the human heart is God's spirit, enlivening us and enabling us to cry out, "Lord, Lord." Thus the Holy Father concludes his reflections on catechetics with this statement: "I invoke on the catechizing Church this Spirit of the Father and the Son, and I beg him to renew catechetical dynamism in the Church" (72.10).

Perhaps our own reflection on this apostolic exhortation, and the subsequent application of it, should also conclude by asking for the gift of the Holy Spirit on everyone who faithfully passes on the story of Jesus and helps others to encounter the living Christ.

Chapter 3

God's Mercy

Dives in Misericordia

ENGLISH TITLE:	**Rich in Mercy**
DATE ISSUED:	**November 30, 1980**
TYPE OF DOCUMENT:	**Encyclical Letter**

A dramatic scene often appearing in various forms in movies and television dramas is the moment when the guilty person "throws himself on the mercy of the court" and begs forgiveness, pardon, and a lighter sentence from the judge. What heightens the drama is the uncertainty of the response. The judge does not always temper justice with mercy. The court and the law are not always prone to forgiveness.

Perhaps one of the reasons we are easily caught up in this type of story is because each one of us knows that at different times in our lives, we have failed and done what is wrong. Presumably we have not been engaged in the type of activity that is so much a part of the entertainment industry and that brings the guilty person before a court of law. But nonetheless, we are sympathetic because each one of us knows in our own heart that we, too, from time to time have failed and have sinned.

We know that every time we turn our attention to our relationship with our good and loving God, we also come with a plea for mercy. The great difference between the mitigated, contextualized, and limited mercy of the courtroom-drama judge and divine mercy is the unconditional and unlimited depth of God's forgiveness.

On the first Sunday of Advent in 1980, in the third year of his pontificate, Pope John Paul II published his second encyclical letter, *Dives in Misericordia* (Rich in Mercy). In the introduction the pope tells us:

> Following the teaching of the Second Vatican Council and paying close attention to the special needs of our times, I devoted the encyclical *Redemptor Hominis* to the truth about man, a truth that is revealed to us in its fullness and depth in Christ. A no less important need in these critical and difficult times impels me to draw attention once again in Christ to the countenance of the "Father of mercies and God of all comfort" (2 Corinthians 1:3). (1.2)

God's Mercy Is Visible

In turning our attention to the mercy of God, John Paul first reflects on the revelation of God's mercy—the fact that God is always rich in mercy and that he is always generous in his loving kindness. This chapter includes a reflection on Jesus as the very incarnation of God's mercy, because it is in Christ—God with us—that we come to know God. The pope points out that it is precisely in our encounter with Christ that God's invisible nature becomes in a special way visible, "incomparably more visible than through all the other 'things that had been made': it becomes visible in Christ and through Christ, through his actions and his words, and finally through his death on the cross and his resurrection" (2.1).

Jesus is the incarnation of mercy. He makes the mercy of God physically and visibly present to us. When he stretched forth his hand, touched a person, and said, "Your sins are forgiven you," the power of God and the love and mercy of God took on human form. So it is today. In the Church the loving mercy of God continues to be visibly present because Jesus takes the gentle forgiveness of an all-powerful

God and moves it from the realm of human abstraction to something as real and as concrete as the priest's hand raised in absolution.

The Church is the living continuity with Jesus and makes him present in our world. There is a parallel between God's Word taking on flesh and becoming a man—one of us—and the new body of Christ, his Church, taking form among us as visible, structured, and tangible. Thus we can say that Christ sent the apostles, and the apostles and their successors continue Christ's work in the organized Church with visible and tangible sacraments.

What a blessing it is to know that God is truly with us! There is something in our human nature that calls out for the assurance that our sins are truly forgiven. We need to know that God's mercy is at work in us. The Sacrament of Penance or Reconciliation is the visible manifestation of God's mercy that assures us, in human terms, that we have clear access to the mercy of God.

There is a long-standing Catholic tradition, not only in our churches but also in Catholic homes, schools, and institutions, of hanging a crucifix on the wall. On the cross we see the body of Christ in the moment of his death, and we also see our salvation. His outstretched arms are a powerful, visible, and clear sign of the depth and breadth of God's mercy. Every time we pass by a crucifix, we are reminded that God's love is at work in our lives—not as an abstraction, but every bit as real as the presence of the crucifix.

In the second part of *Dives in Misericordia*, the pope calls our attention to the messianic nature of Christ and his saving action among us:

Christ, then, reveals God who is Father, who is "love," as St. John will express it in his first letter (1 John 4:16); Christ reveals God as "rich in mercy" as we read in St. Paul (Ephesians 2:4). This truth is not just the subject of a teaching; it is a reality made present to us by Christ. Making the Father present as love and mercy is, in Christ's own consciousness, the fundamental touch-stone of his mission as the Messiah." (3.4)

Jesus' coming among us had a specific goal. He was to redeem us from our sin and ransom us by his blood. The very unfolding of Jesus' messianic mission includes an outpouring of God's mercy on us.

The much beloved American spiritual "Were You There When They Crucified My Lord?" captures something of the longing to be present to God and know that God is truly present to us. That is what the sacraments are all about; that is the essence of the power of a sacrament. In the visible, audible, or tangible sacramental sign, God's Spirit is at work, not only showing us or symbolizing what is happening, but actually effecting and making the reality come to be. We do not just hold on to a nostalgic longing to have Christ and his saving death present in our lives; we have the sacramental action reassuring us that Christ is truly at work with us here and now.

The Church is able to profess belief in the sacramental forgiveness of sins while being fully aware that only God forgives sins. Our proclamation of faith states that Jesus, through his death, washed away all sin, and after his resurrection, gave to the Church the power and authority to apply to us the redemption he won on the cross—that is, God's forgiveness of our sins.

The Old Testament Experience

In part three, our attention is turned to the Old Testament and the concept of God's mercy in the covenant with the Hebrew people. Perhaps nowhere are the fidelity, generosity, and patient nature of God's love more visible than in the story of God's effort to win over and hold the allegiance of his chosen people. No sooner has God led the Israelites out of Egypt through the power of his strong arm and mighty works than they fall into idol worship. No sooner has God formed them into a people and turned over to them a land flowing with milk and honey—a land they had not planted or cultivated—than they abandon him in the pursuit of other gods. No sooner has God offered to be their king and to speak to them through the voice of the judges than they clamor for a king just like all the other nations.

The eighth chapter of the First Book of Samuel is a recounting of the establishment of the monarchy in Israel. From the time of their entrance into the promised land until that moment in the First Book of Samuel, God had led his people and guided them through his chosen agents, called judges. But in chapter eight, we read how the people wished to become like all the other people around them. They wished to look like other nations, be structured like other nations, and therefore have a king just as everyone else did. The clamor of the people for a king is echoed sometimes in our own culture, when political correctness and the desire to be in conformity with society often supplant the moral obligation found in the commandments of God. Sentiment becomes the new touchstone, and truth takes second place.

There is poignancy in God's response to the people of Israel in granting their wish to have a king. He says to Samuel, "Grant the people's every request. It is not you they reject, they are rejecting me as their king" (1 Samuel 8:7).

The people ask for a king, and God gives them one. The history of the kingdoms of Judea and Israel is marred with recurring incidents of betrayal, denial, infidelity, and failure. Only God stands firm in his allegiance and faithfulness. I could not help but think of our mottos, "In God We Trust" and "One Nation under God"—and yet how shy we are today to recognize our historic rootedness in God. A recent front-page news story related how one school district, by an overwhelming majority, voted to remove from all the classrooms a placard showing the American flag over which is superimposed "In God We Trust." The reason, according to the news report, was the fear of offending someone who may not believe in God. In the same vein, I read about a Catholic university that was hesitant to have a crucifix in each classroom lest it offend the sensitivity of those who are not Christian.

In concluding this section, John Paul reminds us: "Connected with the mystery of creation is the mystery of the election. . . . That mystery of election refers to every man and woman, to the whole great human family. 'I have loved you with an everlasting love, therefore I have continued my faithfulness to you' (Jeremiah 31:3)" (4.12). The reason we know that the mercy of God is so readily available to us is because God has chosen us. We are those whom God has brought "out of darkness into his wonderful light" (1 Peter 2:9). As Peter asserts in his first letter, the whole Church is to be "a royal priesthood, a holy nation, a people of his own" (2:9).

We must never lose the perspective that John Paul refers to as "a perspective both temporal and eschatological." We have been called and continue to be called by God each day to live out, here and now, the plan for us that will reach fulfillment in heaven. Because God wants us to achieve the goal, he makes available to us his mercy and forgiveness at every turn in the road. We are never abandoned, never left to ourselves, no matter how long we have gone down the wrong path and in the wrong direction.

The Prodigal Son

This brings us to chapter four and the beautiful reflection on the parable of the prodigal son. Perhaps no story in the New Testament from the lips of Jesus is more beloved than the parable of the son described as the "prodigal" who squanders his portion of the inheritance and then returns to beg, but who ends up receiving the warm and full-hearted embrace of his father's mercy. In his reflection the pope reminds us that what took place in the relationship between the father and the son in Christ's parable is not to be evaluated "from the outside." We need to look at our relationship with God in the context of our graced bond with him as one of his adopted children.

How faithful the father in the parable must have been! The story says that as the prodigal son came near, the father "caught sight of him, and was filled with compassion. He ran to his son, embraced him and kissed him" (Luke 15:20). Obviously, the father was waiting. We can envision the rise of the hill with the loving father pining for the return of his son—even this prodigal son. This is the image the encyclical holds out for us. The father is waiting patiently, lovingly, forgivingly. All we have to do is turn to him, and he will rush to embrace us.

Dives in Misericordia paints a beautiful picture of God's mercy. First of all, the God who created us in love brought us into being so that we could one day be with him forever. Planted deep in the recesses of our hearts and emblazoned on our human nature are the marks of our sublime destiny. Thanks to the gift of our human intellect, we are capable of understanding the yearnings of the human heart and our natural orientation toward God. This we have come to name the "natural moral law." None of this is extraneous to who we are. By our very creation, we have an intrinsic relationship to God. He is our Creator, we are his creatures.

In the very beginning of creation, God set within the works of his hand a law that would govern creation. The natural physical law expressed in something as simple as the law of gravity or the law of physics is built into creation. So it is with the natural moral law. We as human beings are rational and capable of understanding God's plan for us and how we ought to act. Since the natural moral law exists within our human nature, and since all of us share that nature, the moral law applies to everyone. It is the common primeval norm that calls us to allegiance.

Adopted Sons and Daughters

But the story does not end there. Our relationship with God was to be raised to a whole new level in Jesus. The pope points out in chapter four that our relationship with God must be evaluated at the highest possible level of intimacy with God—as adopted sons and daughters. St. Paul, writing to the Romans in chapter eight and to the Galatians in chapter four, reminds us, as does the Holy Father in *Dives in Misericordia*, that our relationship with God the Father is radically altered because we have received the gift of the Holy Spirit.

What identifies us as Christians is the joyful awareness that we can pray with childlike confidence and tender intimacy to a loving father, to "Abba." Just as the prodigal returned to his father aware that there was an intimate bond of father and son even if he had abused his father's love, so each one of us is urged to return to the loving embrace of our Father because of the intimate bond of adopted sonship that is ours, even if we have abused it. No wonder this encyclical is entitled *Dives in Misericordia*, since that is what our Father is. Boundless in forgiveness, he works his ways among us with loving kindness.

But where do we find the fullest possible revelation of God's mercy? How is it manifested to us? These questions bring us to the chapter entitled "The Paschal Mystery." Here we are reminded that the true depth of God's mercy is revealed in the cross and the resurrection: "The Paschal Mystery is the culmination of this revealing and effecting of mercy, which is able to justify man, to restore justice in the sense of that salvific order which God willed from the beginning in man and, through man, in the world" (7.4).

In the final commendation at a funeral Mass, the celebrant tells us that "the love of Christ, which conquers all things, destroys even death itself" (Funeral Liturgy). Before the power of sin and death, we can sometimes feel helpless. Evil seems so often to triumph, and certainly death awaits each of us. How can we hope to restore what is lost in our own spiritual life through our personal sin; and how, even more, can we hope to restore the right balance in our communal and societal life in a world wounded by sin and its consequences? Where do we turn for the possibility of healing? Is it "tilting at windmills" to dream of a world of justice and peace and to work for a truly good and just society?

The cross of Christ calls us to a realism that recognizes our own weakness but also our capacity to accomplish something unthinkable and wondrous—the kingdom of God. John Paul writes, "The cross of Christ on Calvary is also a witness to the strength of evil against the very Son of God, against the one who, alone among all the sons of men, was by his nature absolutely innocent and free from sin, and whose coming into the world was untainted by the disobedience of Adam and the inheritance of original sin" (8.1).

Yet it is precisely in this cross, which appears to triumph over Christ, that the ultimate victory of God over the power of darkness appears. On September 14 we celebrate the Feast of the Triumph or Exaltation of the Holy Cross. The beautiful Christian hymn "Lift High the Cross" is a testimony to the victory of Christ's death and resurrection over sin and failure. Precisely through this action that we call "the paschal mystery," you and I—and every Christian baptized into the death and resurrection of Christ—have the hope of forgiveness and ultimate victory.

It is Jesus who invites us to reconciliation with God. It is Christ the Good Shepherd who offers us forgiveness and the power to turn away from sin. In writing to the Corinthians, St. Paul reminds us that just as sin came into the world through Adam and Eve, so too grace and a new creation come to us through Jesus Christ. Just as in Adam all people die, so in Christ all shall be brought to life—a new life in grace (cf. 1 Corinthians 15).

The Sacrament of Reconciliation

In establishing his Church, Christ passed on to her the power to forgive sins. Just as he forgave sins, so would those chosen by him to be his apostles have the extraordinary power to forgive sins. In the priesthood today, the visible, external sign of Christ's mercy and forgiveness is exercised in the Sacrament of Penance, also called the Sacrament of Reconciliation or confession.

It is the faith of the Church that in baptism all our sins are forgiven. In this sacramental action, we are buried into the death of Christ and rise with him to new life. Yet the mercy of God is not exhausted in this one action. Our personal lives bear testimony to the countless failings that mar our relationship with God. Though we cannot be rebaptized, we do have access to the same loving mercy of God, who is prepared to wash away all of our personal failures.

How is this possible? The answer to the question "How does God's mercy continue in the world today?" brings us to chapter seven, where we encounter the mystery of God's mercy alive in his Church today. The Sacrament of Reconciliation is the story of God's love that is always available to us. It endures even our own selfishness and limitations. Like the father in the parable of the prodigal son, God waits, watches, and hopes for our return, even when we continually walk away. Like the son in the parable, all we need to do to return to our Father is to recognize our failings, our faults, our sins, and above all else, God's love.

The lesson of the parable of the prodigal son is twofold: God's immense and never-failing mercy and the son's contrition and humility. Without his turning back to the father, he would never have experienced the father's loving embrace.

Jesus continues to call us to holiness and to his ever-present loving forgiveness. He offers us reconciliation. But we need to ask for it. The saving, healing, and restoring action that takes place in the Sacrament of Reconciliation is available to each of us, but we need to ask for the mercy of God and open our hearts before we can receive it.

To understand the fullness of God's mercy, its availability to us today, and the importance of the Sacrament of Reconciliation, we need to understand clearly the extent of Jesus' saving action. I believe that is why the Holy Father devoted so much time in the encyclical *Dives in Misericordia* to highlighting God's mercy at work in us.

Christ's Atonement for Our Sin

The man Jesus Christ, who is also God's true Son, is the only one who could offer the Father a fitting atonement for sin. Here we see the immensity of God's saving mercy. Not only does God save us, but God brings about salvation in a generous way, in a manner that honors the humanity it saves. In Christ, God allows a human being to bring gifts worthy of salvation. St. Paul puts it this way: "For if by that one person's transgression the many died, how much more did the grace of God and the gracious gift of the one person Jesus Christ overflow for the many" (Romans 5:15).

Jesus became the new Passover. He is the unique and final sacrifice by which God's saving plan was accomplished and by which we were saved from sin and damnation. In God's holy plan, it was determined that the word of God made flesh in Jesus would be the one great expiatory sacrifice that would take away the sins of the world. We continue at the celebration of every Eucharist to proclaim, before we receive the body and blood of Christ in Communion, that this is "the Lamb of God who takes away the sins of the world."

It is in this recognition—this act of faith—that we find our forgiveness. Because Jesus willed that in the Eucharist and in the other sacraments, his saving work would continue throughout history, we can avail ourselves of God's forgiveness. Just as God sent Jesus, and Jesus sent his apostles, so the saving mystery of the forgiveness of our sins continues because the Church continues to exercise the forgiveness of God as God has ordained.

The mystery of God's mercy includes the Sacrament of Penance. Here Christ continues to be available. It is in the person of Christ that the priest hears the confession of guilt. Such a confession is made with the full expectation of mercy, compassion, and ultimately, absolution.

As we approach the confessional, which is a foreshadowing of the judgment seat of God, we do so aware of our own failings yet fully expecting the mercy of God. God does not fail us. The priest speaks the judgment of the Savior's mercy as he invokes the power of Jesus: "I absolve you from your sins in the name of the Father and of the Son and of the Holy Spirit."

Since the Sacrament of Reconciliation restores us to our baptismal innocence, theologians sometimes speak of it as our "second conversion." Obviously, our first conversion was in baptism and is not repeated. However, thanks to the mercy of God, reconciliation can be repeated over and over, even "seventy times seven." If this were not the case, few of us would stand much chance of being saved.

St. Ambrose, the fourth-century bishop of Milan and teacher of St. Augustine, reflected once on these two "conversions," pointing out that in the Church, "there are water and tears, the water of baptism and the tears of repentance." Other Church fathers have spoken about the Sacrament of Penance as a "laborious kind of baptism"—the idea being that in baptism, all sin is washed away, and we are restored to new life, while in the Sacrament of Reconciliation, we strive once again to restore that pristine baptismal state. In its discussion on reconciliation, the Council of Trent (1545–1563), which devoted great energy to clarifying how the mercy of God is applied to us in the sacramental economy, cites St. Gregory of Nazianzen and St. John of Damascus and asserts that penance is a sacrament distinct from baptism. It can be called a kind of baptism because it restores baptismal holiness, but it is referred to as laborious because it cannot do this "without many tears and labors on our part."

The Need for Regular Confession

As we reflect on the mercy of God and as it is presented in the pope's encyclical *Dives in Misericordia*, we need to speak about how you and I approach the Sacrament of Penance. This wondrously generous gift of mercy is available to each and every Catholic. All we need to do is go to confession and ask for God's forgiveness. What more honest and yet humble step can a person take, then, but to kneel down for God's forgiveness in this sacrament of his mercy? The practice of our faith should include regular sacramental confession.

A Catholic who has committed a grave sin is obliged to ask for forgiveness for it in this sacrament. Once we do, and we receive sacramental absolution, we are restored again to holiness—to an innocence before God. So powerful is the grace of this sacrament that the Rite of Penance tells us: "Frequent and careful celebration of this sacrament is also very useful as a remedy for venial sins. This is not a mere ritual repetition or a psychological exercise, but a serious striving to perfect the grace of baptism so that, as we bear in our body the death of Jesus Christ, his life may be seen in us ever more clearly" (Introduction, 7b).

The Church has long identified four aspects of the Sacrament of Penance: contrition, confession, absolution, and satisfaction (some act of penance). The Rite of Penance states:

The follower of Christ who has sinned but who has been moved by the Holy Spirit to come to the Sacrament of Penance should above all be converted to God with his whole heart. This inner conversion of the heart embraces sorrow for sin and the intent to lead a new life. It is expressed through confession made to the Church, due satisfaction, and amendment of life. God grants pardon for sin through the Church, which works by the ministry of priests. (Introduction, 6)

Once we have sorrow for our sins, we are obliged to confess them to the priest who stands in the person of Christ and his Church. At the judgment of the priest, we receive absolution and the imposition of a penance by way of satisfaction. These familiar steps are the elements of the Sacrament of Reconciliation. At the very heart of the sacrament are the confession of our sins and the absolution of the priest.

Reconciliation with Others

As Pope John Paul II concludes *Dives in Misericordia*, he writes that the love of God involves the love of people. It is God's love for us that is the example and driving force of what our love for others should be. It is clear that John Paul here is appealing to the world—even to those who do not accept our belief in Christ and the infinite mercy of God—that the proclamation of God's mercy is essential and is truly dictated "by love for man, for all that is human and which, according to the intuitions of many of our contemporaries, is threatened by an immense danger" (15.5).

Pope John Paul has once again returned to a theme that permeates all of his writings: Christ truly is the redeemer of mankind. His way is the way that brings reconciliation, peace, and unity among peoples. To dismiss any aspect of God's revelation is to move forward in peril because we will miss a significant portion of the true vision of human life's worth, purpose, and goal. In concluding, the pope reminds us that "the reason for [the Church's] existence is, in fact, to reveal God, that Father who allows us to 'see' him in Christ" (15.7).

Our world, which at times can seem so harsh, unforgiving, and unrelenting, can be greatly served by the realization that just as God is rich in mercy, and just as that mercy and forgiveness are available to all of us, so should each of us be open to one another with the same consideration and loving forgiveness.

What a world we could bring about if such a vision, rooted in God's revelation and proclaimed by St. John Paul II in *Dives in Misericordia*, were accepted as the starting point for how we deal with one another in our families, in our communities, in our nation, and in the world at large. Nothing less than this is the message of the pope's second encyclical letter, *Dives in Misericordia*.

Chapter 4

A "Gospel" of Work

Laborem Exercens

ENGLISH TITLE: **On Human Work**
DATE ISSUED: **September 14, 1981**
TYPE OF DOCUMENT: **Encyclical Letter**

C atholic social teaching has played a significant role in the development of much public policy and legislation that affect how we work and live. For over a hundred years, the teaching of the Catholic Church on work and the dignity of workers has provided the backdrop, or social context, for much of what has emerged and for what we now take for granted in our public policy.

To contrast the condition of workers at the end of the nineteenth century with conditions today is to see great and vivid differences. Given what we now experience, it is hard to remember—even though it is very important to do so—that there was a time in the history of our country when workers were treated little better than chattel and were considered far more expendable than horses and mules. Images of children working in factories or in mills and mines—uneducated, uncared for, and lacking access to health care—are a real part of any collage that would depict the 1800s and early 1900s in the United States. The same depiction of those times is true around the world.

Catholic social teaching has traditionally marked as a milestone the publication of the encyclical letter *Rerum Novarum* in 1891 by Pope Leo XIII. This was the first focused and concentrated articulation of the Church's understanding of the dignity of workers and their rights. It also provided a rationale for explaining the worth of labor itself—although this was not completely new. Over many centuries, commentators on the Book of Genesis have talked about the importance of human work and its place in God's plan.

The Impact of Pope Leo XIII's *Rerum Novarum*

Early Church fathers saw in the Book of Genesis a relationship between the creative power of God and the ability of human beings to produce, through human skill and work, all kinds of goods that benefit the human race. The reason *Rerum Novarum* is highlighted so regularly is because it was the beginning of a long series of papal encyclicals and statements developing the constant theme that work is an integral part of the human experience and that workers have an innate dignity.

Not everyone praised Pope Leo XIII's first social encyclical. Many found it an intrusion of the Church into the marketplace. Some commentators of that era called upon the pope and bishops to stay inside the sanctuary and leave the marketplace to them. Their cry was "separation of church and workplace." Economics, we were told, were predetermined by laws and forces about which the Church knew little and should say even less.

We must also remember that this was the time of a freewheeling capitalism that had a theological justification rooted in the teaching of many reformed churches. A "counter-theology," contrary to Catholic teaching, proclaimed that wealth was a sign of divine predilection and that the condition of many workers was predestined in God's plan. This vision of two classes of human beings created by God—one to serve the other—was articulated with great gusto from many non-Catholic pulpits across our land. This theological justification for the exploitation of brother and sister human beings was a strong force in the molding of laws and the creation of much public policy. This was so precisely because the authentic teaching coming out of Catholic inspiration was not yet well articulated.

The origin of the Knights of Columbus is rooted in the social and economic conditions that motivated Pope Leo XIII to write *Rerum Novarum*. Fr. Michael J. McGivney, serving at St. Mary's Church in New Haven, Connecticut, was aware of the many hardships and dangers that Catholics faced in his day, and this inspired him to establish a fraternal fellowship to support its members and their families. At the time, no other type of social security or assistance was available. A huge international fraternal order developed to serve the needs of struggling Catholic families whose breadwinners often died relatively young and in tragic circumstances because of harsh working conditions. The nation's political system had yet to evolve a sense of social consciousness and political conviction to address the needs of women and children widowed and orphaned. In fact, Fr. McGivney died a year before *Rerum Novarum* was issued. Yet his vision grew out of the same matrix of concern and social awareness.

For many historians and scholars of the late nineteenth and early twentieth centuries, the upheaval that eventually led to improved conditions for the working class—of which so many of our parents and grandparents were a part—was as much a theological and philosophical struggle as it was an economic and political one. The gradual triumph of Catholic social teaching over the theology of economic predestination was no small part of the background of the victory of legislation guaranteeing decent working conditions, living wages, tolerable working hours, and the banning of the exploitation of young people.

Remembering the Past

We can begin to see something of the success of Catholic social teaching in creating a more just society when we look back at the conditions that surrounded and permeated the lives of the working class. We may be tempted today to ask how it was possible to justify such squalid and miserable living and working conditions. How could one turn a blind eye to child labor and to twelve-hour working days? For those who controlled the levers of power and who also benefited from these conditions, justification was as close at hand as the opinion makers of the day and the pulpits that sought the soothing balm of "predestination" as an explanation for the glaring social injustices of the time.

The same is true today; we have merely changed the words. The atrocity of abortion on demand and its consequences hides behind the theoretical justification of "freedom of choice." A few hundred years earlier, forcing human beings into bondage as slaves was justified under the claim of economic choice. While it may be hard to believe that adult human beings were shackled and beaten simply to extend the economic advantage of their "masters," so it should be equally difficult for us today to comprehend that this was done under the banner of "choice." The politicians who guided the nation then and the judges who ruled on the meaning of its laws had little difficulty arriving at what they considered a reasonable political compromise that protected the "economic rights" of slave holders with the "differing commercial interests" of non-slave states.

Today we look back aghast that the cultural climate permitted the exploitation of workers or the slavery of peoples. I suspect that someday future generations will look back at our age equally appalled that under the banner of "choice," we justifed incredibly evil acts. When we look at the Church's social teaching and the papal encyclicals in which it is articulated, we can take great comfort in the leadership that the Church has provided and also draw courage to support that same teaching office as it confronts equally grave injustices today.

The History of the Church's Social Teachings

Pope John Paul II's *Laborem Exercens* (On Human Work), published on September 14, 1981, the Feast of the Exaltation of the Holy Cross, is one more in a line of teaching documents over decades intended to more deeply penetrate the mystery of human work and its value and the dignity of those who labor. Before Pope John Paul II, Pius XI had written a letter on the fortieth anniversary of *Rerum Novarum* entitled *Quadraegesimo Anno*—logically enough, "The Fortieth Year." Extending the vision of *Rerum Novarum,* Pope Pius XI held up the principles of individual worth, value, and dignity as well as the right of people to come together collectively to defend their rights and bargain for their vindication.

In 1961 Pope John XXIII published his encyclical *Mater et Magistra.* Some in the political and economic world rejected the wisdom of John XXIII on the grounds that the Church, when it entered into the world of labor, economics, business, and the social order, was a better mother than teacher. The years had passed since *Rerum Novarum,* but the oppositional refrain was pretty much the same: "separation of church and economics" or "separation of social and moral teaching from business."

Pope Paul VI, on the eightieth anniversary of *Rerum Novarum,* published the encyclical *Octogesima Adveniens,* which renewed and extended the Church's ongoing analysis of the dignity of the human person, the value and quality of work, and the relationship of both to the social, economic, and political orders.

In this book, in addition to a reflection on *Laborem Exercens,* we will also encounter Pope John Paul II's social encyclical *Sollicitudo Rei Socialis,* published February 19, 1988, and *Centesimus Annus,* issued on May 1, 1991, on the hundredth anniversary of Leo XIII's *Rerum Novarum.* A tradition has grown up over the past century of commemorating anniversaries of significant social encyclicals with a new one extending the teaching and applying it to new situations. Thus the body of Catholic social teaching continues to grow and be ever more fruitful.

One Sows, Another Waters

If we were to use the image of the planter and the garden, then Pope Leo XIII was the one who planted the seed. His encyclical was a groundbreaker. Successive popes tilled the soil, watered, pruned, and cared for the growth of Catholic social teaching until in our own day, we have that fully grown tree in whose branches so many have found comfort, support, and guidance.

When we turn our attention to *Laborem Exercens*, we find the encyclical divided into five chapters. In part one, which serves as an introduction, John Paul explains why he wrote this letter and speaks about the organic development of the Church's social action and teaching, thus placing *Rerum Novarum* in a wider ecclesial and magisterial context.

In part two, the pope turns to the Book of Genesis and develops an understanding of the meaning of work by drawing on biblical teachings, describing what it means to address work in "the subjective sense"—that is, placing man at the center as the subject of work. Many readers will recall that the pope had previously directed his attention to the Book of Genesis in a whole series of Wednesday audience talks that developed and analyzed the biblical account of creation, touching upon, among other things, the subjective definition of man and the dignity of the human person. Echoes of the 1979 and 1980 catecheses on the Book of Genesis reverberate throughout *Laborem Exercens*.

Part three addresses the conflict between labor and capital in the present moment of history. John Paul shows himself to be intimately aware of the philosophical foundations of much of the current attitudes toward labor. As a master teacher, the pope takes the wisdom of God's revelation and casts the current conflict in a new light. He brings fresh direction and meaning to the tensions and dynamics of the struggle—to the dialectic, if you will—but this time viewed under the guidance of God's word.

The rights of workers and the implications of those rights in so much of our modern culture form the content of part four. The question of employment takes on significance in this chapter. The pope discusses work as the way in which individuals participate in the equitable distribution of the goods of the earth. Here he underscores the need for "rational planning and the proper organization of human labor in keeping with individual societies and states" in order to discover "the right proportions between the different kinds of employment: work on the land, in industry, in the various services, white collar work and scientific or artistic work, in accordance with the capacities of individuals and for the common good of each society and of the whole of mankind" (18.5). Each area of human need is satisfied through the efforts of those whose energy and talent produce some product or service. In return, a person shares in the goods necessary for a full life. Work is the means or key to access this pattern of human development.

The encyclical concludes with part five, which speaks of the "elements for a spirituality of work." In this section the pope returns to the theme of the integral nature of work as a part of God's creative plan rather than as something extraneous and incidental to it. Particularly enlightening is the reflection on human work in the light of the cross and the resurrection of Christ:

The Christian finds in human work a small part of the cross of Christ and accepts it in the same spirit of redemption in which Christ accepted his cross for us. In work, thanks to the light that penetrates us from the resurrection of Christ, we always find a glimmer of new life, of the new good, as if it were an announcement of "the new heavens and the new earth" in which man and the world participate precisely through the toil that goes with work. (27.5)

The Church, by its very nature, is the continuing presence of Christ in the world. Her message is always spiritual and pastoral. Yet the voice that proclaims Jesus' gospel must do so in a way that touches us where we live and act. The call to conversion to God's way will always bring the teaching office of the Church into an encounter with the lived realities of the human condition. For some, this is not popular and engenders criticism. Nonetheless, such action is necessary if the Church is to be true to her mission. Pope John Paul II fruitfully moves forward the role of Catholic social teaching in the "marketplace" in *Laborem Exercens*.

A Natural Moral Order

Laborem Exercens is addressed not only to the Catholic faithful but also "to all men and women of good will." When the Church turns its attention to the moral order—and social justice is a part of the moral order—it does so with the conviction that it speaks not only about revealed truth but also out of the human experience. What the Church has to say on the natural moral order, and therefore on the right ordering of people among themselves and as a community, is rooted in human nature.

Thomas Jefferson once wrote of "the laws of nature and nature's God." This was in justification for the acts that led to our independence as a nation. But the reference point is the same: the recognition that there is such a thing as human nature and that from it follows a natural moral order that we are all obliged to recognize, accept, and follow.

In the past, when we have read of The Hague tribunal's efforts to prosecute people—even heads of state—for crimes against humanity, we recognize that there are boundaries for human action and that an awareness of those boundaries is built into human nature. Classical philosophy and theology speak of the *jus gentium* ("law of nations"). This is the recognition that a law of nations—a law built into the hearts of all people—is recognized everywhere. In addressing this social encyclical to the Church and to the wider community, the pope asserts that he is acting as a spokesperson not only for the revealed word of God but also for the natural moral law—the work and gift of God the Creator.

The God of creation is the God of revelation. Thus the truth of the created moral order is as much the responsibility of the teaching office of the Church as is the truth revealed directly by God in his intervention in human history. The *Catechism of the Catholic Church* speaks of the Decalogue (the Ten Commandments) containing "a privileged expression of the natural law." It quotes St. Irenaeus: "From the beginning, God had implanted in the heart of man the precepts of the natural law. Then he was content to remind him of them. This was the Decalogue" (CCC, 2070).

One of the reasons that the Church has not been hesitant to enter into the social, economic, and political orders in matters of human life and dignity is because the Church has been charged by her divine Founder to address matters of faith and morals. The foundation for the moral order is God's creative action; human beings are created in the image and likeness of God and called to form a good and just human society in which each person can achieve the fullness of his or her potential.

A part of this vision is the realization that the goods of the earth are created for everyone's use. No one person or group of people has a hegemony on what God has created. The resources of this world are entrusted to all for the benefit of all. Thus the Church can speak of the common stewardship that is the responsibility of every person.

For example, in defending the right of private property, the Church argues that all are entitled to goods sufficient to be able to carry out

God's will for them. We can lay claim to what we work for and what is thus ours. But the Church's social justice teaching has always insisted that property does not take precedence over human life and worth. Rather, the goods of this earth are seen as a means to a much larger end than the mere acquisition of wealth. Material things are meant to advance human dignity, not degrade it.

The essential outline of social justice teaching has emerged over the decades since the first social encyclical, *Rerum Novarum*, with the basic foundation of the Church's teaching being respect for persons— individual human beings and their God-given dignity. It includes the recognition of human solidarity and our obligation one to another because we all share a common destiny and should be able, through our human work, to access our fair share of the goods of the earth. The social doctrine of the Church also calls us to respect the goods of others so that "to each his own" becomes an operative principle, but always within the context of the common human enterprise and human solidarity.

Man and Work

Having addressed the organic development of the Church's social action and teaching in part one of *Laborem Exercens*, John Paul turns to the relationship of "man" and work. Obviously, through-out the text, the pope uses the word "man" in the inclusive sense of all members of the human race, male and female. In quoting from this encyclical letter and from other papal documents, I use the term in the same collective sense.

It has been pointed out more than once that Pope John Paul II brought his own specific philosophical and theological expertise to the transmission of the Church's teaching. Nowhere is this more evident than in *Laborem Exercens*. In part two, where the pope describes work, he invites us to look at it under two dimensions:

in the objective sense, as technology, and in the subjective sense, as man, the subject of work. In other words, work is not just something we produce; it is also an expression of who we are. "Man has to subdue the earth and dominate it, because as the 'image of God' he is a person, that is to say, a subjective being capable of acting in a planned and rational way, capable of deciding about himself, and with a tendency to self-realization. As a person, man is therefore the subject of work" (6.2).

When we speak of man being made in the image and likeness of God, we sometimes tend to confine our reflection to the analysis of the component parts of human nature—intellect and free will. Thus it is often said that we are made in the image and likeness of God because we can think and love. We have intellect and a will, just as God has and is intellect and love.

But there is more to our mirroring God. Our capacity to work is a reflection of the creative power of God. True, ours is much more limited. But on a scale of finite to infinite, what we do that transforms this world and brings forth what we need to grow, develop, and flourish reflects the action of God that brought forth all that is. Thus we can say that labor is not just production but an action expressive of our very humanity.

This certainly casts a richer light on "earning our daily bread by the sweat of our brow" (cf. Genesis 3:19). As we approach our work, whatever it may be, we can now define it in new terms. All human labor, remunerated or not—the household variety of a wife or mother, or the structured version of a fixed salary or pay by the hour—takes on fuller meaning. According to John Paul, work is not just tasks to be completed but a very expression of our ability to bring into being what was not yet fully realized:

Through this conclusion one rightly comes to recognize the preeminence of the subjective meaning of work over the objective one. Given this way of understanding things, and presupposing that different sorts of work that people do can have greater or lesser objective value, let us try nevertheless to show that each sort [of work] is judged above all by the measure of the dignity of the subject of work, that is to say the person, the individual who carries it out. (6.6)

Solidarity and Workers' Rights

One of the words that emerged over and over again in the writings of John Paul's pontificate is "solidarity." In one sense, solidarity as a virtue is the practical manifestation of unity and communion. On the ecclesiastical level, solidarity reflects our most profound communion in Christ; it initiates our unity and is manifested practically and pastorally when we work together to create ministries. In the temporal order, and particularly in the area of human work, solidarity is reflected in the coming together of workers who react "against the degradation of man as the subject of work, and against the unheard-of accompanying exploitation in the field of wages, working conditions, and social security for the worker" (8.2). Today the word "solidarity" is identified with workers' rights to come together, to organize and to speak collectively against injustices, and at the same time, to further enhance the dignity of human work and the worker.

Chapter four, "The Rights of Workers," begins with the recognition that work is a source of rights on the part of the worker. But this right, John Paul notes, must be examined "in the broad context of human rights as a whole, which are connatural with man, and many of which are proclaimed by various international organizations and increasingly guaranteed by the individual States for their citizens" (16.1).

Rights do not exist in a vacuum. Too often we experience the isolation of individual rights to such an extent that an individual's civil right or legal right takes precedence over a God-given right. While slavery may have been legal in our country a hundred and fifty years ago, it was not moral. It was a legal, civil right divorced from and outside the context of basic human rights. The pro-life effort in our country constantly reminds us that not everything that is legal is moral and that we need to find the proper moral context against which to evaluate legal "rights."

In our complex society today, in which we are increasingly interdependent, each segment of society needs to look to the other and to have a meaningful dialogue with one another to consider what is at the service of the common good—of all of society. Yet even this parameter must be contextualized by the more important norm of our God-given rights rooted in our dignity as human beings.

The Spirituality of Work

Laborem Exercens is a powerful, thought-provoking encyclical. Not only does John Paul present a masterful teaching on the dignity of the worker, the priority of labor, workers' rights, and the spirituality of work, but he does so in a way that elevates the entire discussion to a spiritual level. We are a graced people. Christ is the redeemer of humankind. We are not simply carrying out activities aimlessly as we make our way through life.

The concluding chapter of *Laborem Exercens* presents the "elements for a spirituality of work." I found particularly intriguing the section that describes the many individual professions exercised by man as recorded in the books of the Old Testament. These are listed in paragraph 26.2, together with a list of passages in Scripture where Jesus alludes to various occupations.

As he concludes the encyclical, the pope calls us to see human work in the light of the cross and the resurrection of Christ. "The final word of the Gospel on this matter, as on others, is found in the paschal mystery of Jesus Christ. It is here that we must seek an answer to these problems so important for the spirituality of human work" (27.2). Our daily work should present us with an opportunity to see how we share in the work of Christ, which reached its culmination on the cross.

The more I reflect on these words, the more it becomes apparent that this encyclical is calling each of us to see in our daily activity and in the work we do a spiritual dimension that parallels the redeeming action of Jesus as he took up his cross, carried it, and died on it for us. Nothing we do is meaningless if it is done with the love of God and motivated by Christ's grace. Our daily activity, "the sweat of our brow," takes on deeper and fuller meaning—and permanent value—when it is seen as part of Christ's effort to renew the face of the earth.

There is a plan. We are a part of that plan. Christ has redeemed us. The power of the Holy Spirit is at work in us transforming our world. Our work can be a part of the establishment of the new creation—the new heavens and the new earth. This is possible because we are a new person—new in grace, new in the gift of the Holy Spirit. It is within this vision that Pope John Paul II addresses human work and presents us with an extraordinary and life-giving vision of the dignity and value of human work and of the worth of each person in God's eternal plan.

Chapter 5
·····················

THE FAMILY AS FOUNDATION

Familiaris Consortio

ENGLISH TITLE: **The Christian Family in the Modern World**
DATE ISSUED: **November 22, 1981**
TYPE OF DOCUMENT: **Post-Synodal Apostolic Exhortation**

At the heart of every marriage is human love—a love so strong that it brings together a man and a woman who commit themselves to each other in a lifelong journey. Marital love is expressed in commitment. That is why the centerpiece of the wedding ceremony is the exchange of promises that the bride and groom make to each other. The mutual pledge to be with and for each other "for better or worse, richer or poorer, in sickness and in health until death do us part" is an expression of the permanent and irrevocable partnership—the family—that both are now establishing. While the words are one expression of their commitment, the love that radiates from the faces and the eyes of the soon-to-be husband and wife as they pronounce these promises proclaims forcefully and eloquently what marriage is all about.

This is not only the ideal that we strive day in and day out to sustain, but it is also the lived experience of generations of people all over this planet. In every culture and at all times, we have witnessed the coming together of a man and a woman in a permanent union to sustain each other in love and to bring forth new life in children. While the form of the public recognition of this commitment may vary, the reality is that marriage and family are an intrinsic part of the human condition.

As is done in so many dioceses across this land, once a year I have the privilege of presiding at the fiftieth-wedding-anniversary celebration of couples from all of the parishes of our diocesan Church. In recent years we have had as many as five hundred couples, surrounded by their children and grandchildren, who joyfully and solemnly renew their wedding promises. This event is a testimony not only to the enduring quality of human love but also to the value of commitment.

Contrasting sharply with this view of the importance of marriage and the sacred quality of commitment is a much more casual approach to marital love. The front page of a local newspaper recently featured an article relating national trends and statistics and noted how many young people have chosen to live together without being married. The mentality behind this approach to life was summed up by one young man pictured on the front page, who said, "This works just fine because if either one of us gets tired of it, we can just walk away."

Committed Love

At the heart of human commitment—certainly at the heart of marriage vows—is the realization that we do not just walk away. The power of human love brings a man and a woman together. That love needs to be nurtured and fostered so that the couple can maintain their personal commitment to each other. Only in the context of lifelong mutual self-giving do all the daily challenges and ups and downs of living together and raising a family become not only bearable but also fruitful. To start with the presumption that, at the first note of discord, one can simply "walk away" is to empty marital commitment of both its beauty and integrity.

In response to the many pressures on family life today in our world and culture, a synod of bishops was convened in 1980 under the direction of Pope John Paul II. It was the first synod at which he would preside as supreme pastor of the Church. On November 22, 1981, the Solemnity of Christ the King, the fruit of that synod was published as the post-synodal apostolic exhortation entitled *Familiaris Consortio* (The Christian Family in the Modern World). It is no surprise that much of the interest and concern of John Paul in promoting and sustaining family life is found throughout this doctrinal and pastoral presentation on the meaning of marriage and family.

At the very core of this message is the recognition that God has a plan for marriage and the family, especially the Christian family. As we look back at this exhortation from the vantage point of thirty years of experience, we soon realize that the concerns that impelled the pope to write about the family then are still very much with us today.

A brief introduction of the exhortation places the 1980 synod in continuity with the preceding synods and highlights the intention of the document to underscore the "precious value of marriage and of the family" (3.1). The body of the text is divided into four chapters. The first describes the positive and negative dimensions of contemporary family life, while the second reflects on the nature of the family as a community whose foundation is love. The third provides an in-depth analysis of the work, or tasks, of the family. The final chapter calls for the Church to develop strenuous initiatives on behalf of families, especially those that are struggling today.

Because it is the duty of the Church to proclaim the true nature of marriage and family life, she needs to be aware of the context in which that proclamation takes place today. "Since God's plan for marriage and the family touches men and women in the concreteness of their daily existence in specific social and cultural situations, the Church ought to apply herself to understanding the situations within which marriage and the family are lived today, in order to fulfill her task of serving" (4.1).

Marriage Today

The pope begins by recognizing both the positive and negative aspects of the situation in which the family finds itself today. The positive aspects are "a sign of the salvation of Christ operating in the world," while the negative aspects are "a sign of the refusal that man gives to the love of God" (6.1). He first addresses the positive aspects:

> On the one hand, in fact, there is a more lively awareness of personal freedom and greater attention to the quality of interpersonal relationships in marriage, to promoting the dignity of women, to responsible procreation, to the education of children. There is also an awareness of the need for the development of interfamily relationships, for reciprocal spiritual and material assistance, the rediscovery of the ecclesial mission proper to the family and its responsibility for the building of a more just society. (6.2)

We recognize this insight as positive direction and development in the human experience of how we relate to one another and how we see ourselves. The emphasis within our American culture on the freedom of the individual and our responsibility for the success of interpersonal relationships only enriches the understanding of what it means to be truly and fully human and what it means to say that there is a social dimension to human life.

We are not islands in the vast sea of humanity. We are created by God to relate to one another and to do so in love. To the extent that our culture emphasizes human freedom and responsibility, the dignity of the person, and the need for responsible interpersonal relationships, to that extent it supports the Church's vision of the dignity of the human person and of marriage and family life as revealed in God's word. But there is also a darker side. Here the pope reminds us:

> On the other hand, however, signs are not lacking of a disturbing degradation of some fundamental values: a mistaken theoretical and practical concept of the independence of the spouses in relation to each other; serious misconceptions regarding the relationship of authority between parents and children; the concrete difficulties that the family itself experiences in the transmission of values; the growing number of divorces; the scourge of abortion; the ever more frequent recourse to sterilization; the appearance of a truly contraceptive mentality. (6.2)

Using the motif of light and shadows, the pope calls us to appreciate the value of what we see around us when we address developments in our culture. At the same time, he challenges us not to do this blindly. We need to critically evaluate what is presented by our modern society as a development against what God calls us to be and what Jesus and his Church present to us as God's plan for human living.

It is no surprise to anyone aware of current developments in our culture that family life is undergoing a breakdown and that in the wake of its collapse, we face the unraveling of the fabric of our society at every level. The argument can be made that there have always been failed marriages and irresponsible parents. This is true. What we are witnessing in our day—what the Holy Father highlights in *Familiaris Consortio*—is that it is now the very institution of marriage and the family that is under assault.

In the past, marriage and family life were held up as the ordinary way of life and the expected manner of expression of marital love, but today, to an increasing extent, the opposite is true. Made-for-television morality and media hyping of so-called alternative lifestyles have created a backdrop against which marriage, family life, fidelity, concerned care, and formation of children are often ridiculed.

Our world today is vastly different from the world in which those who just celebrated their fiftieth wedding anniversary were married. In contrast to what we see around us, the Church presents a vision of the partnership of man and woman, the communion of marriage, the beauty of family life, and the goodness of marital commitment to love and life. We discover this vision as we turn to the second chapter of the exhortation.

Scriptural Foundations

Beginning with an exegesis of the Book of Genesis, which is reminiscent of his first prolonged series of Wednesday audience talks, John Paul reminds us that God created us in his own image and likeness, brought us into existence through love, and calls us to love. "Christian revelation recognizes two specific ways of realizing the vocation of the human person, in its entirety, to love: marriage and virginity or celibacy. Either one is, in its own proper form, an actuation of the most profound truth of man, of his being 'created in the image of God'" (11.4).

The initial plan of creation called for man and woman to come together and form a society of mutual support. "Their bond of love becomes the image and the symbol of the covenant which unites God and his people" (12.2). In God's plan, the family, which comes into being in the love and commitment of a wife and husband, is not just meant to *be* but is also called to *do*: "The family finds in the plan of God the Creator and Redeemer not only its identity, what it is, but also its mission, what it can and should do" (17.1).

The image of family life that emerges from chapter three, the role of the Christian family, is one that includes the following: personal commitment of the partners in the marriage, openness to the generation of new life if it is God's plan for the marriage, and the joyful acceptance of the responsibility and privilege of raising children and helping them to grow in wisdom, grace, and age. The pope also addresses the recognition of the rights and role of women both in the family and in society, the special role of men as husbands and fathers, the rights of children, and the elderly in the family (cf. 18.1–27.3).

Chapter three is the core of the teaching of *Familiaris Consortio*. It offers us a vision of family life sorely needed today and obviously rooted in God's created plan. Love is from God. We are called to love one another. The mutual love of a man and a woman brings them together in an act that sets in motion a dynamic responsibility for family and eventually for both the human society and the growth of the Church. Such life-giving love is intended to be permanent, faithful, fruitful, and mutually supportive.

In God's plan, the wonder of human love is raised to the level of a sacrament so that among the baptized, marriage becomes a covenant committing the man and the woman to live with one another in a bond of love whose charter was established by God. This covenant is a symbol of the undying covenant love established by Christ with his Church in the paschal mystery. It is an encounter with Christ that makes effective the graces it signifies—the graces needed to make human love enduring, faithful, and fruitful, and therefore a suitable image of the love between Christ and his Church.

The Importance of the Family

The pope concludes *Familiaris Consortio* with this now well-known and oft-repeated statement: "The future of humanity passes by way of the family." This is a particularly powerful statement that is self-evident once we reflect on it. Into the family are born those who constitute the next generation. Thus it has been from the beginning, and so it shall be throughout human history. What is passed on is the heritage of each successive generation. If we are successful in teaching the faith, forming character, and nurturing virtue, then the culture and society that we create will be all the better. To the extent that we fail, so shall it be reflected in our culture.

It is not an exaggeration to say that the future of humanity passes by way of the family. Each individual believer today has within his or her power the ability to model what true family life really is and to advocate it for the good of the nation. *Familiaris Consortio*, then and now, is essentially an encouraging call to reflect upon and reaffirm marriage and family life and to defend it at all times. In doing so, we guarantee the strength and richness of marriage and family for ourselves, our nation, our society—and most important, for our children and their children.

Chapter 6

SIN AND FORGIVENESS

Reconciliatio et Paenitentia

ENGLISH TITLE: **Reconciliation and Penance**
DATE ISSUED: **December 2, 1984**
TYPE OF DOCUMENT: **Post-Synodal Apostolic Exhortation**

Things do not always work out the way we wish they would. Only in children's stories does everyone "live happily ever after." In the moral order, in our relationship with God and our neighbor, we often fail. "Sin" is the name we give to such failures.

Human history is marked by deep suffering and grief. Much of sacred Scripture is a record of human sorrow, failure, and sin. Though the books of the Bible recall the infinite mercy of God, they are also starkly realistic in describing the tragedies and afflictions that are part of the human condition. In helping us to understand something of the consistency of human failure and sin, St. Paul turns to the experience of original sin (Romans 5).

The account of the fall in the Book of Genesis, in language somewhat figurative in all its details, presents the reality of the first human rebellion against God. We do not know the exact nature of the first human sin. Scripture suggests that the malice of that sin rests chiefly in its elements of pride and disobedience. For St. Paul, the contrast is between the disobedience of Adam and the obedience of Christ (Romans 5:19).

The Church has always taught that from Adam, original sin has been transmitted to every member of the human family. Not only do people tend to imitate the sinfulness that surrounds them, but each individual is born into a condition of sin and can be freed from that condition only by the merits of Jesus Christ.

The Second Vatican Council's *Gaudium et Spes* (The Pastoral Constitution on the Church in the Modern World) confirms that we are born into a sinful state:

> Examining his heart, man finds that he has inclinations toward evil too, and is engulfed by manifold ills which cannot come from his good Creator. Often refusing to acknowledge God as his beginning, man has disrupted also his proper relationship to his own ultimate goal, as well as his whole orientation toward himself, toward others, and toward all created things. Therefore, man is split within himself. (GS, 13)

It is the split we feel within us—when we fail to do the good we want and do the evil we do not want (Romans 7:19)—that cries out for reconciliation. Healing begins first with our reconciliation with God but also includes the right ordering of our relationships with others and all human creation.

At the very beginning of the post-synodal apostolic exhortation *Reconciliatio et Paenitentia*, Pope John Paul II cites Jesus' call to repent and believe in the gospel:

> To speak of reconciliation and penance is, for the men and women of our time, an invitation to rediscover, translated into their own way of speaking, the very words with which our Savior and Teacher Jesus Christ began his preaching: "Repent, and believe in the gospel" (Mark 1:15), that is to say, accept the good news of love, of adoption as children of God, and hence of brotherhood. (1.1)

If we are going to right what is wrong and heal what is wounded, if we are going to restore the correct order and right relationship with God, others, and all of creation, we need to be reconciled.

In addition to an introduction and conclusion, *Reconciliatio et Paenitentia* has three principal chapters. Part one, entitled "Conversion and Reconciliation: The Church's Task and Commitment," affirms the mission of the Church to bring about the conversion of hearts. In part two, "The Love That Is Greater Than Sin," we find a reflection on sin as the root cause of all that afflicts the relationships of individuals with one another, with God, and with all of creation. It is in this section that John Paul also discusses both the personal and social dimensions of sin. In the third and last part, "The Pastoral Ministry of Penance and Reconciliation," the document considers the ways by which the Church is to foster reconciliation. Finally, in the conclusion, the pope calls us to a unity of spirit that avoids evil and is zealous for what is right.

Our Need to Recognize Our Sin

The opening chapter begins with the story of the prodigal son. In Luke's gospel (15:11-32), we find the story of the younger of two sons who ask for and receive his portion of the inheritance and then goes off and squanders it. It is the loving, forgiving, ever-vigilant father who awaits the son and who embraces him when he recognizes his foolishness and returns. The pope sees in both the prodigal son and the elder brother who stayed at home every human being:

This prodigal son is man—every human being—bewitched by the temptation to separate himself from his father in order to lead his own independent existence; disappointed by the emptiness of the mirage which had fascinated him; alone, dishonored, exploited when he tries to build a world all for himself; sorely tried, even in the depth of his own misery, by the desire to return to communion with his father. (5.3) . . .

Man—every human being—is also this elder brother. Selfishness makes him jealous, hardens his heart, blinds him, and shuts him off from other people and from God. The loving-kindness and mercy of the father irritate and enrage him; for him the happiness of the brother who has been found again has a bitter taste. From this point of view he too needs to be converted in order to be reconciled. (6.2)

However, we cannot even begin to be reconciled if we do not know that we need forgiveness. One of the great tragedies of our modern age is the refusal to recognize the existence of sin. The pope points out that "when the conscience is weakened, the sense of God is also obscured, and as a result, with the loss of this decisive inner point of reference, the sense of sin is lost. This explains why my predecessor Pius XII one day declared, in words that have almost become proverbial, that the 'sin of the century is the loss of the sense of sin'" (18.3).

We seem intent today on justifying everything we do. The manipulation of language serves to facilitate this end. Killing is now described as "facilitating the conclusion of the biological process." Abortion is now defined as a procedure that "terminates in demise." One is reminded of the embezzler who pleaded before the judge that he was not guilty of a crime but was simply "participating in the equitable distribution of the goods of the earth in a private and personal manner."

Our age may be like every other previous age in its share of sins of passion. But our age seems to exceed previous generations in our need to sin against the light. Too many who form the opinions and guide the discussions and debates in our nation on major issues seem intent on manipulating rather than presenting the truth. For example, discussing stem-cell research, a syndicated columnist, like many of her colleagues, was quite content to brush aside all scientific data to the contrary and declare that since what "we are dealing with is not human, there can be no moral consequence" to whatever is done to an embryo.

If we use our energies to redefine reality, we delude ourselves. *Reconciliatio et Paenitentia* calls us to realize that the starting point for all reconciliation is the recognition that we have done something wrong. First comes an awareness of our failure, our sin. Then comes a sense of contrition or sorrow for what we have done. This prompts us to ask for forgiveness. Absolution is the final step in the process, but all of this dynamic is a part of true reconciliation.

Forgiveness Freely Given

The Sacrament of Penance is available to each one of us. In chapter three of this encyclical, Pope John Paul observes:

> To evoke conversion and penance in man's heart and to offer him the gift of reconciliation is the specific mission of the Church as she continues the redemptive work of her divine Founder. It is not a mission which consists merely in a few theoretical statements and the putting forward of an ethical ideal unaccompanied by the energy with which to carry it out. Rather, it seeks to express itself in precise ministerial functions, directed toward a concrete practice of penance and reconciliation. (23.1)

One would think that with all the emphasis on the difficulties of our human condition and our regular failing and falling into sin, we could easily become depressed and despondent. Yet the opposite is true. While the Church recognizes sin, it also proclaims forgiveness. The Church's pastoral ministry, admirably reflecting the richness of

God's wisdom and mercy, not only has the capacity of naming sin but also of forgiving it. There is a sense in which our approach to reality is much more wholesome because we can name sin and see it for what it is and does.

At the same time, we are not abandoned in the misery of human failure, but we receive in full abundance God's rich mercy in the Sacrament of Penance. The God who calls us to holiness makes it possible for us to attain it:

> From the revelation of the value of this ministry and the power to forgive sins, conferred by Christ on the Apostles and their successors, there developed in the Church an awareness of the sign of forgiveness, conferred through the Sacrament of Penance. It is the certainty that the Lord Jesus himself instituted and entrusted to the Church—as a gift of his goodness and loving kindness to be offered to all—a special sacrament for the forgiveness of sins committed after baptism. (30.1)

For all those who have committed mortal sin after baptism, it is necessary to receive this sacrament so that they may recover the grace and friendship of God. A worthy reception of this sacrament is "the primary way of obtaining forgiveness and the remission of serious sin committed after Baptism. . . . It would therefore be foolish, as well as presumptuous, . . . to claim to receive forgiveness while doing without the sacrament which was initiated by Christ precisely for forgiveness" (31.2).

The Sacrament of Penance is not optional in the Church. We are not free to claim that we bring our sins directly to God to be forgiven. Christ has established this means to ensure that we are not only forgiven but also know that we are forgiven. We need to hear the words. That is what absolution—and the Sacrament of Penance—is all about.

Reconciliatio et Paenitentia devotes considerable space to the description of the Sacrament of Penance and its celebration. All of this is supported by the exhortation's teaching on repentance. We cannot really expect forgiveness of our sins if we are not sorry for them. Sorrow, if it is to be true, must be interior, that is, from the heart, and not merely something we express on our lips. Our sorrow should also include repentance for all of our sins and anything that would exclude us from the friendship of God.

Our Sins Affect the Whole Community

In concluding these reflections on *Reconciliatio et Paenitentia*, I want to touch on what the document calls "social sin." "To speak of social sin means in the first place to recognize that, by virtue of human solidarity which is as mysterious and intangible as it is real and concrete, each individual's sin in some way affects others" (16.5). Just as we do not make our way through life alone but rather as part of God's family, and just as that family is affected by what we do, so too is it harmed by our failure or sin. This exhortation reminds us that some sins constitute a direct attack on one's neighbor. "They are an offense against God because they are offenses against one's neighbor. These sins are usually called social sins" (16.6).

In the Rite of Reconciliation at the beginning of the Eucharistic liturgy, we ask forgiveness for all the ways in which we have sinned in our thoughts and words and in what we have done and failed to do. Others are affected by what we say and do and by what we omit. The consequences of our actions as they touch others bring us face-to-face with the reality that we do not make our way through life alone.

To speak of social justice—our obligation to one another as part of social structures—brings us into a highly complex area of relationships and obligations. While the specific consequences of social justice are not always as clearly defined as perhaps our personal obligations in relation to individuals, nonetheless, they are real. This exhortation draws attention to this area for our examination as we look around us to see if we are truly in right relationship with God, our neighbors, and all of God's creation.

With pastoral insight, John Paul brings his exhortation *Reconciliatio et Paenitentia* to a conclusion by encouraging us to make greater use of the Sacrament of Reconciliation. He encourages not only greater availability of the sacrament but also additional catechesis about it. How often we experience that some of those at Sunday Mass are only vaguely aware of the rich gift of sacramental absolution and need to be both catechized in its fruitfulness and invited into its exercise. As I read this portion of the exhortation, I thought of the young man waiting ahead of me in line at the airport ticket counter in a major Midwestern city. At a certain point, he turned and asked if I were a Catholic priest. Satisfied with my answer, he then asked, "What is that thing we Catholics use to get rid of the excess baggage we carry around?" It was clear he was not referring to his luggage. When I responded, "Confession," he said, "Yes, that's it. How do you do that?"

Each of us can, in turn, do our part. We should encourage those we know who may have drifted away from the practice of this wonderful sacrament to consider it once again. God is merciful and loving. All we need to do is "repent and believe in the gospel" (Mark 1:15).

Chapter 7

MODELS OF EVANGELIZATION

Slavorum Apostoli

ENGLISH TITLE: **The Apostles to the Slavs**
DATE ISSUED: **June 2, 1985**
TYPE OF DOCUMENT: **Encyclical Letter**

If you stand in St. Peter's Square in Rome before the great basilica in honor of the chief of the apostles, you see two great statues, one of St. Peter and the other of St. Paul, the apostles whom the Church of Rome venerates in a special manner. In the basilica itself, the high altar and the confessional altar under it mark the burial place of St. Peter—the fisherman from Galilee whom Jesus chose to be the rock on which he would build his Church.

How quickly the center and focus of the Church moved from Jerusalem and Galilee to Rome, the center of the sprawling empire of the Caesars! In God's providence, both Peter and Paul, princes of the apostles, journeyed to the Eternal City.

We are told that the twelve apostles set out from what we now call the Holy Land to carry the faith to different parts of the world. Constantinople claims the special role of Andrew; Spain traces a tradition back to James, and the Church in India follows its lineage back to Thomas. Yet it was from Rome that the successors of Peter—the bishops of Rome who were the popes—sent forth missionaries to the entire world.

In his encyclical letter *Slavorum Apostoli* (The Apostles to the Slavs), his fourth, Pope John Paul II commemorates the evangelization of the

Slavic people by Sts. Cyril and Methodius. In this letter addressed to the whole Church, the pope singles out for our attention and veneration the two evangelizers who are credited with bringing the faith to Central and Eastern Europe and to the Slavic people. The apostles to the Slavs followed in the great tradition of going forth from the center of the Church—Rome—to ensure that the saving gospel of Jesus Christ would be proclaimed and embraced by an ever-growing number of faithful.

We are all familiar with the history of the sending forth of missionaries from Rome: Augustine to England, Boniface to Germany, Ansgar to Scandinavia, and Patrick to Ireland. The list goes on, since many groups of people and territories honor those who first brought them the Catholic faith. In Central and Eastern Europe, Cyril and Methodius are especially recognized as the ones who brought the faith to the Slavic people. The pope uses this eleven-hundredth anniversary of Methodius' death as an occasion for the whole world to honor these extraordinary evangelizers.

Preparation for the Task Ahead

In the second chapter of this encyclical letter, Pope John Paul II recalls the life of St. Methodius and that of his brother, St. Cyril. Cyril and Methodius were brothers born in Thessalonika, today a part of Greece, then a part of the Byzantine Empire. Methodius was the elder brother whose baptismal name "was probably Michael." He and his younger brother, Constantine, "who came to be better known by his religious name, Cyril," both undertook secular careers before dedicating themselves to monastic life (4.3). As John Paul points out, "The event that was to determine the whole of the rest of their lives was the request made by Prince Rastislav of Greater Moravia to the Emperor Michael III to send to his peoples 'a Bishop and teacher . . . able to explain to them the true Christian faith in their own language'" (5.1).

Early in his life, Cyril felt a call to monastic life. He entered a monastery and discovered that he was a very good student. As time went on, he became proficient in philosophy and eventually became an excellent teacher. Methodius began with a slightly different career path. First, he entered the world of politics and quickly became familiar with the political structures of his time. However, after a while, he was inspired to set aside his political career and devote his life more fully to the service of God.

Looking back, we can see the hand of God at work forming Cyril and Methodius for the task that lay ahead. Both were pious, devout men who wished to serve God. One had a monastic background, was well-grounded in philosophy, and was an accomplished teacher. The other was more versed in the ways of the world, with political and diplomatic skills. They were chosen and commissioned to undertake the task of preaching the gospel in Greater Moravia, a state then including various Slavic peoples of Central Europe at the crossroads of the mutual influences between East and West. Combining their gifts, the two brothers ventured into a whole new uncatechized world to introduce it to Christ.

At a certain point in their ministry, both Cyril and Methodius traveled to Rome to receive confirmation of their work and particularly to enjoy papal approbation of their efforts at enveloping the faith in the culture of the Slavs and making it a Christian culture. At the time that Cyril and Methodius started out for Rome, the Church still enjoyed unity. This was before there were any divisions, when the whole Church was one and the successor of Peter guided the ministry of the universal Church.

It was logical that both Cyril and Methodius would head to Rome. First of all, it was their desire to receive a blessing on what they were already accomplishing and on what they intended to do. Their vision was to bring the good news of Jesus, his salvation, his love, the grace of the sacraments, and the teaching of the Church into the world of the Slavs—into the whole world of Eastern Europe. But more than that, they hoped to see the Church well established so that their work of evangelization would continue, and future generations would be blessed by the truth of Jesus' gospel and the power of the Church's sacraments.

John Paul tells us that in Rome, Pope Hadrian II "received them very cordially" (5.3). He approved the Slavonic liturgical books, which he ordered to be solemnly placed on the altar in the Church of St. Mary Major, and recommended that Cyril and Methodius begin ordaining priests. It was during this visit to Rome that Cyril died. Methodius, now consecrated an archbishop, returned to continue his work as "Papal Legate *'ad gentes'* (for the Slav peoples)" (6.2). The rest, as we say today, is history.

Cyril was buried at the Church of St. Clement in Rome. On the walls of that church, frescoes dating back centuries show Cyril and Methodius as they are receiving a commission from the pope to carry on their ministry. That was what Methodius did. He returned to the East as a bishop and successor to the apostles, possessing the power to ordain priests and bishops, which enabled him to stabilize the fruit of the work that he and his brother had already accomplished.

Heralds of the Faith

The extraordinary work of Cyril and Methodius is described by John Paul in subsequent chapters of the encyclical. They were heralds of the faith and planted the Church of God in the hearts of the Slavic peoples. In addition, they recognized what John Paul calls the "catholic sense of the Church," a unity that exists even with great diversity—the incarnating of the gospel in the native culture of the Slavonic people. The pope closes his encyclical with a recognition of the significance and influence of the Christian millennium in the Slavic world.

Legend tells us that it was Methodius who provided the Slavonic translation of the Bible. Until this time, the Bible was available in Greek and then in the Vulgate, the Latin, thanks to the work of St. Jerome. Methodius provided a translation for all of the Slavic people. At the same time, he wrote a compilation of Byzantine ecclesiastical and civil law, putting together a framework of religious and civil laws that would guide the Slavic people as they began to develop and would enrich their lives and their culture.

Cyril and Methodius are venerated in the West and in the East as apostles to the Slavs. They were true apostles. They taught the faith and lived the faith they taught. But they also established the Church through the ordination of bishops and priests to ensure that the sacraments were administered and the gospel proclaimed. In this way the whole Slavonic culture was permeated with God's word and the presence of the Holy Spirit.

Christ's One Church

It is clear as we read the pope's encyclical that a number of points deserve to be highlighted. These include the understanding of the unity of the Church and the communion of all the particular or local churches with each other, while at the same time recognizing the unique place of the Church of Rome in sustaining and manifesting this communion.

Christ's one Church is manifested throughout the world in what we call today diocesan churches. Everything that Christ has brought to us for our transformation into the new creation is present to us in a diocesan church gathered around the bishop. The pope as successor to Peter and chief shepherd of the whole universal Church exercises a unique and particular role in the Church. Cyril and Methodius manifested this understanding of the central and determining role of Peter with their decision to "go to Rome" to have their mission, ministry, and work approved and confirmed.

This same dynamic is at work in the Church today. Each diocesan church gathered around the bishop, a successor to the apostles, makes present to the faithful the saving power of Christ's gospel and the life-giving sacraments, particularly and most especially the Eucharist. Yet for each of these churches to fully express the universal Catholic Church, each must be related in faith and charity with the successor of Peter—the bishop of Rome, the pope. While today there may be discussions on the intricacies of this relationship and how it is best implemented, nonetheless, it is the belief of the Church that Peter and his successors speak for the universal Church and confirm the authenticity of the faith and ministry of the local or particular churches.

Cyril and Methodius journeyed to Rome to have their work affirmed. They were caught up in one of the great efforts of the Church in every century—the imbuing of the culture with the gospel of Jesus.

Transforming Human Culture

Church documents today speak of "inculturation." The term indicates the successful enlivening of a culture with the imperatives of the gospel. As yeast permeates the dough and causes it to rise, so must the gospel enter into the very fabric and fiber of human culture, not to empty it of its value and uniqueness, but rather to help it rise to a whole new level of meaning and worth. John Paul put it this way:

The Church is catholic also because she is able to present in every human context the revealed truth, preserved by her intact in its divine content, in such a way as to bring it into contact with the lofty thoughts and just expectations of every individual and every people. Moreover, the entire patrimony of good which every generation transmits to posterity, together with the priceless gift of life, forms as it were an immense and many-colored collection of tesserae that together make up the living mosaic of the Pantocrator, who will manifest himself in his total splendor only at the moment of the Parousia. (18.1)

Obviously, Cyril and Methodius are patrons and models of evangelization. They are reminders to us that we are not idle bystanders in the history of God's grace at work in our world. We are called to be participants in the drama of the new creation. Some Christians, such as Cyril and Methodius, achieve the work in a dramatic and exemplary manner. Yet each of us is challenged to share the good news.

While *Slavorum Apostoli* may focus on the Slavic peoples, their culture, history, and faith, and while it may highlight Cyril and Methodius as patrons of evangelization, it also challenges every reader. We are to hear with our own inner ear and heart the call to transform the culture in which we live and make it just a little bit more Christian. We can all do this in some small way, with our own works of faith and charity and our own witness to the Lord. As we do, we will see the beginnings of that new creation that Jesus established, that Cyril and Methodius proclaimed, and that each of us is called to manifest.

Chapter 8

LORD AND GIVER OF LIFE

Dominum et Vivificantem

ENGLISH TITLE: **The Holy Spirit, Lord and Giver of Life**

DATE ISSUED: **May 18, 1986**

TYPE OF DOCUMENT: **Encyclical Letter**

How is it that the work of Jesus, which includes our salvation, continues in the world today? After all, Jesus is no longer with us. Following his resurrection, he ascended to his Father in glory.

The answer to this question—"How is Jesus still at work with us?"—is found in Jesus' "farewell discourse" in chapters 14–16 of John's gospel, where Jesus promises and at the same time reveals the Spirit, the Paraclete. In fulfillment of his pledge that he would not leave us orphans (14:18), Jesus explains to his apostles, before he undergoes his passion and death on the cross, that he will empower them with the gift of the Holy Spirit. Pentecost marks the fulfillment of this promise and the initiation of his Church, the beginning of the new creation.

Pope John Paul II's encyclical letter *Dominum et Vivificantem* (The Holy Spirit, Lord and Giver of Life), published on Pentecost Sunday, May 18, 1986, presents the Church's teaching on the Holy Spirit. This encyclical completes the trilogy on the Most Holy Trinity, begun with his first letter, *Redemptor Hominis*, on the Lord Jesus Christ and developed in his second encyclical on the mercy of God the Father, *Dives in Misericordia*. In this third Trinitarian exposition, the pope turns his attention to the Holy Spirit as the Lord and Giver of Life.

It is clear that the Holy Father does not intend to present a textbook exposition of the doctrine of the Holy Spirit. Rather, he invites us to reflect on the importance of the Holy Spirit in the life of the Church and in our own lives. The Spirit is our source of encouragement in our efforts to renew both the Church and the wider society in which we live.

"The way of the Church passes through the heart of man, because here is the hidden place of the salvific encounter with the Holy Spirit, with the hidden God, and precisely here the Holy Spirit becomes 'a spring of water welling up to eternal life' (John 4:14)" (67.1). The pope uses these words to conclude the encyclical, in effect challenging us to take a look at the power of God's Spirit at work within us. We must determine if we have opened our hearts to God's gracious gift of the Spirit, which urges us to live the gospels in such a way that we actually bring about in our world some manifestation of the new creation, the kingdom of God.

The Work of the Spirit

"Do you not know," asks St. Paul, "that you are the temple of God, and that the Spirit of God dwells in you?" (1 Corinthians 3:16). The Holy Spirit works in God's people collectively as the Church, but his inspiration and love are directed also to each individual Christian. With personal concern, God's Spirit wills to sanctify and lead each and every one of us to perfection. In all of us who thirst for the life-giving waters of grace, the Holy Spirit desires to make both our faith and our love personal and strong.

Indeed, only the presence of the Spirit binds the believer intimately to Christ. "Whoever does not have the Spirit of Christ does not belong to him" (Romans 8:9). "And the way we know that he [Christ] remains in us is from the Spirit that he gave us" (1 John 3:24).

At the heart of the work of the Holy Spirit within the souls of the faithful is an outpouring of self to make us holy. The process of becoming holy—perfect as our heavenly Father is perfect—begins at baptism when the Holy Spirit initiates his dwelling in the soul to endow it with sanctifying grace, to implant in it faith and love and other rich gifts. "Whoever loves me," Jesus said, "will keep my word, and my Father will love him, and we will come to him and make our dwelling with him" (John 14:23).

Convincing the World of Sin

In addition to an introduction and a conclusion, *Dominum et Vivificantem* has three chapters. In the first, the pope addresses Jesus' gift of the Spirit to the Church and the gradual understanding of the Holy Spirit as a distinct, divine Person. The Spirit, one with the Father and the Son, is now the life-giving force of the Church. By his communion with the Father and the Son, he makes present the Trinitarian life in each believer.

While we may be in awe of the mystery of God's Holy Spirit at work within us, and while the Church's teaching on the life-giving power of the Spirit may uplift us, we are also sadly aware of our own human failings. Concurrent with the energizing, renewing, restoring, and sanctifying force of the Holy Spirit are the continuing and perduring effects of both original sin and our own personal sin.

In chapter two, John Paul turns our attention to the mission of the Holy Spirit, which is "to convince the world concerning sin" (28). Conversion begins with a recognition that we are caught in the grasp of sin. One of the principal works of the Holy Spirit, as the pope unfolds for us, is the awakening in human hearts of a sense of our own sinfulness in order to prepare the way for our conversion and our ability to live in the truth.

In the celebration of the Eucharist, we pray in the Roman Canon that we might be recreated "in Spirit and in truth." As we gradually become a part of this new creation—a new being with new life in Christ—we take on more and more the transforming gift of the Spirit, which touches our hearts and opens our minds to the fullness of the truth.

Because we have been made in the image and likeness of God and have an intellect and a free will—with the power to know and to choose—God the Father, Son, and Holy Spirit are able to dwell within us as the truth that fulfills our intellect and the Spirit of love that completes the yearning of our will. But from the earliest moment of God's creative plan for us as the human family, sin has inserted its ugly face:

> The spirit of darkness is capable of showing God as an enemy of his own creature, and in the first place as an enemy of man, as a source of danger and threat to man. In this way, Satan manages to sow in man's soul the seed of opposition to the one who "from the beginning" would be considered as man's enemy— and not as Father. Man is challenged to become the adversary of God! (38.1)

The power of darkness continues to sow seeds of division, striking at the very heart of our relationship with God in order to alienate us from him. We see this effort around us every day. For example, the teaching of the Church is presented as antiquated and archaic. Those who would foster a vision of human life centered on self and driven primarily by personal satisfaction and aggrandizement paint the voice of the Church—the Spirit's proclamation—as foolish. The public debate over abortion reveals how devious these attacks are. The banner "pro-choice" flies over the buildings where death is meted out to unborn children. Abortion is described as a "reproductive right," and the consequences of the exercise of this right are masked in rhetoric and denial.

What is under attack in so much of this "civilization of death," as it is aptly described by John Paul in his encyclical *Evangelium Vitae*, is first of all the truth. Words are used to hide, distort, mask, and deform the truth. The taking of the life of helpless elderly persons is no longer called euthanasia or even mercy killing. We now read about "facilitating the natural conclusion of the biological process." Infanticide, the killing of a newborn child, is guised as the "termination of the product of extended gestation." An unborn baby is killed under the banner of its "prefunctional dependency."

"The Spirit who searches the depths of God was called by Jesus in his discourse in the Upper Room the Paraclete. For from the beginning the Spirit 'is invoked' in order to 'convince the world concerning sin'" (39.1). Here the pope is reminding us that the redemptive, salvific work of Christ's death and resurrection becomes operative in us to the extent that we recognize our own sin and turn from it. In the logical dynamic of our communion with God, first comes our recognition of our sinfulness and then our turning to God for healing and new life.

It is in the chapter on the Spirit convincing the world of sin that the pope not only reiterates the Church's ancient teaching that it is the Spirit who enlightens our minds to recognize right from wrong. He also emphasizes that it is the healing power of the Spirit that makes us one with God, who forgives our sins and restores us to new life. It is the Spirit who gives life.

The Holy Spirit Is the Source of New Life

In the third chapter of *Dominum et Vivificantem*, John Paul reminds us: "Man's intimate relationship with God in the Holy Spirit also enables him to understand himself, his own humanity, in a new way. Thus that image and likeness of God which man is from his very beginning is fully realized" (59.1). Each of us is called to a sublime destiny. What awaits us at the end of this long struggle through life is the glory of God. The Spirit comes, not only to convince us of sin, but also to provide us with an awareness of who God is, and therefore who we are, and to give us a share in the life of God himself. There is no greater gift than God's gift to each of us of the Holy Spirit who elevates us to new life in God.

At the same time, the encyclical recalls that we do not make the journey through life to the Father by ourselves. We are not islands in a sea of time and space. We are members of a family—God's family. The Church is the sacrament of intimate union with God. In his reflection on the role of the Church and our salvation, the pope reminds us that the "new coming of Christ by the power of the Holy Spirit and his constant presence and action in the spiritual life are accomplished in the sacramental reality" (61.2).

The great sacramental presence of Christ is his Church. The manifestation of Christ in a life-giving manner takes place in the seven sacraments, which bring us into an immediate and grace-filled encounter with Christ, and this happens most clearly in the Eucharist. "The most complete sacramental expression of the 'departure' of Christ through the mystery of the cross and resurrection is the Eucharist," John Paul writes. "In every celebration of the Eucharist, his coming, his salvific presence, is sacramentally realized: in the Sacrifice and in Communion. It is accomplished by the power of the Holy Spirit, as part of his own mission" (62.1).

This masterful encyclical is a reaffirmation of the Church's faith conviction that the Holy Spirit is the gift of the Father and the Son, given to us to help us enlighten our minds so that we can recognize the truth of our human condition and our need for God's grace. At the same time, the Spirit is the source of our new life, so that not only our minds but also our hearts are changed, elevated, and made capable of union with God. Finally, the pope confirms what we as Catholic faithful know intuitively: The Spirit of God is at work in his Church, and we access this marvelous gift through our participation in the life of the Church.

Much of what the Holy Father teaches is challenged by currents in our culture and society today. *Dominum et Vivificantem* is not an exercise in redundant catechesis; rather, it is an exhortation to renew some of our most important beliefs. For example, in a culture that increasingly sees truth as relative and in which the sentiment is "My opinion is as good as yours," the encyclical reminds us that even when it comes to determining God's revelation and right from wrong, there *is* such a thing as truth.

The human intellect is capable of knowing and therefore living by the truth. The natural moral order and God's revelation in the Ten Commandments of how we are to make our way through life are not options among many. The path through life is not directed by multiple-choice selections, all of which are more or less correct. And yet our culture thrives on this vision of multiple truths and conflicting opinions, and the result is moral paralysis.

The Spirit Active and Present in the Church

We make our way through life as God's family. The Spirit is poured out on the apostles and through them on all who hear the word and allow it to take deep root in their hearts. When the Advocate descended on the apostles at Pentecost, Peter was able to testify to the Spirit in order to explain the charisms that accompanied the Pentecost event. Addressing the crowd that had gathered, Peter spoke first of Jesus. "God raised this Jesus; of this we are all witnesses. Exalted at the right hand of God, he received the promise of the holy Spirit from the Father and poured it forth, as you both see and hear" (Acts 2:32-33).

The Acts of the Apostles tells us that the people in the crowd were deeply moved, and they asked Peter what they should do. He told them, "Repent and be baptized, every one of you, in the name of Jesus Christ for the forgiveness of your sins; and you will receive the gift of the holy Spirit" (Acts 2:38). The rich outpouring of the

Holy Spirit foretold by Jesus in his farewell discourse came to fruition in the Pentecost event. The decisive coming of the Spirit on Pentecost is described in Acts, which chronicles much of the early life of the Church and has been called by some the "Gospel of the Holy Spirit."

Guided by the Holy Spirit in the light of the Pentecostal event, the apostles and the early followers of Jesus identified Christ with his Church—his new body. This explains why we turn with such confidence to the Church, not only to encounter Christ sacramentally, but also to hear his voice reflected in its teaching.

"I will not leave you orphans" (John 14:18). The fulfillment of this pledge by Christ is the gift of the Holy Spirit, and the gift of the Holy Spirit is identified with the constitution of the Church. Thus with confidence, you and I can turn to the Church to hear God's word even when it challenges us beyond our comfort level. And in the same Church, we find a living presence of Christ, not only in the proclamation of the word, but also in the sacraments, most especially the Eucharist. In concluding his encyclical, John Paul notes:

> The Church with her heart which embraces all human hearts implores from the Holy Spirit that happiness which only in God has its complete realization: the joy "that no one will be able to take away" (John 16:22), the joy which is the fruit of love, and therefore of God who is love; she implores "the righteousness, the peace and the joy of the Holy Spirit" in which, in the words of St. Paul, consists the Kingdom of God (cf. Romans 14:17; Galatians 5:22). (67.5)

Not only did Jesus give us the Spirit so that we would not be left orphans, he also gave us the gift of the Holy Spirit, present and active in his Church, so that our joy might be complete.

Chapter 9

BEHOLD YOUR MOTHER

Redemptoris Mater

ENGLISH TITLE: **The Mother of the Redeemer**
DATE ISSUED: **March 25, 1987**
TYPE OF DOCUMENT: **Encyclical Letter**

The most majestic church dedicated to Mary in our country is the Basilica of the National Shrine of the Immaculate Conception in Washington, D.C. The architectural style of this huge structure has been described as "American Byzantine." With its strikingly beautiful bell tower reaching into the heavens, it stands in our nation's capital as a visible and imposing witness to the role of Mary in the life of Jesus and his Church, and therefore in the unfolding of God's salvific plan.

Adjacent to the Catholic University of America, the shrine proclaims in its own way one of the central mysteries of our faith—that God sent his only begotten Son to become one of us so that we in turn might become adopted children of God. In every side chapel, in every facet and niche, this message is repeated: "The Word became flesh and made his dwelling among us" (John 1:14).

Pope John Paul II begins his encyclical letter *Redemptoris Mater* (The Mother of the Redeemer) with St. Paul's proclamation to the Galatians: "When the time had fully come, God sent forth his Son, born of a woman, born under the law, to redeem those who were under the law, so that we might receive adoption as sons. And because you are sons, God has sent the Spirit of his Son into our hearts, crying,

'Abba! Father!'" (4:4-6; 1.1). Even the date of the encyclical—March 25, 1987, the Solemnity of the Annunciation of the Lord—speaks to us of the focus of the pope's message.

The Pope's Marian Devotion

John Paul's devotion to Mary was no secret. Throughout his pontificate, he over and over again lifted up for our attention and veneration the person of Mary—Mother of Jesus, Mother of the Church, Mother of God, our mother. His coat of arms carried a large "M" under a cross and bore his motto, *Totus Tuus*, "All Yours," in reference to his relationship to the Mother of God. Why such devotion to Mary? The same question can be asked of the whole Church: Why such worldwide and millennia-long devotion to Mary?

In every part of the world, in every land where the Church has taken root, there are chapels, churches, shrines, and sanctuaries dedicated to Mary. No architectural style has been left out of this praise of the Mother of God, whether in stone, brick, wood, steel, or glass. The same is true for the symphony of praise in hymns sung in every language across the globe. From the earliest days of the Church's worship in Greek and later in Latin, to the hundreds of vernacular languages now used in the liturgy, hearts and lips have given voice to the role of Mary, the Mother of the Redeemer.

Redemptoris Mater helps us understand more fully why it is that Mary holds such an important role in the hearts of the faithful and the life of the Church. In addition to the introduction and conclusion, the encyclical is divided into three chapters. In the first, the pope describes the many New Testament texts that speak of the Mother of Jesus. The second chapter relates Mary to the ongoing work of Christ in his Church. Here we see the reason for the title "Mary, Mother of the Church." The final chapter is a moving reflection on the Marian dimension of Christian life and includes a meditation on the meaning of the 1987 Marian year, which commemorated the twelfth centenary of the Second Council of Nicea, held in 787.

Chapter one begins with the divine plan of salvation. Here we are reminded that the eternal design of God the Father includes his plan of man's salvation in Christ:

> It is a universal plan, which concerns all men and women created in the image and likeness of God (cf. Genesis 1:26). . . . In fact, the God who is the "Father of our Lord Jesus Christ . . . chose us in him before the foundation of the world, that we should be holy and blameless before him. He destined us in love to be his sons through Jesus Christ, according to the purpose of his will, to the praise of his glorious grace, which he freely bestowed on us in the Beloved. In him we have redemption through his blood, the forgiveness of our trespasses, according to the riches of his grace" (Ephesians 1:4-7). (7.1)

To understand God's plan for our salvation after our fall from grace demands that we reflect on the role of Mary. When we turn to the pages of sacred Scripture, we see unfolding the dynamic of this divine mystery. God was to come among us so that he could be one with us in a way that would give unique meaning to the cross of Calvary and the empty tomb of Easter. At the heart of our faith is the recognition that God came among us. Jesus is truly God and truly man.

The gospels proclaim with profound directness the events surrounding the conception and birth of Jesus. The archangel Gabriel proclaimed to Mary that she was to be the Mother of God. In her great faith, she accepted his words. Her faith and openness to God's word are intimately tied together with the event we call the incarnation— the taking on of our human nature by God's eternal Word. The child born of Mary in Bethlehem was truly the eternal Word made flesh.

The Gospel of Luke tells us that Mary "gave birth to her firstborn son. She wrapped him in swaddling clothes and laid him in a manger, because there was no room for them in the inn" (Luke 2:7). These two events, the annunciation and the nativity, are defining moments in the entrance into our human history of God as one of us.

While the New Testament does not speak at great length about Mary, the essential truths concerning her place in the mystery of Christ and his Church are clearly rooted there. For centuries Christians have prayerfully reflected on all that sacred Scripture says about the Mother of God. The pope begins his meditation on Mary and the mystery of Christ in the pages of sacred Scripture by reflecting on the Second Vatican Council's teaching on the role of the Blessed Mother. *Lumen Gentium* (The Dogmatic Constitution on the Church, 52–69) offers insight into the profound mystery of how it is that God would come among us and how that enduring presence remains today.

A World-Changing Encounter

St. Luke's account of the archangel Gabriel's message to Mary that she was to be the Mother of God sets the stage for everything else that will happen. Here Mary emerges as the "favored one" who is "full of grace" (Luke 1:28) because of her unique role in God's saving plan as Mother of the Redeemer. Luke thus discloses to us that Mary is "full of grace" as a result of her messianic motherhood, her divine maternity. She is "most blessed . . . among women" (1:42) because she is so highly favored by the Lord's presence within her.

In the dialogue between Mary and the archangel, Mary's faith and openness become evident. Mary's words "How can this be, since I have no relations with a man?" (Luke 1:34) recall her commitment to serve the Lord with an undivided heart. In God's plan, however, a human father was not necessary for the eternal Son: "The holy Spirit will come upon you, and the power of the Most High will overshadow you" (1:35). Once God's plan was made clear to her, Mary freely gave her consent in an act of humble faith and loving obedience: "Behold, I am the handmaid of the Lord. May it be done to me according to your word" (1:38).

In a sense, all time stood still as this conversation between Mary and the archangel took place. From all eternity, God's plan called for his only begotten Son to come among us as one of us so that we might rejoice in a level of oneness with God that is described as "adopted sonship." In the preface for the Christmas liturgy, we pray, "In the wonder of the Incarnation, your eternal Word has brought the eyes of faith a new and radiant vision of your glory. In him we see our God made visible and so are caught up in the love of the God we cannot see."

All of this hung on Mary's response. As St. Augustine once remarked on the importance of our participating in God's plan, "God created us without our help, but he would not save us without our help." In a way, all creation held its breath while the archangel Gabriel announced to Mary that she was being asked to undertake a unique and essential role in the salvation of all of us. On her answer would depend the fulfillment of God's plan. Perhaps sensing her confusion, the divine messenger says to her, "Do not be afraid, Mary, for you have found favor with God. Behold, you will conceive in your womb and bear a son, and you shall name him Jesus. He will be great and will be called Son of the Most High" (Luke 1:30-32).

Continuing to quote from St. Luke's gospel, the pope reminds us that "when the Virgin, disturbed by that extraordinary greeting, asks: 'How can this be, since I have no relations with a man?' she receives from the angel the confirmation and explanation of the preceding words. Gabriel says to her: 'The Holy Spirit will come upon you, and the power of the Most High will overshadow you. Therefore the child to be born will be called holy, the Son of God' (Luke 1:35)" (9.2).

A New Creation

Thus we have the beginning of a whole new order—the new creation. Mary's response, "Behold I am the handmaid of the Lord. May it be done to me according to your word" (Luke 1:38), sets the stage for all those events that are to follow: Jesus' death, resurrection, and ascension; the outpouring of the Holy Spirit; the establishment of his Church; and the ongoing work of redemption in which you and I are caught up today by the grace of the Holy Spirit. The Holy Father describes it this way: "The Annunciation, therefore, is the revelation of the mystery of the Incarnation at the very beginning of its fulfillment on earth. God's salvific giving of himself and his life, in some way to all creation but directly to man, reaches one of its high points in the mystery of the Incarnation" (9.3).

In this opening chapter, John Paul reflects on the varied ways in which Mary appears in the pages of the New Testament. While these vignettes of her life are few, they are extremely significant. Moving through them, the encyclical letter brings us to the reflection on Mary as our mother. In a relatively long meditation on the marriage feast of Cana, the pope points out that the gospels clearly speak of a new dimension: the meaning of Mary's motherhood that extends beyond her relationship to Jesus, which is reflected in her instruction to the servants to "Do whatever he tells you" (John 2:5).

John Paul writes, "The description of the Cana event outlines what is actually manifested as a new kind of motherhood according to the spirit and not just according to the flesh, that is to say Mary's solicitude for human beings, her coming to them in the wide variety of their wants and needs" (21.3). At the foot of the cross, Jesus consigns Mary to John and asks John to assume the care of Mary: "Woman, behold your son" and "Behold, your mother" (John 19:26, 27).

The pope draws our attention to the significant change that is taking place in Mary's relationship with all of us: "It emerges from the definitive accomplishment of the Redeemer's Paschal Mystery. The Mother of Christ, who stands at the very center of this mystery—a mystery which embraces every individual and all humanity—is given as Mother to every single individual and all mankind" (23.2).

Mary, the Mother of Jesus, is the Mother of God because Jesus is God with us. Mary, the Mother of God, is also our mother because we are caught up through the power of the Holy Spirit in adopted sonship with God. She is Mother of the Church, to whom we turn in intercession in asking to become more closely identified with her son—God's Son—our Lord and Savior.

Mary and the Pilgrim Church

This brings us to the second chapter of *Redemptoris Mater*, "The Mother of God at the Center of the Pilgrim Church." It was God's plan that the saving work of Jesus would not end with his ascension into heaven. Every generation would have access to the wonder of God's love and the generosity of God's forgiveness. How does this happen? The answer is the mystery of the Church.

In the outpouring of the Holy Spirit, Jesus established his Church. In doing so, he fulfilled his promise that on Peter, the "rock," he would build his Church (Matthew 16:18). Now Peter would be empowered to fulfill the charge that he received from the risen Jesus on the shore of Galilee: "Feed my lambs. . . . Feed my sheep" (John 21:15, 17). Each person who will be baptized in the power of the Spirit will become a member of the body of Christ, of which Christ is the head, as St. Paul says (Colossians 1:18).

Not as individuals or isolated persons do we make our way through time and history to our eternal home in heaven. Rather, we do so as part of God's family—his Church. John Paul writes:

Built by Christ upon the Apostles, the Church became fully aware of these mighty works of God on the day of Pentecost, when those gathered together in the Upper Room "were all filled with the Holy Spirit and began to speak in other tongues, as the Spirit gave them utterance" (Acts 2:4). From that moment there also begins that journey of faith, the Church's pilgrimage through the history of individuals and peoples. (26.1)

As the new creation began to take form, and as the beginnings of the kingdom of God began to be manifested in a way that would endure century after century, Mary was present. As the pope points out, "We see her in the midst of the Apostles in the Upper Room, 'prayerfully imploring the gift of the Spirit' (LG, 8)" (26.1). And, he says, "At the first dawn of the Church, at the beginning of the long journey through faith which began at Pentecost in Jerusalem, Mary was with all of those who were the seed of the 'new Israel'" (27.1).

What we learn in this section of *Redemptoris Mater* is in part an answer to the question "Why do Catholics give so much devotion and attention to Mary?" As Mother of the Church, she is truly our mother. To her we turn with filial affection and devotion, anticipating her intercession for us with confidence because she has already received us as her children.

Obviously, Christ is the one eternal mediator between God and man. It was in his death and resurrection that we were ransomed from sin and granted new life in Christ. Yet as Christ became our adopted brother, so we presume to turn to his mother, whom he shares with us so that we can beg her intercession with her divine Son.

Maternal Mediation

The final chapter of *Redemptoris Mater*, "Maternal Mediation," calls our attention to this unique role of Mary under the titles

"Advocate," "Auxiliatrix," "Adjutrix," and "Mediatrix." "Through her mediation, subordinate to that of the redeemer, Mary contributes in a special way to the union of the pilgrim Church on earth with the eschatological and heavenly reality of the communion of saints, since she has already been 'assumed into heaven' (LG, 62)" (41.1). Christ stands alone as the mediator between God and his people. Mary stands in relationship to Jesus and to us as one to whom we can turn, who will place before her Son, the true mediator, her pleas on our behalf.

Throughout Christian history, devotion to Mary represents and manifests the Christian recognition of the intimacy of the bond between Mary and her son Jesus and her unique and determining role in the unfolding of God's plan. Catholics do not worship Mary, but we truly venerate her because she is the Mother of Jesus, the Mother of God, the Mother of the Church—and our mother.

The pope concludes this encyclical with an expression of wonder at the mystery of a God who so loves us that he sent his Son to us so that we might share in his divine life. "At the center of this mystery, in the midst of this wonderment of faith, stands Mary" (51.4).

Chapter 10

BUILDING A BETTER WORLD

Sollicitudo Rei Socialis

ENGLISH TITLE: **On Social Concern**

DATE ISSUED: **December 30, 1987**

TYPE OF DOCUMENT: **Encyclical Letter**

"If you want peace, work for justice." This familiar and often-quoted statement of Pope Paul VI highlights how important it is to understand the interrelated nature of Catholic teaching and not isolate any one element from its God-given context. The longing of the human heart for peace and stability is intimately tied to the human desire for justice—social justice at every level of our society.

On February 19, 1988, Pope John Paul II issued his encyclical letter *Sollicitudo Rei Socialis* (On Social Concern), which was signed on December 30, 1987, and marked the twentieth anniversary of Pope Paul VI's 1967 social encyclical *Populorum Progressio*. In both these documents, there is a beautifully articulated vision of a world social order rooted in justice and bearing the fruit of peace.

The Christian Worldview

For the Christian, there is only one specific worldview in which peace can be found, and it is based on revelation. It rests upon the conviction that the God of creation has given life to all men and women and therefore is their Father. It accepts the redemption of Christ as the means to solidarity among all people. It looks to the Spirit of peace and reconciliation as the bond enabling all to live together. Within this context, the Christian speaks of the progress of people, social justice, and peace.

The doctrinal and theological explanation of the world for the Christian is the human condition in the face of God's salvific plan. Original sin, personal guilt, redemption, grace, and the hope of final reconciliation with God are supernatural realities. For a person of faith, these are the facts against which the struggle for peace and social justice in our day must be seen. With this view, the follower of Christ recognizes that the only real and lasting reconciliation will be the peace that rests upon God's revealed plan.

In *Sollicitudo Rei Socialis*, John Paul takes up this theme of Pope Paul VI and insists that because of the ethical and religious dimensions of human life, questions of social concern and justice fall within the competence of the Church's teaching office. Jesus brought into this world an understanding of human existence. It is precisely this understanding that the Church, in her magisterium, must continue to promote as gospel values, which have an impact on human development and all the economic, social, cultural, and political aspects of life. Repeatedly, Pope John Paul II calls us to recognize the Church's duty to defend and promote human dignity. At a later moment in his pontificate, John Paul would devote an entire encyclical, *Evangelium Vitae*, to this very point.

The pope reminds us that Catholic teaching on social justice is rooted in the Church's need to teach the moral law. The Church is not called upon to analyze social conditions from a sociological or historical perspective but rather, from their moral dimension. The authority to teach in areas of social justice is rooted in the Church's mandate to express the natural moral law, which is God's law found written in the hearts of all people. The *Catechism of the Catholic Church* speaks not only of the foundational nature of the natural moral law but also of the commandments themselves as privileged expressions of the natural law (2070–2071).

Yet the Church moves us beyond just the implications of the natural moral order and brings us face-to-face with the direction Jesus has given to the human enterprise. By involving all of us in a new ethical situation that contradicts our own limited human experience, Jesus challenges us to work out a social order in this world that more closely manifests the justice and peace of his kingdom. In contrast with the pragmatic calculations and reasoned positions of the Greeks and the Romans of antiquity, Jesus spoke of a personal commitment to charity toward all people. So revolutionary and demanding is this commitment that it depends utterly on a perspective offered only by divine revelation. Thus the gospels can remind us that Christ's peace and world order are not the peace of this world (Luke 12:51-53).

In his gospel, St. Matthew outlines in the several chapters that make up the Sermon on the Mount (5–7) some of the essential attitudes that are the result of the new perspective introduced into the world by Jesus. The gospel insists on a vision of men and women as eventual citizens of heaven. For Jesus, the works of the social order unfolding in this world are ultimately directed to the fulfillment of the kingdom in another world. The background is always human life seen as potentially divine and eternal.

High Praise for *Populorum Progressio*

In the introduction to *Sollicitudo Rei Socialis,* the pope gives high praise to the originality of *Populorum Progressio* and the wisdom of Pope Paul VI in tying the Church's social teaching to the reflections of the Second Vatican Council, which had concluded just a few years earlier. John Paul provides three reasons why Paul VI's encyclical is so original.

The first is the point we have just stressed—the pope's exercise of his teaching authority in areas that truly represent "an application of the word of God to people's lives and the life of society, as well as to the earthly realities connected with them" (8.4). The second reason is its breadth of outlook. Both *Populorum Progressio* and *Sollicitudo Rei Socialis* face "the serious problem of unequal distribution of the means of subsistence originally meant for everybody, and thus also an unequal distribution of the benefits deriving from them" (9.6). This brings the Church into the world of economics, social development, and justice among peoples. The third reason that it is so original is the comprehensive manner in which the Church's social teaching is presented and applied "to the very concept of development" (10.1).

In his encyclical, Pope John Paul provides an overview of the whole range of social concerns rooted in social development and social justice or the lack of either throughout the world. In the third chapter, "Survey of the Contemporary World," he makes it abundantly clear that he is well aware of both the efforts for social justice and the failure of social development that nations throughout the world are experiencing. He is obviously keenly in tune with the suffering of people everywhere.

Chapter four, "Authentic Human Development," brings us to what is essentially the theological foundation for the final two chapters: "A Theological Reading of Modern Problems" (five) and "Some Particular Guidelines" (six).

Authentic Human Development

In the section on human development, the pope points out that the "story of the human race described by sacred Scripture is, even after the fall into sin, a story of constant achievements" (30.5). At the heart of this development or growth is the Lord Jesus. "A part of this divine plan, which begins from eternity in Christ, the perfect 'image' of the Father, and which culminates in him, 'the first born from the dead' (Colossians 1:18), is our own history. . . . It thus prepares us to share in the fullness which 'dwells in the Lord' and which he communicates 'to his body, which is the Church' (1:19; cf. Ephesians 1:22-23)" (31.2).

Jesus proclaims peace in the same breath with which he blesses the poor and those in mourning. Believers are reminded of their duties toward those who are poor, afflicted, and downtrodden, but always in terms of the kingdom of heaven. The perspective is that of the call to be a child of God. We are to build up this world because we are the beginning manifestation of the kingdom whose fullness will be reached in glory. Within this vision both God and man have value in themselves.

The Sermon on the Mount requires that the believer see the dignity of his fellow human beings. This dignity, value, and worth come from God, reside in us, and are held sacred because of our ultimate goal—union with God. Such a perspective requires faith. Belief alone makes it possible for us to hold out hope in the life to come. Faith provides the moral climate in which, for the Christian, human dignity can assert itself and human freedom can grow.

The Virtue of Solidarity

It has been said that John Paul brought the virtue of solidarity to a new level of awareness both in the Church and in the wider human community. Solidarity, which the pope speaks of as "undoubtedly a Christian virtue" (40.1), is at the center of practical efforts to achieve human communion, especially when that community is nurtured by grace. It is rooted in the unity of the human race and elevated to a more intense level through the outpouring of the divine life in baptism; and it is articulated in works of generosity, forgiveness, and reconciliation.

Today the translation of Christ's reconciliation into visible, tangible results is being carried on in the area of social justice. It is here that the battle for human dignity and freedom is being waged. *Sollicitudo Rei Socialis* confirms that it is precisely in the works of social justice that the Church is calling us to a new level of commitment and solidarity that will eventually bear the fruit of peace.

Human philosophy or political theory alone cannot provide a true understanding of the human condition. Christ is the answer to our longings and the questions that arise in our hearts, regarding not only our personal path to God, but also our obligations to each other as a society—as a human community. This conviction brings us to chapter six, in what John Paul describes as "Some Particular Guidelines."

The pope reminds us that "the Church does not have technical solutions to offer for the problem of underdevelopment as such" (41.1). Nevertheless, "the Church is an 'expert in humanity' and this leads her necessarily to extend her religious mission to the various fields in which men and women expend their efforts in search of the always relative happiness which is possible in this world, in line with their dignity as persons" (41.2). By meeting practical human problems head on and by attempting to eliminate intolerable situations that breed injustice and division, we are capable of building human solidarity.

The Social Order Is Built on Rights

The social order functions as it recognizes the rights of persons, both moral and physical. It is built and sustained on rights and duties. Yet rights of themselves are secondary to the persons they serve. Rights can be in conflict with the higher values connected with the essential well-being of persons. For example, each person has a right to life, freedom, and the opportunity to develop his or her potential as a human. Property rights, tradition, privilege, and institutional prerogatives, all necessary for the maintenance of the social order, may often contradict the basic rights of the individual. A natural tension exists as the effort is made to highlight first and foremost individual human dignity, values, and rights within the context of a common good.

All rights have to be seen within the context of the inherent dignity of human life according "to the laws of nature and nature's God." The long-accepted precedence of the absolute right of property fell beneath the weight of the objections voiced by the drafters of our own Declaration of Independence. At the origin of our nation, the dignity of the person as created by God according to his law and plan was the starting point. The natural right to life, liberty, and the pursuit of happiness as being God-given and respectful of the basic dignity of each person is written into our nation's founding documents. Thus we should not be surprised that over and over again, John Paul calls for the recognition of such basic human values as the starting point for public policy and social practice.

In concluding this beautiful reflection on social concerns, the pope points out:

The Church well knows that no temporal achievement is to be identified with the kingdom of God but that all such achievements simply reflect and in a sense anticipate the glory of the kingdom, the kingdom which we await at the end of history, when the Lord will come again. But that expectation can never be an excuse for lack of concern for people in their concrete personal situations. (48.1)

The Holy Father reminds us that the kingdom of God in its fullness will only become apparent in the realm of glory. At the same time, we are charged to make every effort to manifest—through works of truth, kindness, justice, and love—the coming of that kingdom in our world. We have the power to make the kingdom of God break out into this world and to begin to transform it into what will, in its fullness, be heaven.

We have a long way to go, but this encyclical teaches us that there are practical, concrete steps that we can take here and now to more fully manifest the kingdom of God in our world.

Chapter 11

SPEAK AND LIVE THE FAITH

Christifideles Laici

ENGLISH TITLE: **The Vocation and the Mission of the Lay**
                          Faithful in the Church and in the World
DATE ISSUED: **December 30, 1988**
TYPE OF DOCUMENT: **Post-Synodal Apostolic Exhortation**

The Second Vatican Council, which has so greatly influenced the Church in the twentieth century and continues to have an impact on us today, concluded in 1965. To commemorate the twentieth anniversary of the conclusion of the Council, in 1985 Pope John Paul II called an extraordinary synod to celebrate, examine, and promote the application of its teachings.

In the light of that important discussion, the next ordinary assembly of the Synod of Bishops, which convened in Rome in the fall of 1987, was devoted to the theme of the vocation and mission of lay-people in the Church and the world. It was not a coincidence. The Second Vatican Council highlighted the role of the laity and challenged us to address more vigorously our baptismal gifts and the obligations that flow from them.

It was in the last session of the Council that *Apostolicam Actuositatem* (The Decree on the Apostolate of the Laity) was approved. It reminded the whole Church that lay Christians—like the clergy and men and women in consecrated life—are entrusted by God with the apostolate by virtue of their baptism and confirmation. They have the right and duty, individually or grouped in associations, to make the message of salvation known and accepted by people throughout the world.

This document was a resounding affirmation of the place of laypeople in the work of the Church. More than 99 percent of the membership of the Church is comprised of laywomen and laymen. The teaching office of the Church emphasized that it is to this vast throng of Jesus' disciples that the work of evangelization and sanctification is entrusted. Imagine what the world would be like if every baptized Catholic accepted the challenge to share the faith and to live out the call to holiness in the midst of the family, at work, and in the public sector—wherever God's grace is experienced.

This is part of the vision that Pope John Paul II communicates in the post-synodal apostolic exhortation *Christifideles Laici* (The Vocation and the Mission of the Lay Faithful in the Church and in the World). He begins the document, published December 30, 1988, on the Feast of the Holy Family, with a reminder of the richness of the teaching of the Second Vatican Council and how "the Council fathers, re-echoing the call of Christ, have summoned all of the lay faithful, both women and men, to labor in the vineyard" (2.5). It is not surprising that Pope John Paul II, who was a Council father and who experienced the outpouring of the Spirit and the energy of the Council deliberations, would turn the Church's attention to something that was a focus of the Council and is intrinsic to the life of the Church.

Sometimes we hear that the increasing emphasis on the role of the laity in the life of the Church today is the result of the shortage of priests and religious. Yet both the Decree on the Apostolate of the Laity and its timing tell us something different. At a time when vocations were at their highest point, the Church called the laity to assume their responsibility bestowed on them in baptism and confirmation to spread the gospel of Jesus Christ. The laity are particularly called to transform the temporal order, which is their special domain.

In this apostolic exhortation, John Paul uses the image of the vineyard, specifically Jesus' words to "go into my vineyard" (Matthew 20:4). This challenge is given not only to priests and religious. The vineyard also awaits cultivation by all who will undertake the task. In the introduction, the pope tells us that "the words 'you go into my vineyard too' . . . were reechoed in spirit once again" at the synod, which "treated in a specific and extensive manner the topic of the vocation and mission of the lay faithful in the Church and in the world" (2.6). The pope also noted that lay faithful, both women and men, were represented at the synod and made valuable contributions to its proceedings.

The Need for Active Involvement

In issuing a reminder to the lay faithful of their important role in spreading the gospel, John Paul underscores the particularly pressing need in the world today for such work. Again, echoing the words of Jesus, the pope asks, "Why do you stand here idle all day?" (Matthew 20:6). He adds, "A new state of affairs today, both in the Church and in social, economic, political and cultural life, calls with a particular urgency for the action of the lay faithful" (3.2).

Oftentimes, when something happens in our community or when laws are enacted that challenge some of our most cherished convictions, Church leaders will be asked, "Why doesn't the Church do something about this?" While it is true that the clergy are called to proclaim the gospel, it is equally true that laywomen and laymen are challenged to apply the gospel to the circumstances of our day. It is not enough to presume that the hierarchy alone will address serious social and moral problems in our society. Everyone has to be involved and take an active role. We sometimes hear politicians say that while they may hear from bishops and priests on specific issues, they do not hear much from significant portions of the Catholic laity. If that is true, we must change it.

The voice and engagement of the laity will ultimately determine the direction of our society. The voice of Catholic physicians needs to be heard in the area of medicine. Catholic lawyers need to speak out on the ethics involved in the practice of the law. Catholic parents should be involved in educational issues. Numerous other examples are available to all of us. This is what the apostolic exhortation *Christifideles Laici* addresses. "It is necessary, then, to keep a watchful eye on this our world, with its problems and values, its unrest and hopes, its defeats and triumphs: a world whose economic, social, political, and cultural affairs pose problems and grave difficulties" (3.6).

Chapter one, "The Dignity of the Lay Faithful in the Church as Mystery," provides the foundation for our understanding of the role of the laity in the life and mission of the Church. As the pope writes, "The voice of the Lord clearly resounds in the depths of each of Christ's followers who, through faith and the sacraments of Christian initiation, is made like Jesus Christ, is incorporated as a living member in the Church, and has an active part in her mission of salvation" (3.5).

Baptism gives each believer an apostolic vocation. "Go, therefore, and make disciples of all nations, baptizing them . . . , teaching them to observe all that I have commanded you" (Matthew 28:19, 20). Spreading the kingdom of God everywhere for the glory of God the Father is a task that derives its mandate, energy, and grace from baptism.

The task of proclaiming and spreading the faith is particularly challenging today because we live in an age of aggressive secularism. Thus we may be tempted at times to view it as an impossible mission. Yet in his exhortation, the pope points out that Jesus never promised that our work would be easy. Like Jesus, the pope warns us that not everyone will have ears to hear the good news. On the other hand, we know that we have the power of God's Spirit to enable us to meet the challenges of the day.

Baptism and the New Life of the Spirit

In chapter one, the Holy Father holds out for us a beautiful vision of Christ present and at work in the world today. Just as the glorified body of Christ sits now at the right hand of the Father, so his new body is present in our world today—his Church. Every person who is baptized into new life becomes a member of the body of Christ. In all the gifts and talents, all the abilities and graces that abound among the laymen and laywomen who make up the Church, everything that is needed to advance the building of the kingdom of God can be found.

In every baptism we recall that three actions take place. The pouring of the water and the action and words of the sacrament both symbolize and realize the washing away of original sin, the outpouring of new life, and the incorporation of the individual into the body of Christ, his Church.

"It is no exaggeration to say that the entire existence of the lay faithful has as its purpose to lead a person to a knowledge of the radical newness of the Christian life that comes from baptism, the sacrament of faith, so that this knowledge can help that person live the responsibilities which arise from that vocation received from God" (10.1). We are baptized not only for our own salvation. Incorporation into the body of Christ is not an action of personal piety. Rather, we are engaged in a new life of the Spirit so that working in and through us, the Spirit might transform the whole world. This is no small gift. In fact, "baptism regenerates us in the life of the Son of God; unites us to Christ and to his Body, the Church; and anoints us in the Holy Spirit, making us spiritual temples" (10.1).

With this as a foundation, John Paul moves into the second chapter and describes the participation of the lay faithful in the life of the Church as communion. He begins with the scriptural image of the branches and the vine: "I am the true vine, and my Father is the vine grower. . . . Remain in me, as I remain in you" (John 15:1, 4). Here we learn that precisely because he or she is an important part of the Church, each individual layperson is called to carry out the mission and work of the whole Church.

The Holy Father completes the image of the Church by reminding us that we make our journey as a family and that God's family has shepherds to lead it. Out of the vast body of those baptized into new life in Christ, Jesus chooses some and configures them to himself through the Sacrament of Holy Orders so that there is leadership for the whole body. Every baptized person is configured to Christ as a member of his body, and every ordained priest and bishop is configured to Christ as head of that body. Together they bring the new body of Christ to fullness as it makes it way through time and history.

To Be a Witness

In chapter three, the pope notes that "it is always the one and the same Spirit who calls together and unifies the Church and sends her to preach the gospel 'to the end of the earth' (Acts 1:8)" (32.4). "Whoever remains in me and I in him will bear much fruit" (John 15:5). It is Jesus who appoints us to go forth and bear fruit, but always in communion with the Church so that what we bear witness to is authenticated by its continuity with Jesus.

"To witness" is to manifest before another the truth of some specific reality. "Witness" in this sense means to make known to others what the Church proclaims. Christ, the eternal Word of the Father, is of course the only witness to the Father. All other witnesses must somehow share in the one eternal testimony offered by Christ. "I know where I came from and where I am going" (John 8:14). "A son cannot do anything on his own, but only what he sees his father doing; for what he does, his son will do also. For the Father loves his

Son and shows him everything that he himself does" (5:19-20). "I do nothing on my own, but I say only what the Father taught me" (8:28).

The Son is the one who has to dispense life to all and does so as a living witness to the Father. His witness is the light, and that light as the knowledge or revelation of the Father is our new life. Therefore to accept Christ is at one and the same time to know him and to live a fuller life in him. This depends on the function of the witness.

It is to the Church that the full office of testifying to all the works of God has been given. In this sense the Church is the only witness to Christ. A person's individual witness can claim to be authentic only to the extent that it reflects the witness of the Church.

Witness essentially relies on continuity between the fact witnessed and the testimony to it. Continuity is absolutely essential to authentic, credible witness. All the authenticity of a witness depends on the witness' relationship to the Church. Thus the Holy Father reminds us of the challenge we have to proclaim God's word and to do it in full continuity, in full communion, with the whole body of Christ.

Not everyone has the same responsibility in the vineyard. In chapter four, the pope outlines for us the various responsibilities of the "laborers" in the Lord's vineyard. Young and old, men and women, religious, ordained, and laity are all laborers in the vineyard, each according to his or her state in life and vocation.

In our land, where increasingly we see the claim of secularism as the only true expression of our national ideals and goals, the voice of committed Catholic lay men and women is all the more necessary. It is the task of each layperson to speak and live the faith today.

Before concluding this apostolic exhortation, John Paul calls our attention in the fifth and final chapter to the formation of the lay faithful. Here we are reminded that formation is not just a practical experience but also a spiritual one. Learning about the faith takes place on many levels, both cognitive and affective. Thus the pope brings this chapter to a conclusion with the reminder that we must develop our prayer life so that we are open to the gift of the Spirit, present to the urgings of God's grace, and alive in our new life in Christ.

Chapter 12

A QUIET MAN WITH MUCH TO SAY

Redemptoris Custos

ENGLISH TITLE: **On the Person and Mission of St. Joseph**
DATE ISSUED: **August 15, 1989**
TYPE OF DOCUMENT: **Apostolic Exhortation**

Father's Day in our country has become a way of recognizing the important place of Dad. While the celebration itself may be focused on a Father's Day card, a gift, or a special meal, at its heart is the recognition that a father plays a singularly important role in the life of a family. Children need a father. Fathers have a God-given responsibility to their children.

There was a time when this was taken for granted. But today we live in a culture in which the family is under tremendous pressure, if not to say assault. Under the banner of "personal freedom," more and more individuals— fathers and mothers—are walking away from their mutual responsibility to their children and leaving them to the care of either one or the other or to a third party. Hollywood movies, television, and sitcoms too often emphasize the single-parent family and increasingly exclude the role of the father.

In some segments of our community, it has even become commonplace for fathers to walk away from their responsibility to the children they have generated. What makes this all the more disconcerting is the silence on the part of so much of our society. This is construed too readily by younger people as approval. The contrast between the dysfunctional culture that beckons us to the future and the family values that are woven into our tradition challenges us to pay more attention to family life today. We need to examine more carefully the role of father and the vocation to fatherhood, with all of its joys and responsibilities.

An Example of Fatherhood for Our Age

On August 15, 1989, during the eleventh year of his pontificate, Pope John Paul II wrote an apostolic exhortation entitled *Redemptoris Custos* on St. Joseph and the Catholic understanding of fatherhood. Aware of the significant cultural changes in societies around the world, including the disintegration of family life, the pope holds up St. Joseph as an example for our age. In doing so, as with all of his writings, the Holy Father helps us to see far more deeply into the meaning of our Catholic faith.

In his introduction to this exhortation on St. Joseph, the pope points out the parallel between Joseph and the Holy Family and Joseph and the Church, which is rooted in the mystery of the incarnation. Just as "St. Joseph took loving care of Mary and gladly dedicated himself to Jesus Christ's upbringing, he likewise watches over and protects Christ's Mystical Body, that is, the Church" (1.1).

As we begin our reflection on St. Joseph, spouse of Mary and patron of the universal Church, we need to examine the relationship of the Church itself to the mystery of God coming among us—the incarnation. In God's eternal plan, he chose to be with us as one of us. At the annunciation the angel told Mary that she would conceive by the power of the Holy Spirit and bring forth a child who was to be both God and man. In the nativity this divine intersection of earth and heaven took place. Jesus, who was the son of Mary, was also the Son of God. "The Word became flesh and made his dwelling among us" (John 1:14).

Because of Mary's role in the incarnation, her place in the Church would be equally significant. The Church continues the mission and presence of Christ in the world. It therefore is made up of human members. Yet it is Christ who heads this body and his Holy Spirit who is its soul.

Just as we call Mary "Mother of the Church" because she is the mother of Jesus who is head of the Church, so we look to St. Joseph, who was foster father of Jesus and his protector, as the patron of the universal Church—protector of the Church.

St. Joseph's Role in Our Redemption

The first chapter of the apostolic exhortation on St. Joseph focuses on his marriage to Mary. This is the foundation of his role in salvation history. Joseph, a son of David, was asked by God to take Mary as his wife. She was to bear a son, conceived by the power of the Holy Spirit, whom he was to call Jesus (Matthew 1:20-21).

The pope points out that the divine messenger "introduces Joseph to the mystery of Mary's motherhood" (3.2), but Joseph was to have a singular role in the unfolding of the mystery of our redemption. He would join Mary in being the "first guardian of this divine mystery" (5.2). Together with Mary and in relation to her, he is intimately involved in this final stage of God's revelation that takes place in Christ.

To accept all of this, Joseph, like Mary, had to be a person of faith. What strikes us when we look at the pages of Scripture and see the figure of Joseph—even if he is sketched somewhat faintly against all the other dominant figures—is his great faith. When the angel comes to him in a dream and says to him that he is to take Mary as his wife, he does not hesitate (Matthew 1:24). When he has to set out with very little provision to Bethlehem where his wife's child will be born, he does so unflinchingly and without complaint (Luke 2:4). And when God tells him to flee with the child for its safety, his response is total and complete (Matthew 2:13-14). Little is said of St. Joseph in the New Testament, but what does come through is the "righteous man" of great faith (Matthew 1:19).

Joseph's role in salvation history is linked to Mary because of Joseph's marriage to her. The pope tells us that this marriage is the "juridical basis of his fatherhood." While Joseph was not the natural father of Jesus, nonetheless, he was the spouse of the Blessed Mother and in that capacity, he assumed responsibility for the child Jesus and for Jesus' mother. The apostolic exhortation refers to "the service of fatherhood" and holds up Mary's marriage to Joseph and their relationship to each other as the starting point for our understanding of Joseph's relationship to Jesus: "The Son of Mary is also Joseph's Son by virtue of the marriage bond that unites them" (7.4).

Because Joseph was spouse of the Blessed Virgin Mary, they formed a family. When a man and a woman come together to exchange vows publicly and have their marriage to each other witnessed, they become a family. Marriage by its nature is indissoluble and intended to provide mutual support to the spouses.

In a society in which family life is collapsing and our social order is unraveling, the Church's teaching on the indissolubility of marriage and the obligation of parents to their children is a necessary and timely remedy. Today we observe the proliferation of gangs and at-risk youth who feel alienated. We experience the growing expectation that somehow the state or society is supposed to assume the responsibilities of the family. In a time like this, the wisdom of the Church's teaching becomes more apparent.

In God's plan for our salvation, the second Person of the Blessed Trinity was to become one of us. That would happen through Mary, who would bring forth her child. St. Joseph would be called by God to serve the person and mission of Jesus Christ "through the exercise of his fatherhood" (8.1). Thus we can rejoice that St. Joseph, through his marriage to Mary, was caught up in the mystery of spiritual fatherhood and became a model of marriage and care of one's child, and an exemplar of the Holy Family.

The family is essential because it is *"the original cell of social life"* (*Catechism of the Catholic Church*, 2207). It is the natural society in which a husband and wife come together in love and give themselves in mutual support. From that "original cell," the whole human community grows in an ever-widening set of relationships. While the generation of Jesus is entirely unique in all of human history, the responsibilities of Joseph remained rooted in his marriage to Mary and therefore in his relationship to Jesus.

The gospels clearly describe the responsibilities of Joseph toward Jesus. In *Redemptoris Custos,* the pope reminds us how these duties were discharged—beginning with the journey to Bethlehem and the protection and care of Mary at the birth of Jesus, which Joseph witnessed. The exhortation goes on to note that Joseph discharged his first religious obligation as a father with his son's circumcision and the conferral of the name "Jesus." The presentation of Jesus in the temple, the flight into Egypt, and the finding of the child Jesus in the temple are all examples in Scripture of Joseph's care for and nurturing of Jesus.

Joseph's Relationship to Jesus

From one perspective, the most telling line in Scripture relative to Joseph's relationship to Jesus is found in Luke's gospel. After Mary and Joseph return to Nazareth after finding Jesus in the temple, St. Luke says that Jesus grew "in wisdom and age and favor before God and man" (Luke 2:52). Here, one's imagination can depict the daily routine of this adolescent, a teenager growing up and coming to know the faith and values of his family, his obligation to God, and his place in the affection of his parents. It is sometimes difficult to realize that Jesus had to learn to speak, read, and write. He had to be taught manners and how to relate to others. He had to learn his prayers and how to do his chores. In all of this, we can envision the role of Joseph. At the same time, Jesus was becoming more fully aware of his deepest inner identity and his mission as redeemer of the world.

Chapter three of the apostolic exhortation is directed to Joseph as a "just man," a husband. Here the Holy Father unfolds for us a picture of Joseph who is enveloped in love—love of God, love of his spouse, and love of the child committed to his care. While married life may bring with it enormous challenges expressed in the day-to-day routines, it is love that makes it a blessing.

How often in wedding celebrations do the Scriptures remind us that a marriage—the coming together of a man and woman—is a part of God's plan as expressed in the Book of Genesis. Very often the second reading in the wedding liturgy is from St. Paul's letter that tells us it is love that makes this possible (1 Corinthians 13). The fulfillment of the plan—God's master plan for a man and woman to come together as husband and wife and as mother and father—requires an enormous amount of effort on the part of both spouses. It is love that brings the effort to the fore every day—day in and day out.

"What God has joined together, no human being must separate" (Mark 10:9). Among the "hard sayings" of Jesus, this one is particularly challenging for many people today. Statistics show that one of every two marriages in this country ends in divorce, and the rate continues to climb. Perhaps what Jesus was saying to us is that it is impossible to sustain a loving permanent relationship through all the difficulties of life without the firm commitment that the partnership will endure, despite all the trials and tribulations. In a society that so lightly sets aside personal commitment, we should not be surprised that marriage is in a state of decline. The Catholic vision of love and marriage continues to offer sound direction and true guidance.

The Work of Family Life

In chapter four, the Holy Father points out that "work was the daily expression of love in the life of the family of Nazareth" (22.1). Something as wondrous and beautiful as a successful marriage and a functioning family does not happen on its own. A mother, a father, and the children need to work at making a family a success. Such effort is an expression of love and can be seen in countless acts of kindness, understanding, and appreciation. After our annual Mass for those celebrating their golden jubilee of marriage, I sometimes ask people in the reception line what the secret is to their success. So often the response is this one: "We work at it every day."

St. Joseph is clearly a patron for fathers and a model of parenting for our day. As the foster father of Jesus, he is a gentle, loving man wise enough to teach a child and caring enough to be present at the important moments to lead by example. The child Jesus had what we would call today a "role model" in his young adolescent life. The *Catechism of the Catholic Church* reminds us that "parents have the first responsibility for the education of their children" (2223). The home should be a center for education in the virtues. It is also to be what is called the "domestic church." A Christian family constitutes a specific manifestation and realization of ecclesial communion. It is a sign and an image of the Father, the Son, and the Holy Spirit, just as the Church itself and every believer are to be manifestations of the love of God within us and at work in the world around us.

In concluding his apostolic exhortation, John Paul recalls that St. Joseph is patron of the Church in our day. "This patronage must be invoked as ever necessary for the Church, not only as a defense against all dangers, but also, and indeed primarily, as an impetus for her renewed commitment to evangelization in the world and to reevangelization" (29.1). St. Joseph, who was responsible for Jesus' human understanding of his relationship with God and his education in the faith, is a model to every believer of the obligation to spread the faith.

Each one of us is called to be an evangelist, and we do not have to leave home to share our faith. All around us are people who should be with us at Sunday Mass. We all know friends, co-workers, and neighbors who do not participate in the sacramental life of the Church. The Holy Father challenges us to reach out to all of them and invite them back to the faith. In this way the ever-widening family of the faith, God's family, will be enriched and renewed.

We should never be passive bystanders in God's great salvific plan. Each of us is called to be an active participant. Through his relationship to Mary as her spouse, to Jesus as his foster father, and to the Church as its protector, St. Joseph is an example to each of us. We are called to be actively engaged in our vocation, our calling from God, in a way that quietly but effectively spreads the faith and extends God's kingdom to every place and age.

Chapter 13

Sowers of the Seed

Redemptoris Missio

ENGLISH TITLE: **The Mission of the Redeemer**
DATE ISSUED: **December 7, 1990**
TYPE OF DOCUMENT: **Encyclical Letter**

In what has become a tradition in the Church to mark the anniversaries of significant magisterial documents, Pope John Paul II issued his eighth encyclical, entitled *Redemptoris Missio* (The Mission of the Redeemer), on December 7, 1990, to celebrate the twenty-fifth anniversary of the Second Vatican Council's Decree on the Church's Missionary Activity, *Ad Gentes*. The purpose of the pope's letter was to remind us of our participation in the missionary activity of the Church.

Sacred Scripture provides us with a clear indication of the intense commitment of the infant Church to missionary activity. There was an urgency about the need to spread the gospel as well as an awareness that the missionary activity and the identity of the Church were intimately linked. Even a cursory glance at the Acts of the Apostles reveals a self-understanding on the part of the apostles that the fledgling Church was missionary by its very nature. The apostles were witnesses of the resurrection and our salvation in and through Christ. The spread of the message was the spread of the Church. The acceptance of the message was the growth of the Church.

Ad Gentes is the foundational document for reflection on the Church's missionary activity. In the introduction, the decree clearly states:

The apostles, on whom the Church was founded, following the footsteps of Christ "preached the word of truth and begot churches." It is the duty of their successors to carry on this work so that "the word of God may run and be glorified" (2 Thessalonians 3:1), and the kingdom of God proclaimed and renewed throughout the world. (AG, 1)

Pope Paul VI followed the lead of the Council and gave even greater emphasis to evangelization, as is evident both in his choosing Paul, the apostle to the Gentiles, as his papal name and in his apostolic journeys to other continents. In his apostolic exhortation *Evangelii Nuntiandi*, he spoke of evangelization in the broadest of terms: "Evangelization is in fact the grace and vocation proper to the Church, her deepest identity. She exists in order to evangelize, that is to say in order to preach and teach, to be the channel of the gift of grace, to reconcile sinners with God and to perpetuate Christ's sacrifice in the Mass, which is the memorial of his death and glorious resurrection" (EN, 14).

The Agent of Mission: The Holy Spirit

John Paul's encyclical *Redemptoris Missio* builds on the doctrine of *Ad Gentes* and *Evangelii Nuntiandi* and devotes one entire chapter (3), entitled "The Holy Spirit, the Principal Agent of Mission," to a discussion of the doctrinal basis for the Church's missionary or evangelizing activity.

Pope John Paul begins his reflection on the missionary activity of the Church in chapter one by raising the following question: "Is missionary work among non-Christians still relevant?" He also asks the ultimate question relative to missionary activity: "Why, then, should there be missionary activity?" (4.3).

The pope notes that in recent years a breakdown of commitment or enthusiasm in missionary work has been widely reported. Those who comment on this breakdown speak of a need to redefine or refocus the missionary activity of the Church precisely in terms of its doctrinal basis, that is, that life in Christ in and through the Church is an essential part of the proclamation that leads to salvation.

In addressing some of the reasons for this breakdown in missionary activity, John Paul says he raises this question for several reasons:

> Nowadays the call to conversion which missionaries address to non-Christians is put into question or passed over in silence. It is seen as an act of "proselytizing"; it is claimed that it is enough to help people to become more human or more faithful to their own religion, that it is enough to build communities capable of working for justice, freedom, peace, and solidarity. (46.4)

In answering the above objections, the pope refocuses the missionary activity of the Church in terms of its profound doctrinal basis:

> What is overlooked is that every person has the right to hear the "good news" of the God who reveals and gives himself in Christ, so that each one can live out in its fullness his or her proper calling. This lofty reality is expressed in the words of Jesus to the Samaritan woman: "If you knew the gift of God," and in the unconscious but ardent desire of the woman: 'Sir, give me this water, that I may not thirst" (John 4:10, 15). (46.4)

The permanent validity of the Church's missionary effort rests on the recognition that Christ is the way, the truth, and the life, and not merely one truth or way or life among others. "Master," said the apostle Thomas, "we do not know where you are going; how can we know the way?" Jesus said to him, "I am the way and the truth and the life. No one comes to the Father except through me" (John 14:5-6). Jesus is the way to God. He is the only Savior and the sole mediator between us and God. To the question "Why mission?" John Paul answers:

> We reply with the Church's faith and experience that true liberation consists in opening oneself to the love of Christ. In him and only in him are we set free from all alienation and doubt, from slavery to the power of sin and death. Christ is truly "our peace" (Ephesians 2:14); the love of Christ impels us (2 Corinthians 5:14), giving meaning and joy to our life. Mission is an issue of faith, an accurate indicator of our faith in Christ and his love for us. (11.3)

Bringing Christ to the World

As he has done many times, beginning with his first encyclical letter, *Redemptor Hominis*, John Paul highlights the unique role of Jesus Christ as the only savior. Christ has redeemed us—this is a fact. St. Paul writes to the early Christians in Corinth, "So whoever is in Christ is a new creation: the old things have passed away; behold, new things have come. And all this is from God, who reconciled us to himself through Christ" (2 Corinthians 5:17-18). But the saving work of Jesus is yet to be received in the lives of many, and the full flowering of its richness is yet to be seen. There is apostolic work yet to be done, and, as St. Paul goes on to say, God has "given us the ministry of reconciliation" (5:18).

Because redemption is a continuing reality, mission continues to be an absolute necessity. To the question "Why mission?" the Holy Father responds with the words of St. Paul: "'This grace was given, to preach to the Gentiles the inscrutable riches of Christ'" (Ephesians 3:8). Newness of life in Christ is the 'good news' for men and women of every age: All are called to it and destined for it. Indeed, all people are searching for it, albeit at times in a confused way, and have a right to know the value of this gift and approach it freely" (11.4).

The Church, and every individual Christian within her, must not hide or keep to itself this newness and richness received from God's bounty. Rather, such good news must be communicated to all mankind:

> This is why the Church's mission derives not only from the Lord's mandate but also from the profound demands of God's life within us. Those who are incorporated in the Catholic Church ought to sense their privilege and for that reason their greater obligation of bearing witness to the faith and to the Christian life as a service to their brothers and sisters and as a fitting response to God. (11.5)

Redemptoris Missio brings us next to the unfolding of Christ's mission in our lives through the work of the Church and the power of the Holy Spirit. In chapter two the pope describes the manifestation of the kingdom of God in and through the Church, and in chapter three, he discusses the role of the Holy Spirit as the principal agent of mission.

The Church Is One with Christ

The Church is not only dear to Christ, but it is also the bearer of all his saving gifts. In a real way, the Church is one with Christ. She is made one with him as his mystical body. Christ often identified himself with his followers and with his Church. As he sent the disciples to preach in his name, he said, "Whoever listens to you listens to me. Whoever rejects you rejects me" (Luke 10:16). To those who did deeds of charity for his little ones, he proclaimed, "Whatever you did for one of these least brothers of mine, you did for me" (Matthew 25:40).

Of St. Paul, who had been vigorously persecuting the Church before his own conversion, Christ asked, "Why are you persecuting me? . . . I am Jesus, whom you are persecuting" (Acts 9:4, 5). At the Last Supper, he spoke of the intense unity that makes him one with those who are united by faith and love to him: "I am the vine, you are the branches" (John 15:5). The vine and branches are one living reality. So it is also with Christ and his Church, with Christ and those who love him. Given this understanding of the identity of the Church and its mission to bring all people to God in Christ, the missionary activity of the Church becomes increasingly clear.

In chapter four the pope deals with the vast horizons of the mission *ad gentes* (to the nations), and in chapter five, he discusses the paths of mission. Here the Holy Father addresses the relationship of witness to evangelization and the Church as the force for evangelization. It is precisely because of the process of salvation, which fills up what is lacking in the ongoing process of redemption and helps bring to fullness the good gift of God's love in the world, that the missionary activity of the Church is also turned inward. It strengthens the faith and facilitates the process of the conversion of each believer.

The Lifelong Process of Conversion

The living sense of the faith of which Pope John Paul speaks includes but is more than just the passing on of doctrine. The Holy Father is speaking of a personal and profound meeting with the Savior. This implies a dynamic and lifelong process of conversion, "which demands a continual turning away from 'life according to the flesh' to life 'according to the spirit' (cf. Romans 8:3-13). . . . Conversion means accepting, by a personal decision, the saving sovereignty of Christ and becoming his disciple" (46.2).

These words again remind us of the pope's first encyclical, *Redemptor Hominis*, in which he spoke so beautifully of our need for a living relationship with the Lord of love. As human beings, we yearn to love and be loved, and this yearning finds its fulfillment only in Jesus as the redeemer of humankind. "Jesus Christ is the chief way for the Church. He himself is our way 'to the Father's house' and is the way to each man" (RH, 13). For John Paul, the essential way to deepen and renew our living encounter with the Lord and one another as Church is through a renewed appreciation and understanding of penance, the Eucharist, and catechesis.

In speaking of the place of the Eucharist in *Redemptor Hominis*, the Holy Father says that at times we may fail to appreciate this awesome gift of God entrusting himself to us. And yet God does entrust himself to us, "as if not taking into consideration our human weakness, our unworthiness, the force of habit or routine, or even the possibility of insult." It is an essential truth, John Paul says in this first encyclical letter, "that the Eucharist builds the Church, building it as an authentic community of the People of God, as the assembly of the faithful, bearing the same mark of unity that was shared by the apostles and the first disciples of the Lord" (RH, 20).

The missionary activity of the Church remains permanently valid because it is identical to the nature of the Church. The missionary activity of the Church is focused as much on those who have heard the gospel but no longer find in it a source of direction and motivation for living as it is on those who have never met Christ.

In the remaining chapters of *Redemptoris Missio*, "Leaders and Workers in the Missionary Apostolate" (6), "Cooperation in Missionary Activity" (7), and "Missionary Spirituality" (8), John Paul speaks of all those who should be involved in missionary activity—that is, every member of the Church, whatever his or her state in life or vocation. He also addresses the need for cooperation among all those within the Church to assure that the Church's missionary activity is carried out in an effective and harmonious way. Finally, the encyclical reminds us that missionary spirituality is rooted in our acceptance of the gift of the Holy Spirit. Our call to holiness is, in fact, deeply and intimately linked with the call to spread the faith.

This encyclical continues to present a vision of an ever-growing, renewing, and all-embracing Church with the forceful reminder that this happens because every Catholic is at heart a missionary—whether reaching out to someone who has never experienced Christ or to someone who has drifted away from practicing the faith. It is in this latter category that each one of us is aware of fertile missionary ground in which we can truly be fruitful sowers of the seed. When these seeds are nurtured and nourished, people will return to the Church, to the sacraments, and to life in Christ.

Chapter 14

A COMMITMENT TO CARE

Centesimus Annus

ENGLISH TITLE: **One Hundred Years of Catholic Social Teaching**

DATE ISSUED: **May 1, 1991**

TYPE OF DOCUMENT: **Encyclical Letter**

The May 1, 1991, encyclical letter *Centesimus Annus* (One Hundred Years of Catholic Social Teaching) by Pope John Paul II was published on the centenary of the first social encyclical letter, *Rerum Novarum* (On the Condition of Workers), by Pope Leo XIII. It provides us with an occasion both to celebrate Catholic social teaching and to reflect on it.

One reason for our joy is the realization that more than a century of articulated Catholic social teaching has shaped and continues to influence much of the development of social justice in large parts of the world. *Centesimus Annus* gives us an opportunity to reflect on the origins of Catholic social teaching and the major principles that guide and form it today.

Catholic social doctrine did not develop in a vacuum. In the decades prior to the encyclical *Rerum Novarum*, the stage was set on which the struggle for social justice and human rights would take place. The backdrop for this drama included a theological-philosophical thesis from outside the Catholic tradition that provided justification for much of what took place under the euphemistic terms "empire building" and "the winning of the West."

The principal elements of this "gospel" of economic leadership included the exaltation of business success as a sign of divine predilection and the recognition of financial gain as visible proof of supernatural approbation. Riches were considered a proof of God's love. This mixture of theology, philosophy, and business acumen provided what was considered a justification for a variety of expressions of greed and avarice. Eventually but only slowly, this view of life was corrected by laws that outlawed child labor and atrocious working conditions, established a forty-hour work week, and at the same time, recognized the right of workers to organize and bargain collectively.

The Principles of *Rerum Novarum*

With the promulgation of *Rerum Novarum* in 1891, the Church sought to confront the terrible exploitation and poverty of European and American workers at the end of the nineteenth century. With this document, the Church applied the principles of her social teaching to the conditions and issues emanating from the Industrial Revolution. The focus of *Rerum Novarum* includes the dignity of work, the right to private property, the principle of collaboration instead of class struggle as the fundamental means of social change, the rights of the weak, the dignity of the poor and the obligations of the rich, the perfecting of justice through change, and the right to form professional or labor associations.

Rerum Novarum also made clear the right of the Church to speak out on social matters, since society affects both religion and morality and in turn is affected by them. Much like our own day, the response of some people to the Church's message of moral imperative was not to confront the issue but rather to try to silence the voice of the Church. Leo XIII, on behalf of the Church universal, and the bishops in the United States had to defend the right of the Church to speak to moral issues and to fight grave societal evils against those who tried to divert the discussion by invoking the idea of separation of church and state.

In *Centesimus Annus*, Pope John Paul II notes that the Church's response to the terrible inhumanities of the Industrial Revolution was deeply rooted in our own Christian anthropology that sees the proper relationship of human beings with God and with one another:

> Pope Leo foresaw the negative consequences—political, social and economic—of the social order proposed by "socialism," which at that time was still only a social philosophy and not yet a fully structured movement. . . . Two things must be emphasized here: first, the great clarity in perceiving, in all its harshness, the actual condition of the working class . . . ; secondly, equal clarity in recognizing the evil of a solution which, by appearing to reverse the positions of the poor and the rich, was in reality detrimental to the very people whom it was meant to help. (12.2, 3)

A Biblical Perspective

To gain a sense of the purpose and meaning not only of *Rerum Novarum* but also of the whole body of Catholic social teaching, it is important to understand that this teaching finds its roots in the revelation of the Judeo-Christian tradition and in the Christian vision of the human person. That vision sees the human person as the unfolding image of God and as a transforming agent of society who is, in turn, influenced by society.

In St. Luke's account of the beginning of Jesus' public ministry, we find Jesus in the synagogue at Nazareth quoting the prophet Isaiah: "The Spirit of the Lord is upon me, / because he has anointed me / to bring glad tidings to the poor. / He has sent me to proclaim liberty to captives / and recovery of sight to the blind, / to let the oppressed go free, / and to proclaim a year acceptable to the Lord" (Luke 4:18-19, quoting Isaiah 61:1-2). Jesus then points out in a most dramatic way that he is the fulfillment of this revealed plan of God. The meaning of his ministry is grounded in the Hebrew people's vision of God present in their midst, of their identity as a community, and of their sense of obligation to God's law and its demands.

Concern for those who are poor, downtrodden, weak, alienated, and marginalized was among the essential qualities that God expected of good and faithful Jews. This regard for the poor had to be more than mere obligation. It was a response of gratitude that flowed from their hearts for their covenant, their deliverance from Egyptian oppression, their being gifted with the promised land, and for many other blessings. Compassion, therefore, was not something over and above the commandments. It was integral to and an expression of the law as a matter of basic justice.

Christ came to proclaim a kingdom that is not yet fully with us but, at the same time, is already unfolding in our midst. He validated his vision by revealing that he was sent by God to reveal God's plan and will (cf. John 1:18). For the follower of Jesus, revelation as the source of truth, the reality of the kingdom of God, and the daily struggle to realize something of the kingdom in this life are all foundational truths. Catholic social teaching is grounded in these truths and the tensions they create. It also rests on the firm conviction that what we do in this life, what justice we realize in this world, endures as a sign of God's presence and the beginnings of God's kingdom (cf. Matthew 25:31-46).

Without this clear Christian anthropology that is rooted in the Scriptures, John Paul says, we would become victims of the fundamental error of socialism:

> Socialism considers the individual person simply as an element, a molecule within the social organism, so that the good of the

individual is completely subordinated to the functioning of the socioeconomic mechanism. . . . Man is thus reduced to a series of social relationships, and the concept of the person as the autonomous subject of moral decision disappears, the very subject whose decisions build the social order. . . . In contrast, from the Christian vision of the human person, there necessarily follows a correct picture of society. (13.1, 2)

From a Christian perspective, the human race has come into conflict with its Creator. Egotism, sin, and the rejection of God have given rise to a world filled with injustice. Yet in the midst of all the confusion of conflicting goals and the rejection of values that make up the modern world, the Christian vision has an answer. It is that Christ came to reconcile all men and women with God and with each other. God in Christ was reconciling all things. Christ offers a new creation, a new world, a new style of life, a new way of love.

From the vantage point of revelation, human life is seen as sacred because it is potentially divine. Each human being is not just another traveler on the journey through life but our sister or brother in Christ. Our final destiny is life eternal with the Father. No one is merely a digit on the state census. None are aliens in this life because all are capable of becoming citizens of God's everlasting kingdom. With this starting point, a whole new approach to human problems is available.

In *Centesimus Annus*, Pope John Paul II proposed a "rereading" of Pope Leo's encyclical by inviting us to look back at the text itself in order to discover anew "the richness of the fundamental principles which it formulated for dealing with the question of the condition of workers" (3.1). Later in his encyclical letter, the pope reminds us that rereading *Rerum Novarum* "in the light of contemporary realities enables us to appreciate the Church's constant concern for and dedication to categories of people who are especially beloved to the Lord Jesus" (11.1). Here we are reminded of the often noted "preferential option for the poor." It is an option that the pope had defined earlier as a "special form of primacy in the exercise of Christian charity" (*Sollicitudo Rei Socialis*, 42).

The Challenge for Christians

When we read the challenge of Christ in chapter twenty-five of Matthew's gospel, we discover something of the intensity of the Christian commitment to care for others and establish a truly just order. Have we fed the hungry, clothed the naked, sheltered the homeless, or visited those who are sick or in prison?

Jesus' intention was carried out by his first followers. In the Acts of the Apostles, we read that the first community was of one heart and one soul. Everything was held in common, and distribution was made to anyone in need (cf. Acts 4:32, 34, 35). St. Paul speaks of the lowly and despised of the world as having a special place in the heart and plan of God (cf. 1 Corinthians 1:26-28).

St. James puts strong emphasis on the incarnational dimensions of faith and charity, speaking of authentic religion as including the visiting of orphans and widows in their affliction (cf. 1:27) and reminding us that "faith of itself, if it does not have works, is dead" (2:17). St. John sums up his own understanding of what Jesus expected of his followers: "If someone who has worldly means sees a brother in need and refuses him compassion, how can the love of God remain in him? Children, let us love not in word or speech but in deed and truth" (1 John 3:17-18). While it would be inaccurate to say that Jesus promoted any particular political, social, or economic program, he did establish basic principles that should characterize any just, humane economic or political system. Among these must be a "preferential option for the poor."

Only faith can provide the conviction that our works of justice endure as part of the plan of God to bring about the kingdom of God.

In *Apostolicam Actuositatem* (The Decree on the Apostolate of the Laity), the Second Vatican Council spoke of the enduring aspect of the works of justice and love as the "renewal of the temporal order" (AA, 7). In fact, at this point, in reference to the Christian apostolate of social action, the Council quotes *Rerum Novarum*, Pius XI's *Quadragesimo Anno*, and a 1941 statement by Pius XII.

Building on the Church's Tradition

Centesimus Annus explicitly builds on this long-standing tradition of Catholic social teaching, which is expanded, developed, and applied in the face of new and different threats to the well-being of the human person. John Paul II writes, "Like Pope Leo and the Popes before and after him, I take my inspiration from the Gospel image of 'the scribe who has been trained for the kingdom of heaven,' whom the Lord compares to 'a householder who brings out of his treasure what is new and what is old' (Matthew 13:52)" (3.3).

In the forty years after *Rerum Novarum*, the ever-growing concentration of economic strength and power in the hands of a few would incite a call to class struggle. In order to give a clearer interpretation and a more precise application of the moral law as it relates to human relations and to promote a social order based on justice and charity, Pope Pius XI issued the encyclical *Quadragesimo Anno* in 1931.

This encyclical begins with an overall view of industrial society and production. Stressing the need for both capital and labor to contribute to production and economic organization, it outlines the conditions for the reestablishment of a just social order. At the same time, it seeks to face the great changes brought about by the new developments of the economy and socialism. *Quadragesimo Anno* outlines the principles of solidarity and collaboration that are necessary for a just social order and warns that failure to respect freedom of association and action would compromise the efforts to arrive at justice.

When the Second Vatican Council met from 1962–1965, it chose in a solemn manner to speak fully and directly about the social and temporal aspects of Christian life. *Gaudium et Spes* (The Pastoral Constitution on the Church in the Modern World) addresses the Church's function to promote the good of the whole person "in his totality, taking into account his material needs and the requirements of his intellectual, moral, spiritual, and religious life" (GS, 64).

Gaudium et Spes makes clear that the demands of the gospel plunge the Church into the "joy and hope, the grief and anguish of the men of our time" (GS, 1). It also declares that the Church is not bound to any particular political, economic, or social system. It is in this frame of reference that the Council turns the light of the gospel on marriage and family life, the development of culture, economic life, the political community, and the avoidance of war.

In 1967 Pope Paul VI advanced the development of Catholic social teaching when he issued an important reflection on social matters. *Populorum Progressio* introduced some significant new elements. The encyclical focused its teaching on integral human development, both personal and societal. Development is presented as the transition from less human conditions to those that are more human. The former are found wherever material and moral deficiencies exist together with oppressive structures. In addition to material needs, more human conditions include acquiring "know-how' and culture, as well as respect for the dignity of others, recognition of supreme values and of God, and the Christian life of faith, hope, and charity.

This is the first encyclical devoted almost entirely to international development. It moves beyond rich and poor classes to rich and poor nations. It grounds full and authentic development in a new humanism that embraces the higher values of love, friendship, prayer, and contemplation.

One purpose for writing *Centesimus Annus*, Pope John Paul writes, is "to show the fruitfulness of the principles enunciated by Leo XIII which belong to the Church's doctrinal patrimony, and, as such, involve the exercise of her teaching authority" (3.5). While the situations change and the teaching needs continuously to be applied in a way that makes it relevant, nonetheless, the principles are rooted in revelation and in our human nature. It is the duty of the magisterium to enunciate the Church's social teaching, not as an option for the believer, but as a guide for his or her life.

Balancing Personal Rights and the Common Good

In chapter two, "Toward the 'New Things' of Today," the pope directs our attention to the competing principles that form the background against which the Church's social teaching had to struggle. The operative competing principle in the free-world economy too often has been "the right to a profit." The profit principle dominates many practical decisions and can be felt at virtually every level of our human enterprise. In some instances, there was an elaborate theological justification for the extension of profits over human rights, which found its articulation in the theory of predestination and the size of one's bank balance as a sign of divine predilection. In that part of the world described as "capitalist," the profit principle, either as property or free enterprise, has often been advanced as an absolute norm.

The operative competing value in the socialist world is "the need of the collectivity." The totalitarian principle in a centrally planned economy, while having a totally different theoretical origin and justification, has the same practical conclusion in terms of human rights and the economic condition of the person, whose rights are subservient to the imposed absolute principle.

What makes the struggle for an acceptance of Catholic social teaching all the more difficult is that both of the principles substituted for Catholic social teaching have elements that are valid and cannot be ignored. The free-enterprise system is emptied of all meaning without its profit incentive. Human society fails without due recognition of the rights of the collectivity—the state.

Catholic social teaching has tried to balance the legitimate needs of both the free-enterprise system and the rightful demands of the state against the more basic human needs of individuals who live and die not in abstraction but in the flesh. In the effort to balance the many competing rights and needs, a clear articulation of permanent principles and values has emerged whose claims must be met before any economic system or government can claim to act in a truly just and humane manner. In the remaining portion of *Centesimus Annus,* John Paul provides examples of the concrete manifestation of the major principles and values that are the foundation of Catholic social teaching.

Dignity of the Human Person

The dignity of the human person does not derive from any achievement, accomplishment, productivity, or external talent or attribute. We are created in the image and likeness of God and are called to a divine destiny, which transcends earthly life. As such, every human from the moment of conception until natural death is to be cherished and considered worthy of reverence and respect. It is for this reason that the Church defends so intensely the dignity of persons against all forms of slavery, exploitation, manipulation, and domination, whether these be inflicted in the field of politics, economics, medicine, science, or from cultural or ideological demands.

Flowing from the God-given dignity of the human person are certain inherent rights that must be protected and defended. Of particular importance is the right to religious liberty because it touches the transcendent core of the person—the spirit—and reveals a point of reference and in a certain sense becomes the measure of the other fundamental rights (cf. 44). Our own Declaration of Independence recognizes the rights, rooted in "nature and nature's God," of life, liberty, and the pursuit of happiness.

No one is an island. We are social by nature. Human development and growth take place in society. Because of the principle of interdependence between the person and society, human society must be the object of the Church's social teaching.

By "common good," we mean all those social conditions that favor the full development of human personality. While the common good is higher than private interests, it is intrinsically united to the good of the human person and commits both the ecclesiastical and public authorities to recognize, respect, regulate, protect, and promote rights and facilitate the fulfillment of their respective duties. The Church must continually stress the human meaning of social structures and foster their in-depth transformation according to the criteria of social justice.

In his first encyclical *Deus Caritas Est* (God Is Love), Pope Benedict XVI continues this line of thought when he teaches that Catholic social doctrine "has no intention of giving the Church power over the State. . . . Its aim is simply to help purify reason and to contribute, here and now, to the acknowledgement and attainment of what is just" (28).

Solidarity and Subsidiarity

The two principles of solidarity and subsidiarity should govern social life. The principle of solidarity recognizes that each person, as a member of society, is interconnected with the destiny of society itself and, from the perspective of the gospel, is also bound up with the salvation of all women and men. Subsidiarity complements the principle of solidarity. By this principle, the individual person, local communities, and intermediary bodies of governance are protected from the danger of losing their rightful autonomy and freedom. The authentic development of socioeconomic, political, and cultural life, ending in just and peaceful coexistence, is only possible with the just and responsible participation of all members and sectors of society.

The goods of the earth are given by God to all people in order that they might satisfy their right to a form of life in keeping with their human dignity. While the right to private property is valid and necessary, it is nevertheless restricted within the limits of its social function. As John Paul says, Christian tradition has never upheld this right as absolute and untouchable. On the contrary, it has always understood this right within the broader context of the right common to all to use the goods of the whole creation; the right to private property is subordinated to the right to common use, to the fact that goods are meant for everyone (cf. 30).

The Church's social doctrine invites us to be grateful for the vitality and ferment of the prophetic voices who speak for the unborn, the poor, the homeless, the victims of racism and sexism, the elderly, and the handicapped. The same teaching challenges us so that we may see our world as the house of God, which calls for our care and our stewardship. The goods of the earth are not without limits, nor can they be squandered without regard for future generations.

At the same time, the Church in her social doctrine calls us to reflect on and affirm the vocation of the laity in the world of business, education, labor, medicine, and politics as transforming agents of society. Especially important today is the vocation of the politician, who is called to represent us in the task of building a just social order.

Above all, the Church's social doctrine points us to Christ, who came among us so that we might have life and have it to the full (cf. John 10:10). The same voice of Christ is echoed again and again in the living tradition of the Church that encourages and fosters opportunities for every human being to actualize their God-given potentials, talents, and aspirations so that we might all realize the glory of God in our lives and in the world. As St. Irenaeus wrote, "The glory of God is the human person fully alive."

As Pope John Paul II states at the conclusion of *Centesimus Annus*, "The present encyclical has looked at the past, but above all it is directed to the future" (62.1). The Church's social teaching continually calls us to recognize in our Catholic teaching not only a guide for the present but also a foundation on which to build as we move into the future and face new and difficult issues.

In this final section, John Paul also expresses gratitude to "all those who have devoted themselves to studying, expounding, and making better known Christian social teaching" (56.1). No one has done that with greater dedication, skill, and devotion than Pope John Paul II himself. As we look back over the history of Catholic social teaching and look forward to its ever more explicit application, we do so with great gratitude to all of the popes who have been voices of social justice—and none more than St. John Paul II.

Chapter 15

FORMING GOOD SHEPHERDS

Pastores Dabo Vobis

ENGLISH TITLE: On the Formation of Priests in the
                     Circumstances of the Present Day
DATE ISSUED: **March 25, 1992**
TYPE OF DOCUMENT: **Post-Synodal Apostolic Exhortation**

T he post-synodal apostolic exhortation *Pastores Dabo Vobis* takes its name from a passage in the Book of Jeremiah: "I will appoint over you shepherds after my own heart" (3:15). In these words from the prophet, God promises his people that he will never leave them without shepherds to gather them together and guide them. The exhortation, in English entitled "On the Formation of Priests in the Circumstances of the Present Day," is the fruit of the eighth ordinary assembly of the Synod of Bishops, held in Rome in October 1990.

This synod, in which I was privileged to participate, was devoted to priestly spirituality and the ongoing formation of priests. It addressed two major areas of this lifelong spiritual growth: pre-ordination formation (seminary life), and post-ordination formation (ongoing priestly spiritual renewal).

There is probably no one subject that has been so studied, examined, and reflected upon by the bishops than our system of seminaries and the program of priestly formation preparing a candidate for ordination. And while we devote great energy and resources to preparing a priest for ordination, we do not always, with the same resolve and expenditure, assist the priest after ordination in his daily call to draw closer to Christ.

The first chapter of *Pastores Dabo Vobis* considers the circumstances of the present day in which the priesthood is lived and the background against which it is exercised. Discussing some positive trends, John Paul notes an increased love of Scripture and a growing vitality in the younger churches. He also speaks of "the splendid witness of martyrdom provided by the churches of Central and Eastern Europe, as well as that of the faithfulness and courage of other churches which are still forced to undergo persecution and tribulation for the faith" (6.3).

However, the pope also discusses problems and obstacles in society that affect the priesthood. "A desperate defense of personal subjectivity" renders people "incapable of true human relationships" (7.3). Other obstacles are rationalism, materialism, the practical and existential atheism of our society, as well as the breakup of the family and the obscuring or distorting of the true meaning of human sexuality. Much of this has led to the phenomenon of "subjectivism in matters of faith":

An increasing number of Christians seem to have a reduced sensitivity to the universality and objectivity of the doctrine of the faith, because they are subjectively attached to what pleases them, to what corresponds to their own experience, and to what does not impinge on their own habits. . . . This situation also gives rise to the phenomenon of belonging to the Church in ways which are even more partial and conditional, with a resulting negative influence on the birth of new vocations to the priesthood, on the priest's own self-awareness, and on his ministry within the community. (7.8, 9)

In sketching out these present-day circumstances, the Holy Father has addressed issues with which all of us are quite familiar. We live in a world whose guiding norm has become the individual person and personal experience. We live in a society in which increasingly, the objective nature of the Church's teaching and the binding power of such teaching are denied, if not explicitly then certainly implicitly. Growing out of a theological subjectivism that has characterized much of the writings of the last three decades, many Catholics feel free to pick and choose which teachings they accept and which they reject.

The Unchanging Priesthood

The second chapter of the exhortation is devoted to the nature and mission of the ministerial priesthood. With exemplary conciseness, the perennial teaching of the Church on the nature and mission of the priest is summarized. Building on the Christian identity that has its source in the Blessed Trinity, *Pastores Dabo Vobis* places the priest's identity, like every Christian identity, in the communion of God as Trinity.

In the fullness of time, the eternal Word was sent into the world and human history, marking the beginning of redemption and the Church. The incarnation of Christ and the paschal mystery of his death and resurrection are also the source of the sacramental life and the universal priesthood of the new covenant.

For the sake of this universal priesthood of the new covenant, Jesus gathered disciples during his earthly mission (cf. Luke 10:1-12) to carry out publicly in the Church a priestly ministry (14.1). They were to minister in a special way to those with whom they were united in the body of Christ, a body in which "all members have not the same function" (Romans 12:4; Pope Paul VI, *Presbyterorum Ordinis*, 2). While all the baptized participate in the priesthood of Christ, some are called and ordained to minister to all of the faithful. In the Sacrament of Holy Orders, priests are especially configured to Christ to act in his person as head and pastor of the Church and in the name of the whole people of God (Vatican II, *Lumen Gentium*, 10; *Presbyterorum Ordinis*, 2). Priests are ministers of Christ; they receive their sacred authority from Christ through the Church.

Conferred in the Sacrament of Holy Orders, "the priesthood, along with the word of God and the sacramental signs which it serves, belongs to the constitutive elements of the Church" (16.2). Although the reality of priestly ministry emanated from Christ, its differentiation and precise naming occurred in successive generations of the Christian community under the guidance of the Holy Spirit.

The figure of the good shepherd, who calls each by name and lays down his life for his flock, stands as a sign of that special configuration to Christ that belongs to priests by virtue of the Sacrament of Holy Orders. "The ministry of the priest is entirely on behalf of the Church; it aims at promoting the exercise of the common priesthood of the entire people of God" (16.2).

Configured to Christ

Configured to Christ, head of the Church, and intimately united as co-workers of the bishops, priests are commissioned in a unique way to continue Christ's mission as prophet, priest, and king. Their primary duty is to proclaim the gospel to the whole world by word and deed. This mission extends to all people, even those for whom the gospel has ceased to be a message of hope or a challenge to right action.

The preaching of the gospel finds its source and culmination in the Eucharist. Priests exercise the office of sanctifying the Christian people in the celebration of the sacraments of the Church. As members of one presbyterate gathered around the bishop, priests serve to unite the local Church in one great act of worship of the Father.

Finally, priests exercise the office of shepherd. Called to gather the family of Christ, priests act with a spiritual authority that enables them to lead the people of God along right paths. In these and similar ways, priests are servants of Christ present in the Church as mystery (actuating Christ's presence in the sacrament); as communion (building up the body of Christ); and as mission (heralding the gospel) (16.5).

Pastores Dabo Vobis speaks of the priest as "configured to Christ." In this sense the priesthood is a permanent part of the priest's being. "Priestly character" is in some way introduced into the life and being of the priest. The purpose of the exhortation is to express the fact that Christ associated the Church with himself in an irrevocable way for the salvation of the world. Priesthood is not just for the service of God's people at this stage of development of the kingdom; it exists also to reflect the permanent and transcendent union of Christ with his kingdom and to be a sign of the final fulfillment of the kingdom according to Christ's wish. In this sense the eschatological nature of the priesthood touches every aspect of the priest's work and life. The priest is configured to Christ in a manner that affects his very being for the specific purpose of testifying to the world that the fullness of Christ's kingdom is yet to come but has already begun in our midst.

Because of sacred ordination, the priest stands in the midst of the Church as its leader—its head. He also functions in the name of the whole Church specifically when presenting to God the prayers of the Church and, above all, when offering the Eucharistic sacrifice. As we identify the work of the priest, we realize that it is completely tied to the continuation of the unique work of Christ. That work is preeminently achieved in Christ's death and resurrection, which won our redemption. Hence the priesthood is intimately tied to the Eucharist, which continues to make present the life-giving effects of the great Passover. On the same first Holy Thursday on which he instituted the Sacrament of the Eucharist, Christ conferred priesthood on the apostles: "Do this in remembrance of me" (Luke 22:19).

All of this is the plan of God unfolding in Christ. Priesthood is not an afterthought of the Christian community but the explicit will of Christ. Because of this belief, the Church teaches that holy orders does not take its origin from the community, as though it were the community that "called" or "delegated" priests. The sacramental priesthood is truly a gift for this community that comes from Christ himself, from the very fullness of his own priesthood.

Priestly Formation

To understand fully the importance of *Pastores Dabo Vobis,* it is necessary to see its consequences and offspring. Nearly half of the document is devoted to what might be considered more technical aspects of the life of the Church: the formation of candidates for the priesthood (chapter five) and the ongoing formation of priests (chapter six). In these areas, which have an immense impact on the life of the Church because they deal with the priesthood, the exhortation became normative for a number of documents that direct priestly formation and ongoing formation of priests in the United States.

The *Program of Priestly Formation* (PPF) is published by the United States Conference of Catholic Bishops and oversees the preparation and formation of candidates to the priesthood. The fourth edition, approved by the conference and the Holy See in 1992, was completely rewritten after the publication of *Pastores Dabo Vobis* so that it could include both the experience of the papal seminary study that had taken place in seminaries and houses of formation throughout the United States in the 1980s and the wisdom and direction of the Holy Father in *Pastores Dabo Vobis.* The current *Program of Priestly Formation* (the fifth edition was issued in 2005) continues throughout to reflect the direction and teaching of *Pastores Dabo Vobis.* Another direct consequence of the 1990 Synod of Bishops that followed the exhortation was the *Directory for the Life and Ministry of Priests,* published by the Vatican Congregation for the Clergy in 1994, and the USCCB's *Basic Plan for the Ongoing Formation of Priests,* approved by the bishops in 1999.

In *Pastores Dabo Vobis*, John Paul addresses priestly formation under four basic headings or areas of formation: human, spiritual, intellectual, and pastoral. He affirms the sentiment of the synod that priestly formation needs suitable human formation. Because the priest is called to be a living image or icon of Christ who is head and shepherd of his Church, he should seek to reflect in himself as far as possible the human perfection that was so visible in the incarnate Son of God. Since it is the task of the priest to proclaim the word, to celebrate the sacraments, and to guide the Christian community in charity in the name and in the person of Christ, he must seek to do this in a way that makes him an effective minister to other human beings. *Pastores Dabo Vobis* reminds us that while the priest acts in the name and in the person of Christ, "all this he does dealing always and only with individual human beings" (43.1).

The human formation of priests has a special importance when dealing with those who will carry on Christ's ministry to other human beings. "In order that his ministry may be humanly as credible and acceptable as possible, it is important that the priest should mold his human personality in such a way that it becomes a bridge and not an obstacle for others in their meeting with Jesus Christ the Redeemer of humanity" (43.1).

At the heart of human formation is the quest for maturity. If a priest is going to freely undertake a life of self-giving ministry in obedience to his bishop and in committed celibacy for the sake of the kingdom, he must be mature enough to recognize the implications of his actions, the significance of his choices, and the obligations of his commitments. The challenge today, as it has always been, is to provide an education for sexuality that recognizes the validity, value, and gift of celibacy. Here again, the pope cites one of the propositions of the synod: "A love for Christ, which overflows into a dedication to everyone, is of the greatest importance in developing affective maturity. Thus the candidate, who is called to celibacy, will find in affective maturity a firm support to live chastity in faithfulness and joy" (44.4).

When the Holy Father turns to spiritual formation, he notes that all believers, not only priests, are called to grow in communion with God. In God's wonderful plan, each person should be open to the realization that there is beyond us an all-encompassing Absolute and that, as St. Augustine pointed out, our hearts are restless until they rest in God. "The educational process of a spiritual life, seen as a relationship and communion with God, derives and develops from this fundamental and irrepressible religious need" (45.2).

Those called to serve the Church in the leadership capacity of priesthood must recognize that they are to lead not only by word but also by example. In the realm of spirituality, the priest should be a leader. People should be able to turn to him for counsel and encouragement as they develop their own spiritual lives. In the priest they should see a level of prayer, a spirituality focused on the priest's sacramental ministry, and a communion with God that both inspire and encourage them.

Friendship with Christ

The pope alludes to the Second Vatican Council's Decree on Priestly Formation, *Optatam Totius,* which takes account "of the absolute transcendence of the Christian mystery" but also "describes the communion of future priests with Jesus in terms of friendship" (46.4). To achieve this, the Holy Father points again to the Council's decree, which "indicates a triple path to be covered: a faithful meditation on the word of God, active participation in the Church's holy mysteries, and the service of charity to the 'little ones.'" These are "three great values and demands," the pope says, "which further define the content of the spiritual formation of the candidate to the priesthood" (46.6).

It is obvious, then, that a healthy rhythm of life centered on the Eucharist and involving prayer, the Sacrament of Penance, spiritual reading, and quiet meditative time are all elements of ongoing priestly spiritual formation. To this, the pope adds, "Spiritual formation also involves seeking Christ in people. . . . The priest is, therefore, a man of charity and is called to educate others according to Christ's example and the new commandment of brotherly love (cf. John 15:12)" (49.1, 3).

The next element of priestly formation is described as intellectual formation: understanding the faith. The intellectual formation of candidates for the priesthood is rooted in the necessity that the newly ordained be prepared to take on the challenge of the new evangelization to which the Lord is calling the Church. Quoting the synodal fathers, *Pastores Dabo Vobis* says:

> If we expect every Christian to be prepared to make a defense of the faith and to account for the hope that is in us (cf. 1 Peter 3:15), then all the more should candidates for the priesthood and priests have diligent care of the quality of their intellectual formation in their education and pastoral activity. For the salvation of their brothers and sisters, they should seek an ever deeper knowledge of the divine mysteries. (51.2)

The priest is called to pass on the apostolic tradition. To do this, he must know it. The priest has to be exposed to the two-thousand-year teaching tradition of the Church guided by the Spirit so that he, in his turn, may give an account of what we believe and pass it on with understanding, joy, and commitment.

Finally, *Pastores Dabo Vobis* addresses pastoral formation. Here we are reminded that a priest's formation "must have a fundamentally pastoral character" to prepare him "to enter in communion with the charity of Christ, the Good Shepherd" (57.1). The training of candidates for the priesthood should make them true shepherds of souls after the example of our Lord Jesus Christ, teacher, priest, and shepherd. It is precisely in the pastoral application of the wondrous gifts given to the Church in her sacraments and teaching that the priest becomes a bridge of grace to those whom he serves. *Pastores Dabo Vobis* points out:

> The seminary which educates must seek really and truly to initiate the candidate into the sensitivity of being a shepherd, in the conscious and mature assumption of his responsibilities, in the interior habit of evaluating problems and establishing priorities and looking for solutions on the basis of honest motivations of faith and according to the theological demands inherent in pastoral work. (58.1)

Priestly ministry is sometimes envisioned as hands-on, direct, and person-to-person, and to some extent it still is and always will be. Yet pastoral ministry encompasses more than simply direct sacramental ministry, counseling, or one-on-one teaching. In fact, each priest is called to be a teacher and an administrator as well as a dispenser of the sacraments. The key to pulling all this together is the recognition that all of the above—teaching, administering, and sacramental action—is priestly ministry. All of it is pastoral.

The Need for Ongoing Priestly Formation

I now turn our attention to ongoing priestly formation, which John Paul includes in the understanding of effective priestly ministry. In the past, documents spoke about pre-ordination formation and its importance in preparing a man to undertake priestly ministry. Many documents have spoken about the nature of priesthood and its importance in the life of the Church. *Pastores Dabo Vobis* is the first apostolic exhortation to integrate ongoing or continuing priestly formation into the overall picture of effective pastoral ministry. Here the pope cites the reflections of the synod: "The synod fathers explained the reason justifying the need for ongoing formation, while at the same time revealing its deep nature as internal 'faithfulness' to the priestly ministry and as a 'process of continuing conversion'" (70.9).

Ongoing formation is another way of speaking about personal growth, intellectual and spiritual development, and whatever helps priests to be continually converted to the way of the Lord. Priestly formation, of its nature, must be "increasingly perfected throughout the whole of a priest's life" (*Ratio Fundamentalis*, 100). It is not surprising that such formation is a lifelong process—a way of life. Christ speaks of himself as the way as well as the truth and the life (John 14:6)

The priest's spiritual journey begins with his first personal contact with Christ through the sacraments of initiation and on through preparation for and ordination to the priesthood. It continues throughout his ministry, which when exercised "sincerely and tirelessly," will allow the priest to acquire holiness "in his own distinctive way" (*Presbyterorum Ordinis*, 13). The pilgrimage culminates in the ultimate conversion to Christ in glory.

Christ calls us to a perfection that is not quickly reached, to an intense living of all his gifts, especially love, which binds everything together in perfect harmony (Colossians 3:14). Ongoing priestly formation involves continued growth and development of the person as well as the constant conversion of mind and heart. "If we have the duty of helping others to be converted, we have to do the same continually in our own lives" (Pope John Paul II's 1979 Holy Thursday Letter to Priests, *Novo Incipiente*, 10).

Ongoing formation is an expression of the priest's universal call to holiness, a response to the primal and essential call of God. The call to seek perfection even in the midst of weakness is rooted in the Lord's word: "So be perfect, just as your heavenly Father is perfect" (Matthew 5:48).

The decreasing number of priests in many parts of the world calls our attention to the increased importance of ongoing formation. Where more is being asked of fewer priests, the spiritual and intellectual resources necessary to continue in ministry in a fruitful and positive manner need to be constantly replenished and developed. The need of the world for a new evangelization makes the ongoing formation of priests all the more urgent as heralds of the gospel and witnesses to the kingdom unfolding in the world.

The individual priest has the obvious primary responsibility to pursue his own growth and conversion to the Lord. At the same time, the diocesan bishop is to "exercise the greatest care in the progressive formation of the presbyterate" (*Christus Dominus*, 16). He should be a model for the diocesan priest in the care he takes regarding his own ongoing formation. In addition, it is under his direction that the diocese provides resources and develops clear policies and expectations for the ongoing formation of priests (cf. *Ecclesiae Sanctae*, 7). The magnitude of this task requires collaboration at the level of the episcopal conference in addition to individual episcopal efforts (cf. *Optatam Totius*, 22).

Assisting the diocesan bishop in his task, a diocesan director of ongoing priestly formation can provide the systematic and programmatic support needed for the priest to continue the process of personal spiritual renewal and ongoing formation. The model of continuous professional updating provided by other groups, including doctors, accountants, and other licensed practitioners, is instructive also for priestly continuing formation.

As I mentioned previously, in consequence of *Pastores Dabo Vobis* and also following the requests of numerous bishops during the synod of 1990, the Vatican Congregation for the Clergy issued the *Directory for the Life and Ministry of Priests*. In a way it is a logical extension of both the 1990 synod and *Pastores Dabo Vobis*. Here we are reminded that our challenge now is to devote the same resources to ongoing formation for priests that we do to the pre-ordination formation. Programs articulated in seminaries and houses of formation and based on the documents of the Church provide a model for the development of post-ordination formation programs. While there is no one model or comprehensive plan for formation, there are key elements that emerge from all of the above-quoted documents. The following are the essential ingredients to a wholesome program of ongoing priestly formation:

- Spiritual direction and sacramental reconciliation
- Annual retreats
- Sabbaticals
- Programs for recently ordained priests
- Programs at other times of transition
- Opportunities for priests to meet regularly in a small group
- Workshops and clergy convocations
- Ministerial review

It seems appropriate to conclude these reflections with the final words of the exhortation itself:

"I will give you shepherds after my own heart" (Jeremiah 3:15). Today, this promise of God is still living and at work in the Church. At all times, she knows she is the fortunate receiver of these prophetic words. She sees them put into practice daily in so many parts of the world, or rather, in so many human hearts, young hearts in particular. On the threshold of the third millennium, and in the face of the serious and urgent needs which confront the Church and the world, she yearns to see this promise fulfilled in a new and richer way, more intensely and effectively: She hopes for an extraordinary outpouring of the Spirit of Pentecost. (82.1)

Chapter 16

THE TRUTH SETS US FREE

Veritatis Splendor

ENGLISH TITLE: **The Splendor of Truth**
DATE ISSUED: **August 6, 1993**
TYPE OF DOCUMENT: **Encyclical Letter**

In *Veritatis Splendor* (The Splendor of Truth), an encyclical letter published on August 6, 1993, and addressed to all the bishops of the Catholic Church, Pope John Paul II upholds the conviction that not only is there fixed, absolute objective truth but that we are also capable of knowing it. *Veritatis Splendor* brings us face-to-face with one of the transcendent joys of Christ's Church—its capacity to proclaim the truth clearly, unequivocally, and pastorally. This encyclical letter addresses one of the great issues of our day: human morality. It offers us the Church's perennial response to the question "How shall I live?"

Is it possible to know what is true and what is not? Can we actually determine what is right and what is wrong? These seem to be easy questions to answer. From time immemorial, we have responded as human beings that we are capable of knowing right from wrong and that there is such a thing as objective truth. Two plus two equals four. While someone may dispute this if they got the wrong answer, no one seriously challenges the validity of the statement.

Yet when it comes to the essential questions of right and wrong and "How shall I live?" today we hear more and more that there are no correct answers. Objective truth, we are told, does not exist, and the best we can hope for is a concurrence of opinions. Anyone who has had at least minimal experience with human logic recognizes the impossibility of the situation. If every opinion is true but some contradict each other, then not every opinion can be true. Do we really wish to live our lives in a vacuum of ambiguity, uncertainty, ignorance, and confusion? Most of us answer no. There has to be some fixed star against which we can measure our course through life. God's word offers that permanent beacon of light.

The Importance of Truth

Perhaps the most reassuring part of this letter is its insistence that the truth—God's revelation to us in Jesus Christ—continues to be the way that leads us to everlasting life. *Veritatis Splendor* reaffirms the ancient and ever-new understanding that, in revelation and through human reason, we are capable both of knowing objective truth and of clinging to that truth in a way that will lead us to God, who is not only love but also life and truth itself.

In an age of relativism, with many voices speaking varying opinions—all of which claim to be capable of directing conscience and human life—*Veritatis Splendor* shines in the midst of the gloom of confusion. It says that there is truth, that it is accessible, and that it has a practical pastoral dimension that must be applied each day in our lives.

The pope has addressed this encyclical specifically to the bishops. As those who share with the successor of Peter and under his primate authority the responsibility of preserving "sound doctrine" (2 Timothy 4:3), bishops must be vigilant in ensuring that the word of God is faithfully taught. This is part of the mandate originally given by Jesus to the apostles (Matthew 28:19-20), and it is one that must be constantly taken up anew, in the power of the Holy Spirit, for the promotion of ecclesial communion and evangelization as well as for that dialogue about the truth and the good that the Church seeks to carry on with all individuals and peoples.

This encyclical is divided into three parts. It begins with a biblical meditation on the dialogue between Jesus and the rich young man (Matthew 19:16-22), which helps to bring out the essential elements of Christian morality (8–27). The middle chapter is doctrinal in nature; it is a critical discernment of certain trends in contemporary moral theology in the light of sacred Scripture and the Church's living tradition, with particular reference to the Second Vatican Council (28–83). The third and final chapter, which is pastoral in nature, points out the relevance of Catholic teaching on the moral good for the life of the Church and the world (84–120).

The Heart and Spirit of Christian Morality

The question asked of Jesus by the rich young man is a question present in the heart of everyone: "Teacher, what good must I do to have life?" (Matthew 19:16; 1.1) At the deepest level, the question about good and evil is also about happiness and the meaning of life. The Church was willed by Christ precisely for this purpose: so that people in every age might come to know him and discover in him the only answer fully capable of satisfying all their questions about life.

Jesus responds to the young man, "Why do you ask me about what is good? There is only one who is good. If you wish to enter into life, keep the commandments" (Matthew 19:17; 9.1). This response concisely expresses the very heart and spirit of Christian morality, bringing out the essential elements of Old and New Testament revelation with regard to moral action.

First, it shows the subordination of human action to God, to the One who alone is good. Second, it illuminates the close relationship between the moral good of human actions and eternal life, since the commandments of God, which Jesus confirms and takes up into the new law of love, are the path to life. Third, it reveals the way of perfection, which consists in a readiness to leave everything in order to follow Jesus, in imitation of his own gift of self to God the Father and to his brothers and sisters in service and in love. Christian morality is thus revealed as the complete fulfillment of the law, made possible by the free gift of the Holy Spirit, the source and means of the moral life of the "new creation."

The Church's living tradition, which includes her magisterium, her growing doctrinal understanding, her liturgy, and the lived holiness of her members, has always preserved the harmony between faith and life. In particular, the magisterium of the Church's pastors, with the guidance of the Holy Spirit, has developed an authoritative interpretation of the law of the Lord over many centuries and amid changing historical situations. Encouraged by the papal magisterium of the last two centuries, the Church has continued to develop her rich tradition of moral reflection on many different spheres of human life. That heritage is now confronted by the challenge of a new situation in society and in the Christian community itself.

Alongside praiseworthy attempts at the renewal of moral theology in accordance with the wishes of the Second Vatican Council, doubts and various objections with regard to the Church's moral teaching have arisen, even within Catholic moral theology. It has become increasingly evident that there is no longer a matter of limited and occasional dissent from certain specific moral norms, but rather a general and systematic calling into question of traditional moral doctrine as such, on the basis of certain anthropological and ethical concepts.

Specifically, in certain currents of theology, the traditional doctrine with regard to the natural law and the universality and the permanent validity of its precepts has been rejected. It is called into question whether the magisterium is competent to intervene in matters of morality and to teach authoritatively the binding requirements of God's commandments. Moreover, it is maintained that one can love God and neighbor without being obliged always and everywhere, in all situations, by the commandments taught by the Church. Doubt is raised about the intrinsic and unbreakable bond between faith and morality, to the extent of theorizing the possibility of forms of pluralism that are in fact incompatible with ecclesial communion.

As these ideas become more widespread, no one can fail to see that they have extremely important repercussions for the Church, for the life of the faithful, and for human coexistence itself. The pastoral and social problems that have emerged on every level make it possible to speak of genuine crisis. For this reason, the papal magisterium has deemed it necessary to clarify the points of doctrine crucial for the successful resolution of this crisis.

Contemporary Moral Theology

As part of this task, the pope undertakes a critical discernment of certain trends in contemporary moral theology. First of all, he reaffirms the constitutive relationship between freedom and truth. Genuine moral autonomy, as understood by Catholic doctrine, means that human freedom and God's law meet each other and intersect. Indeed, the "natural" law—the participation of God's eternal law in the rational creature—implies that reason, and the moral precepts that derive from it, are essentially subordinate to divine wisdom.

In opposition to every kind of relativism, the pope points out that the precepts of the moral law possess a universal and permanent character. They express the original truth about the good of the person, indicating the path that leads to the authentic realization of freedom. These precepts are ultimately grounded in Jesus Christ, who is always the same, yesterday and today and forever (cf. Hebrews 13.8; *Gaudium et Spes*, 10).

While acknowledging that there are certain choices in life that are fundamental, particularly the choice of faith, the encyclical rejects any separation between a "fundamental option" of a transcendental character and the deliberate choices of concrete acts. The fundamental choice that characterizes and sustains the Christian's moral life is revoked every time the person uses his freedom in conscious and free choices contrary to the fundamental choice where a morally grave matter is concerned (mortal sin).

The morality of an act, while certainly taking into account both its subjective intention and consequences, depends primarily on the object of the choice that reason grasps and proposes to the will. Consequently, it is affirmed that it is possible to hold as "intrinsically evil" certain kinds of behavior opposed to the truth and the good of the person. The choice by which they are made can never be good, even if that choice is made with a subjectively good intention and with a view to positive consequences. It is not licit, even for the most grave reasons, to do evil that good may come of it (cf. Romans 3:8; *Humanae Vitae*, 14). There thus exist "negative" moral precepts (precepts, in other words, forbidding certain kinds of behavior), which have universal value and are valid without exception.

At the root of the dissent mentioned above, and of solutions which are at odds with Catholic doctrine, is the influence of currents of thought that ultimately separate the exercise of human freedom from its essential and constitutive relationship with truth. An extreme notion of the autonomy of freedom tends to make freedom into an absolute—a source of values—apart from any dependence on truth.

Even more radical, the acceptance of a certain concept of autonomy has called into question the intrinsic connection between faith and morality. Faith, it must be said, is not merely an intellectual assent to certain abstract truths; it also possesses a moral content. Faith gives rise to and calls for a consistent life commitment; it entails and brings to perfection the keeping of the commandments.

"Not everyone who says to me, 'Lord, Lord,' will enter the kingdom of heaven, but only the one who does the will of my Father in heaven" (Matthew 7:21).

The Message of Christian Freedom

In view of these problems and the urgent need of a discernment aimed at safeguarding the deposit of Catholic doctrine, the pope turns to Jesus Christ, the "light of the nations" (*Lumen Gentium*, 1). Christ has shown us the way of authentic freedom: "The truth will set you free" (John 8:32). He himself has told us: "I am the way and the truth and the life" (14:6). Contrary to all those distortions and misrepresentations—which under the guise of exalting freedom actually empty it of meaning—authentic freedom is only discovered in relation to the truth, to that truth which was present "in the beginning" and shines forth in all its splendor (*"veritatis splendor"*) on the face of Jesus Christ (cf. 2 Corinthians 3:5-18).

The purpose of this encyclical, then, is not merely or even principally to warn against error so much as to proclaim anew, in all its power, the message of Christian freedom. At the heart of this message is the conviction that only in the truth does man's freedom become truly human and responsible. But the encyclical also desires to speak to all people of goodwill so that in the present moment of history, it can shed the light of faith on the path of freedom toward the good, the road to an authentically good human life in its personal and social dimensions.

By looking always to the Lord Jesus, the Church comes to discover the authentic meaning of freedom: the gift of self, inspired by love, for the sake of serving God and one's brothers and sisters. She discovers that God's law expresses, in the commandments and in their absoluteness, the demands of love. Universal and unchanging moral norms are at the service of the person and society.

The profound renewal of social and political life, which is increasingly desired by people today, can occur only if freedom is once more linked to truth. Ethical relativism, despite its appearances, inevitably leads to a totalitarianism that denies the truth about man. To promote morality is to promote man and his freedom, but this can never take place in opposition to the truth and in opposition to God.

The Preaching of Christian Morality

In the history of salvation, the martyrs, by preferring death to sin, have borne witness to the inviolable holiness of God's law and the unconditional respect that is due to the requirements of the dignity of each person. In bearing this witness, Christians are not alone; they are supported by the moral sense present in peoples and by the great religious traditions of East and West.

The concrete possibilities of acting according to moral truth, despite the weakness of human freedom caused by sin, are entirely found in the mystery of Christ's redemption. In Christ, God the Father offers us not only the truth about the good (the commandment of love, which sums up in itself the Ten Commandments), but also that "new law" that is his Spirit within us—his grace, which enables us to love and do good. In Christ we encounter the mystery of God, who understands our human weakness, yet never falsifies the standard of good and evil by accepting compromises that would adapt it to particular situations.

For this reason, the preaching of Christian morality, so closely linked to the new evangelization, must heed the warning of the apostle Paul "that the cross of Christ might not be emptied of its meaning" (1 Corinthians 1:17). In the task of proclaiming in all their fullness the justice and mercy that shine forth from the cross, the ministry of moral theologians is crucial; they perform a genuine ecclesial service, in communion with the bishops. Bishops themselves have the task of being vigilant that the word of God is faithfully proclaimed and applied to life, whether in preaching addressed to the faithful, in efforts at evangelization, in teaching imparted in seminaries and faculties of theology, or in the practices of Catholic institutions.

At the conclusion of his encyclical, the Holy Father turns to Mary, Mother of Mercy and model of true Christian freedom. He prays that through her intercession, the truth of her son will shine forth in the moral life of the faithful, "for the glory of God." John Paul recalls, in this final section, the "extraordinary simplicity" of Christian morality, which consists in "following Christ" and letting oneself be transformed by his grace and renewed by his mercy, which comes to us in the communion of his Church (119.1).

Chapter 17

A PEOPLE OF LIFE
AND FOR LIFE

Evangelium Vitae

ENGLISH TITLE: The Gospel of Life
DATE ISSUED: March 25, 1995
TYPE OF DOCUMENT: Encyclical Letter

W hy is the Church so focused on the abortion issue?" Or put another way, "Why is the Church so intensely pro-life?" On numerous occasions these questions have been raised. Those who do not share our pro-life vision or who are uncomfortable with the Church's insistence on the primacy of the right to life tend to label us as "single-issue" people. *Evangelium Vitae* (The Gospel of Life) is a response to these and similar questions as Pope John Paul II sums up the Church's perennial teaching on the worth and sacred character of human life.

On March 25, 1995, Pope John Paul II signed *Evangelium Vitae*— poignantly dated on the day on which the Church commemorates the annunciation, when the Virgin Mary was overshadowed by the Holy Spirit and conceived our Lord and Savior. It brings to our attention how the gift of human life is closely bound to the pledge of eternal life. We are called to a fullness of life that exceeds the dimensions of our earthly existence because it involves sharing the very life of God. In the words of the Holy Father, "Life in time, in fact, is the fundamental condition, the initial stage, and an integral part of the entire unified process of human existence" (2.1).

The pope begins this encyclical with this statement: "The Gospel of life is at the heart of Jesus' message" (1.1). The Sermon on the Mount, extending through three chapters in Matthew's gospel (5–7), is a clear instruction on how Christians are to face life if they are truly to walk in the footsteps of Jesus. Over centuries the Church's social teaching has developed into a highly articulate exposition of human rights based on the dignity of the human person. All this teaching rests on the most profound and basic of all human rights—the right to life. Thus when the pope speaks of the "Gospel of life" as being "at the heart" of Jesus' message, he is stating for us something that we should already clearly understand.

Made in the Image and Likeness of God

Jesus came that we might have life and have it to the full (John 10:10). The new life he brings us presumes the life that reflects the breath of God, so beautifully described in the Book of Genesis as the Creator brings forth the first human life. Forming man out of the clay of the earth, God breathed his breath into man's nostrils, thus making him a living human being. We alone share in the image and likeness of God. The crowning glory of humanity is that we are reflective of the very being of God.

As the first account of the creation of the world reaches a climax in the first chapters of Genesis, God is portrayed as creating man and woman as the crown and glory of all that he has made. "Then God said, 'Let us make man in our own image, after our likeness. Let them have dominion . . .'" (1:26). From the first poetic pages of Genesis, which speak of so many essential truths about humanity, to the gospels, in which we learn in Christ more fully the secret of who we are, Scripture elucidates the meaning of the human person. Since each human person is the "image of God," what we are told about God helps reveal to us who we are; what we learn about humanity, schooled and aided by faith, teaches us not only about ourselves but about God. Thus, to know something about God is to know something about ourselves. To divorce our knowledge of ourselves from our relationship to God is to paint an inadequate and therefore false picture of humanity. "By living 'as if God did not exist,' man not only loses sight of the mystery of God, but also the mystery of the world and the mystery of his own being" (22.4). All we have to do is look around us to see the grotesque image that has emerged as our secular culture has fashioned an image of man and woman divorced from the likeness of God.

As a child at the amusement park, I used to enjoy standing in front of mirrors that deliberately distort your reflection. In one mirror you appear tall and narrow, in another short and squat. Neither image was accurate. If you did not know better, if you took seriously the faulty and distorted reflections, you could easily carry away an entirely different vision of yourself and the world around you. To look at mankind today through the lens of those who see our value and worth based solely in terms of individual convenience, productivity, or career advancement is to create a whole new standard against which to measure the value of human life.

A syndicated columnist once went to great lengths to point out that since an unborn child is "pre-functional," it is expendable. The new image through this distorted lens reflects completely different values against which to measure the worth of a human life. As I read the article, which offered the norm of "pre-function" as the life-or-death determinant, I could not help but think that at some point in my journey through life, I might be declared "post-functional." I shudder at the thought that it is a designation that will serve as a death warrant. The Holy Father describes the consequences of this shift in vision:

The eclipse of the sense of God and of man inevitably leads to a practical materialism, which breeds individualism, utilitarianism, and hedonism. Here too we see the permanent validity of the words of the Apostle: "And since they did not see fit to acknowledge God, God gave them up to a base mind and to improper conduct" (Romans 1:28). (23.1)

John Paul sees what is at the very heart of the new vision of human life and what brings about such a distorted view of life and its horrendous consequences. Here the pope says it all:

The values of *being* are replaced with those of *having*. The only goal which counts is the pursuit of one's own material well being. The so-called "quality of life" is interpreted primarily or exclusively as economic efficiency, inordinate consumerism, physical beauty, and pleasure, to the neglect of the more profound dimensions—interpersonal, spiritual, and religious—of existence. (23.1)

Which of us cannot recognize in our society and in the culture around us the situation as described by John Paul? The term "quality of life" has become the carte blanche for justifying the taking of another's life.

However, the psalmist writes, "What is man that you are mindful of him, / and the son of man that you care for him?" (Psalm 8:4, RSV). Life is of itself a great mystery. Through art and industry, the human family has worked wonders that delight the imagination; at the same time, human history is also a record of sin and sorrow, a series of relentless waves eroding human self-respect. Grandeur and misery, holiness and sin, hopes and fears mark the mystery of our reality. Yet our Catholic faith proclaims that "all things on earth should be related to man as their center and crown" (*Gaudium et Spes*, 12). Even more, human life is touched by the love of God himself. "Yet you have made him little less than the angels, / and you have crowned him with glory and honor. / You have given him dominion over the works of your hands; / you have put all things under his feet" (Psalm 8:5-6, RSV).

The Incomparable Worth of the Human Person

We were made not to be just images of God, knowing and honoring him indirectly and learning of him through things he made. From the very beginning, it was God's plan that human persons should become his children by adoption and share the richness of the life of the Trinity.

Evangelium Vitae reminds us of "the incomparable worth of the human person." The recognition of the value of each human person is grounded in the uniqueness of each of us. Every woman and man is called "to a fullness of life which far exceeds the dimensions of . . . earthly existence because it consists in sharing the very life of God" (2.1). Aside from the unique qualities that every human being has, including the ability to consciously reflect on his existence, the capacity of making free choices, and above all, the possibility of a loving relationship with God, there is the fundamental divine gift that is the call to a life that will "reach its full realization in eternity" (2.1).

The Church has always proclaimed the dignity of each human life. Because we are images of our maker and are called through Christ to share in the personal life of the Trinity, each of us has a transcendent worth. In many ways the Second Vatican Council addressed the special need of our age when it stressed anew how human life must be honored, fostered, and respected:

For God, the Lord of life, has conferred on man the surpassing ministry of safeguarding life—a ministry which must be fulfilled in a manner which is worthy of man. Therefore, from the moment of its conception, life must be guarded with the

greatest care; abortion and infanticide are unspeakable crimes.
(*Gaudium et Spes, 51*)

One can wonder why it was necessary for the pope to write an entire encyclical letter affirming and restating the fifth commandment, "Thou shalt not kill." Yet the answer is all around us. We live in a society that has claimed for itself the right to determine who lives and who dies. In the minds of many, and certainly in some of our legislation, God has been replaced as the Author of life.

How far have we come? The attempt at justifying partial-birth abortion shows how far as a people we have fallen. Now serious journals speak of a "probationary period" when we will have "extended gestation," meaning that after a child is born, it will be allowed to develop for two or three months to see that it meets appropriate standards. If not, the "extended gestation" can be "terminated." We have come a long way from the days when we proudly proclaimed as a nation our commitment to "life, liberty, and the pursuit of happiness." The right to life has fallen victim to the "pursuit of convenience." *Evangelium Vitae* speaks to us in our situation today, in our culture and with our laws.

The encyclical is based on the fundamental assertion of the Christian faith that our lives do not find their fullness and fulfillment in this life but, in fact, are destined to eternal glory and union with God in a life that will never end. Hence, the proclamation of the dignity, value, and sacredness of human life is an integral part of the gospel. The encyclical sharpens this focus by reminding us that the "Gospel of God's love for man, the Gospel of the dignity of the person, and the Gospel of life are a single and indivisible Gospel" (2.4).

New Threats to Human Life

In the introduction, Pope John Paul explains why he wrote the encyclical at the time he did. There are new threats to human life, which are sinister for two very specific reasons. First, they are directed primarily at the life of individuals and peoples, "especially where life is weak and defenseless" (3.2). Second, there is an increasingly concerted effort in broad sectors of public opinion to justify certain crimes against life and to legitimize such threats to human life by bringing the authority of the state to bear in the authorization and even in the exercise of such activity.

The new challenges to the right to life qualitatively change the situation today from previous generations. There have always been threats to human life in the form of poverty, hunger, endemic diseases, violence, and war. Personal animosity, hatred, violence, and killing have always existed. Yet until recently, this condition was viewed as something against which we should struggle individually and collectively as a people. Only in recent years have we seen reflected in laws, court interpretations, and increasingly in public opinion, especially in the communications media, the argument that it is not wrong to take human life as long as we establish politically acceptable parameters that determine who lives and who dies.

One of the most frightening aspects of this new "pro-death" culture, as John Paul often referred to it, is its capacity to cloud and even silence conscience itself so that it becomes increasingly difficult "to distinguish between good and evil in what concerns the basic value of human life" (4.3). Has this generation, with its legalizing of abortion and propagandizing in favor of euthanasia, produced a younger generation that no longer sees life as sacred with intrinsic, enduring value? Are we, in fact, producing a generation that accepts the premise that life has only the value we give to it and that we, individually and collectively, have the right to end human life if it becomes inconvenient? The principle argument used to defend abortion on demand is simply that one chooses to terminate human life for no other reason than that the life of another person is inconvenient to the one with the power to terminate it. As we study and reflect on the increasing violence in our society, streets, schools, and homes—violence manifested throughout our communities—do we not recognize those very principles that place the power over life and death, not in the hands of God, but in the hands of anyone with the power and the public support or means to use it?

John Paul speaks in chapter one of *Evangelium Vitae* about present-day threats to human life in the context of the Genesis account of Cain slaying Abel: "The Lord said to Cain: 'What have you done? The voice of your brother's blood is crying to me from the ground' (Genesis 4:10). The voice of the blood shed by men continues to cry out from generation to generation in ever new and different ways" (10.1).

This encyclical describes with great precision many of the threats to human life, including the increasing spread of euthanasia, whether "disguised and surreptitious or practiced openly and even legally" (15.3). Birth rates rise in poorer countries and drop in richer countries. In the Book of Exodus, Pharaoh, "haunted by the presence and increase of the children of Israel, . . . ordered that every male child born of the Hebrew women was to be killed (cf. Exodus 1:7-22)" (16.3). The pope adds, "Today not a few of the powerful of the earth act in the same way. They too are haunted by the current demographic growth, and fear that the most prolific and poorest peoples represent a threat for the well-being and peace of their own countries" (16.3).

In a section that has proved to be prophetic, not only in the sense of teaching, but also in the sense of anticipatory vision, John Paul writes:

The various techniques of artificial reproduction, which would seem to be at the service of life and which are frequently used with this intention, actually open the door to new threats against life. Apart from the fact that they are morally unacceptable since they separate procreation from the fully human context of the conjugal act, these techniques have a high rate of failure: not just failure in relation to fertilization, but with regard to the subsequent development of the embryo, which is exposed to the risk of death, generally within a very short space of time. Furthermore, the number of embryos produced is often greater than that needed for implantation in the woman's womb, and these so-called "spare embryos" are then destroyed or used for research which, under the pretext of scientific or medical progress, in fact reduces human life to the level of simple "biological material" to be freely disposed of. (14.1)

However, the encyclical does not confine itself to an enumeration of the threats to life. A particularly encouraging part of the letter is the presentation of the positive signs at work, even if "they do not receive sufficient attention in the communications media" (26.2).

One of the casualties of our age is the anticipation of receiving in pubic media a truly balanced presentation of events. One place where this is always evident is the coverage of prol-ife events such as the January March for Life in Washington, D.C. It has long been the practice of major media outlets to give minimal coverage to this event and at the same time, as if to dismiss the event, to present too often an absurdly low number of estimated participants.

On the other hand, many good people, convinced of the worth of human life and the place each one of us has in God's plan for a good and just society, quietly and persistently continue their work and efforts. The pope reminds us, "It is from the blood of Christ that all draw the strength to commit themselves to promoting life. It is precisely this blood that is the most powerful source of hope; indeed, it is the foundation of the absolute certitude that in God's plan, life will be victorious" (25.5).

John Paul speaks of the many married couples who, with a generous sense of responsibility, not only accept children, but also are "willing to accept abandoned children, boys and girls and teenagers in difficulty, handicapped persons, elderly men and women who have been left alone" (26.3). He goes on to speak of movements and initiatives that raise social awareness in defense of life and evidence of a growing public opposition to the death penalty. We are called to address and ultimately change laws and public policy that permit abortion and legalize euthanasia. Clearly, these movements deserve our support "when, in accordance with their principles, such movements act resolutely but without resorting to violence" (27.1).

In a world in which moral parameters are increasingly viewed as determined by public policy and the law, Catholics and all Christians who value the dignity and worth of human life are called upon to express their opposition to legislation and court-imposed interpretation of the Constitution that encourage the destruction of innocent human life. This overriding human right—the right to life—should be a defining factor in the political process.

Life Is Always Good

The second chapter of the encyclical, entitled "The Christian Message Concerning Life," can be summed up in this sentence: "In Christ, the Gospel of life is definitively proclaimed and fully given" (29.3). In this section of the encyclical, the pope offers a masterful summary of the Judeo-Christian tradition that upholds the value and dignity of life and explains why life in itself is good and why God explicitly commands, "You shall not kill" (Exodus 20:13).

In response to the understanding of the worth of human life, which has somehow become so clouded that it is no longer recognized as a value in itself, the pope offers clear direction: "Life is always a good" (34.1). Up until very recently, this statement was universally shared by all. There is an instinctive perception and a fact of experience that life in itself is a great good given to us by God. The understanding that God is the Author of life has gradually changed to a more secular vision that places the sovereignty of human existence in the hands of human beings. This shift is a dramatic and powerful one, unparalleled in our culture. For the first time, we hear around us in academic circles, elitist groups, and legislative caucuses that we—human beings, not God—are the final arbiters of the worth, value, dignity, and therefore extent of human life. To the question "Why is life a good?" the pope reminds us:

> The question is found everywhere in the Bible, and from the very first pages it receives a powerful and amazing answer. The life which God gives man is quite different from the life of all other living creatures, inasmuch as man, although formed from the dust of the earth, is a manifestation of God in the world, a sign of his presence, a trace of his glory (cf. Genesis 1.26-27; Psalm 8:6). (34.2)

"You Shall Not Kill"

Chapter three is a commentary on the commandment "You shall not kill," which begins by pointing out that "God's commandment is never detached from his love: it is always a gift meant for man's growth and joy" (52.2). In this section, John Paul addresses how this commandment is being emptied of its meaning:

> Today, in many people's consciences, the perception of its gravity has become progressively obscured. The acceptance of abortion in the popular mind, in behavior, and even in law itself, is a telling sign of an extremely dangerous crisis of the moral sense, which is becoming more and more incapable of distinguishing between good and evil, even when the fundamental right to life is at stake. (58.2)

It is here that the encyclical addresses with considerable precision the question of euthanasia, suicide, and the ethical relativism "which characterizes much of present-day culture" (70.1).

In this chapter, the pope also addresses the question of intrinsically unjust laws and reminds us that it is never licit to obey an unjust law or to "take part in a propaganda campaign in favor of such a law, or vote for it" (73.3). Nor are we to justify our involvement in such immoral activity by invoking the principle of cooperation. "Cooperation can never be justified either by invoking respect for the freedom of others or by appealing to the fact that civil law permits it or requires it" (74.2).

This encyclical challenges us to accept in practice what we proclaim and to assume the consequences of our personal faith. In effect, the encyclical points out the inconsistency of this often-heard political response: "While I am personally opposed to abortion, I nonetheless favor legislation supporting it." The falsehood of such a proposition has long been evident, particularly since it would never be applied to slavery or concentration camps. The encyclical reminds us that the commandment "You shall not kill" carries with it obligations in the social and political order as well as on the level of personal activity.

A New Culture

Perhaps one of the most engaging chapters of the encyclical is the last one, entitled "For a New Culture of Human Life." Here the Holy Father's message of a culture of life and his description of us as a people of life offer us a grander perspective that is both encouraging and energizing. It is a prophetic vision, one that encompasses our daily struggles to defend human life.

Given the dimensions of the struggle between the culture of death and the civilization of love, we are not free to remain on the sidelines. The pope challenges all of us to be engaged in the promotion of the right to life. Strikingly, he begins the fourth chapter with the reminder that the Church exists in order to evangelize: "The Church has received the Gospel as a proclamation and a source of joy and salvation. . . . Evangelization is an all-embracing, progressive activity through which the Church participates in the prophetic, priestly, and royal mission of the Lord Jesus" (78.1, 2).

All of us have been called to accept and live the gospel. We have also been sent to bear witness to it in our words as well as our actions. "Together we all sense our duty to preach the Gospel of life, to celebrate it in the liturgy and in our whole existence, and to serve it with the various programs and structures which support and promote life" (79.4).

Embryonic Stem-Cell Research

I now want to focus in an extended way on the subject of embryonic stem-cell research—a topic that remains the subject of heated debate today. I believe embryonic stem-cell research has more potential to do harm to our understanding of the value and worth of human life than anything since the widespread acceptance of abortion. *Evangelium Vitae* helps us understand why this is so.

In a dramatization of the conflict between King Henry VIII of England and St. Thomas More—"the king's loyal servant but God's first"—we find this exchange. The king's new first minister, who had obtained his position by perjuring himself, has just offered the king advice on how to resolve a problem. St. Thomas More reminds his young ambitious successor, "You have just made a great mistake. You told the king what he can do. Your task is to tell him what he ought to do."

When we address the question today of medical research in its many developing forms, and when we face the extent of options provided us by scientific technology, we have to ask the question, "Does the end justify any means?" We cannot be content to know what we *can* do, but rather we must ask the more significant question: "What *ought* we to do?"

Early on in the encyclical, where the Holy Father praises the efforts in medical science, particularly among researchers and practitioners, he urges them to be faithful to the Gospel of life. Again as he concludes the encyclical, the pope returns to the theme of the responsibilities and obligations of those engaged in research and health-care services, reminding them of the "unique responsibility" that is theirs (89.2).

Embryonic stem-cell research has all of the potential for good that any legitimate scientific advance brings with it. At the same time, it has an equally huge capacity for moral, spiritual, medical, and human devastation. To the extent that the abortion issue in our country has helped redefine the way many Americans think, to that same extent does embryonic stem-cell research bring with it a whole new way of looking at the human person—a vision incompatible with the Gospel of life.

In the national debate on embryonic stem-cell research, the issue has often been presented in highly emotional terms. Even the language is used selectively so that the scale tips in favor of what seems like a very good end. We hear about all of the wonderful medical advances that might take place as a result of this type of research and eventual therapy. The image of a child struggling with diabetes is placed in the balance against what is described as "just clumps of microscopic cells." One national news magazine some time ago appeared to dismiss the entire ethical and moral aspect of stem-cell research by labeling one side "embryonic research" and the other "pro-life politics."

In order to make an informed moral judgment about one of the most important issues that we as a people are facing today, we need to examine carefully the facts, what exactly is at issue, and why there is a moral prohibition against the use of evil means to achieve a good end.

The Ends Do Not Justify the Means

While stem-cell research may not be at the forefront of the list of concerns that many of us face in our day-to-day lives, it is nonetheless of such significance that we all need to be well-informed about it. Decisions made now could establish a principle that says we are free to use the drastic means of taking another human life, even if it is in its earliest stages, to meet a good end. To concede that the end—even if it is potential relief to long-standing illnesses—justifies the means is to launch our children and grandchildren headlong down a slippery slope on a moral toboggan with neither a steering bar nor brakes.

A stem cell is an unspecified cell that can renew itself and give rise to one or more specialized cell types with specific functions in the body. While it is microscopic in size, it nonetheless contains the elements out of which comes the fully developed human person. The potential of stem cells to develop into a range of tissues is what makes them so attractive to researchers. The science of cell therapy concentrates on ways to replace, repair, or enhance the biological function of damaged tissues or organs by transplantation of isolated or characterized cells. Thus we hear so much about the potential for all kinds of cures and health-care advances.

At the very beginning of human life, after the male sperm cell and female egg come together to form an embryo, there come into being cells that scientists tell us are undifferentiated. Stem cells at this stage are called "embryonic stem cells" because they are located in a human embryo.

Fortunately, embryos are not the only source of stem cells. There are a number of alternative sources of stem cells that hold out realistic hope for cures and treatments of diseases and illnesses. Stem cells from adult tissues, which are committed to differentiating into a limited number of cell types, such as liver (hepatic), brain (neural), or blood (haematopoietic), are called adult stem cells; these too have the capacity to develop into specific tissues. Some scientists today assert that not only are adult stem cells more readily available, but they also are more effective.

Stem cells derived from placenta or umbilical cord blood have also proven to be effective. Originally it was theorized that stem cells from these various sources would be ineffective because they are limited in their ability to become various types of cells. However, alternative sources of stem cells have been successfully differentiated into needed tissue and are already healing human diseases.

The Moral Dilemma

Stem-cell research holds out the promise of a large step forward in the healing process. The Catholic Church is not opposed to the development of these therapies and remedies for a host of ailments and deficiencies that afflict the body. Stem-cell research using stem cells from ethical sources is a continuation of the work that has been done for millennia by physicians and researchers seeking cures for diseases in order to heal the sick.

But the stem-cell process does not take place in a vacuum. It involves human life and the generation of complex, interrelated systems necessary for life. Granted, the life we are speaking about is in its earliest stages and still needs to be greatly developed; nonetheless, it is a member of the human species. We are not talking about a cluster of cells that will develop into a cabbage or a laboratory mouse or a household pet but into a mature adult human being. This brings us face-to-face with the moral dilemma surrounding embryonic stem-cell research.

The Church does not oppose all stem-cell research; it encourages medical development and technological advances. What the Church as the conscience of society calls for is moral and ethical reflection on the use of human embryos for stem-cell research. No scientific, technological, or medical development or advance should take place divorced from human conscience and moral and ethical consideration. Once we admit that we are dealing with the continuum of human life—as all scientists must, given the force of demonstrable physical data—we are not free to treat embryos the same way that we would treat cancer tissue or even a laboratory rat.

At the heart of the moral issue involving embryonic stem-cell research is the fact that the embryo is killed so that the stem cells can be used for research—for the good of someone else. The current literature already speaks about destroying the embryo as useful cells are "harvested" from it. Since there is a continuity from conception through natural death of the human person, at what point do we permit harvesting of parts of that human being for someone else?

We Are Stewards, Not Masters, of Human Life

Embryos are at the very beginning stage of human life. We, as human beings in solidarity with that life, are not free to view an embryo simply as a commodity for our convenience or benefit. When we enter the sacred precincts of human life—when we approach the chamber of life—we are not the masters of the room. We are not the lords of the house of life. God alone has the right to determine who lives and who dies. We are stewards, not masters, of human life. Even when we put on sterilized gloves and work with technologically advanced equipment, we do not take on the mantle of arbiter of human life.

Our basic human obligation to respect the life of another comes into force even when we are dealing with the tiniest form of human life. Once we admit personally or as a society to place into law the presumption that we can take an innocent human life any time we want and at whatever stage we determine, we put into motion a destructive whirlwind that will surely empty all technology and scientific advancement of moral and ethical restraint or true value. If our society announces that it will determine at what point a human life can be used for the benefit of another, then all that is left for the next generation to do is decide when—at what age—that principle is applied.

Already there are those who argue that since the embryo is going to be destroyed anyway, we should feel free to do with it what we will. Would that principle apply to anyone who is terminally ill? It is the same principle that was used to exonerate human experimentation on those in the concentration camps during World War II.

There are those that maintain that scientific advances should not be restrained by moral compunction. We hear over and over the claim that much good will come from this research. The end, we are told, certainly justifies the means that are used. To abandon the long-standing moral presumption that the end does not justify the means puts us on a fast track toward moral anarchy.

There are those who say that the voice of moral restraint, the voice of the Church, should not be heeded in this area of scientific development. In a way, this is a new wrinkle in the overextension of the idea of separation of church and state. It is the separation of moral reflection from scientific studies.

As the Holy Father concludes chapter four of *Evangelium Vitae*, "For a New Culture of Human Life," he reminds us:

> To be truly a people at the service of life, we must propose these truths constantly and courageously from the very first proclamation of the Gospel, and thereafter in catechesis, in the various forms of preaching, in personal dialogue, and in all educational activities. Teachers, catechists, and theologians have the task of emphasizing the anthropological reasons upon which respect for human life is based. . . . We shall find important points of contact and dialogue also with nonbelievers, in our common commitment to the establishment of a new culture of life. (82.1)

The Church Must Speak Out

We cannot proceed down the road of scientific development without moral reflection or ethical judgment. The Church, the voice of Christ applying his gospel to our world today, speaks out of two thousand years of the human experience—and the reflection on that experience in the light of God's word and guided by the gift of the Holy Spirit. It is the task of the Church, as it is of all members of society, to be alert to the wisdom of God when it offers ethical and moral reflection on what we are technologically capable of doing. It is a question not of what we can do but of what we ought to do—what we must do.

The issue of embryonic stem-cell research brings us face-to-face with a fundamental human moral principle and decision. We cannot allow our technology to outstrip our ethical reflection. The two need to go forward together. Our capability to develop and use technology and science must always be done within the context of God's plan—the natural moral order. To be truly human means that we make decisions reflective of the moral order and not based on the emotional appeal of what works for me right now.

The Catholic Church brings a living ethical tradition to this and so many current issues, and it does so with confidence because the Church's moral reflection is guided by a wisdom rooted in God's word and directed by God's Spirit. When we face issues such as abortion, assisted suicide, euthanasia, and other expressions of the culture of death, we have an obligation to resist such encroachments on the civilization of love. In concluding this encyclical, the Holy Father reminds us:

> The Gospel of life is not for believers alone: it is for everyone. The issue of life and its defense and promotion is not a concern of Christians alone. . . . The value at stake is one which every

human being can grasp by the light of reason; thus it necessarily concerns everyone. (101.2)

Evangelium Vitae requires numerous readings. It is a letter about life and for life in the Judeo-Christian tradition. Having read the letter and shared these initial reflections, I encourage you to read again St. John Paul II's words on life, to pray over them, and to rejoice in the Gospel of life that is an intrinsic part of the good news of salvation that Christ announced to us.

Chapter 18

COMMITTED TO CHRISTIAN UNITY

Ut Unum Sint

ENGLISH TITLE:	**On Commitment to Ecumenism**
DATE ISSUED:	**May 25, 1995**
TYPE OF DOCUMENT:	**Encyclical Letter**

On May 25, 1995, the Solemnity of the Ascension of the Lord, Pope John Paul II issued an encyclical letter reaffirming the Church's commitment to ecumenism. The letter derives its Latin title, *Ut Unum Sint,* from Christ's prayer the night before he died: "That they may all be one" (John 17:21). The context against which we see this encyclical letter is the division that plagues the family of those who claim Christ as Lord and call themselves Christians.

For various reasons—some theological, others cultural, and still others political—the Church has struggled with divisions and tensions that tend to pull some members in diverse directions. In the early centuries of the Church, there were doctrinal issues that greatly divided the faithful. In a series of ecumenical councils beginning in A.D. 325 at Nicaea, the Church fathers came together to proclaim clearly and forcefully the unifying faith of the Church.

In the eleventh century, a rupture took place that continues to our own day. A number of Eastern Orthodox churches broke communion with the Apostolic See of Peter. While the creed, the sacraments, and the hierarchical order of the Church were maintained both in the

Catholic Church and in the Orthodox churches, nonetheless, the complete unity enjoyed for over a millennium was disrupted.

In the sixteenth century, a major upheaval took place in the Western church. Today we refer to this as the Reformation. Many ecclesial communities find their inspiration in the events and theologies that developed in Germany, Switzerland, Scotland, and England beginning in 1520. Here we encounter divisions far more substantial than those that plague Catholic-Orthodox relations. Coming out of the Reformation were major doctrinal diversities that touch the very core of our understanding of who Christ is, what he came to do, and our relationship with him and his new body, the Church.

Still later, much closer to our own day, ecclesial bodies have come into being that find their definition in a personal interpretation of the pages of sacred Scripture. Fundamental and evangelical ecclesial communities represent a significant dimension of religious experience today.

In the introduction to *Ut Unum Sint* (On Commitment to Ecumenism), Pope John Paul II calls us to unity. He also recognizes that some substantial progress has already been made, although there is still a long way to go. Nonetheless, we are called to unity, not out of our desire, but by the will of Christ.

The challenge is not peripheral to our mission, nor is it an option. Church unity is obligatory—it is mandated by Christ. Whatever wounds were inflicted on the Christian world, they still need to be healed. We are called to persevere on the path to unity, not for reasons of convenience, but because this is the declared will of Christ who is the head of the Church, his body (Ephesians 5:23). "I thank the Lord that he has led us to make progress along the path of unity and communion between Christians, a path difficult but so full of joy," the pope writes. "Interconfessional dialogues at the theological level have produced positive and tangible results: this encourages us to move forward" (2.2).

In calling us to a commitment to ecumenism, John Paul makes clear his own commitment to the cause: "I intend to promote every suitable initiative aimed at making the witness of the entire Catholic community understood in its full purity and consistency" (3.3). Again, speaking in the first person, the pope tells us:

> This is a specific duty of the Bishop of Rome as the Successor of the Apostle Peter. I carry out this duty with profound conviction that I am obeying the Lord, and with a clear sense of my own human frailty. Indeed, if Christ himself gave Peter this special mission in the Church and exhorted him to strengthen his brethren, he also made clear to him his human weakness and his special need of conversion: "And when you have turned again, strengthen your brethren" (Luke 22:32). (4.1)

The Basis for Ecumenism

In Chapter one, "The Catholic Church's Commitment to Ecumenism," the pope reminds us that it is God's plan that we all be one faith family. The way of ecumenism must be the way of the Church. But even in the face of the lack of unity among Christians and the confident quest for full communion, the Catholic faithful are conscious of being deeply challenged by the Lord of the Church. This challenge can be met only if we are faithful to our own identity and clearly understand our starting point. True ecumenism is rooted, not in compromise, denial of the truth, or a false sense of coming together by leaving behind that which is truly essential to the faith, but in truth, which is its starting point.

The pope notes that during its two-thousand-year history, "the Catholic Church . . . has been preserved in unity, with all the means with which God wishes to endow his Church, and this despite the often grave crises which have shaken her, the infidelity of some of her ministers, and the faults into which her members daily fall" (11.1). Here we find the basis for that outreach to one another that can ultimately bring about true union. The foundation for ecumenical dialogue is first, a clear articulation of what we understand, and then, the recognition that much of our division is the result of human failure and sin. "The elements of sanctification and truth present in the other Christian Communities, in a degree which varies from one to the other, constitute the objective basis of the communion, albeit imperfect, which exists between them and the Catholic Church" (11.2).

What St. John Paul teaches us is essential to the progress in the effort to restore unity among all Christian faith communities. It is not a diminishment of ecumenism to recognize that the Catholic Church claims the fullness of Christ's gifts in an unbroken continuity that establishes a living relationship between the apostles and their successors, the bishops, today. Yet to the extent that some elements of sanctification and truth are found in other Christian communities, the one Church of Christ is effectively present in them (cf. 11). Here the pope refers back to the Second Vatican Council, which speaks of a certain, though imperfect, communion. *Lumen Gentium* (The Dogmatic Constitution on the Church) stresses that "the Catholic Church 'recognizes that in many ways she is linked' with these Communities by a true union in the Holy Spirit" (11.3).

In calling us to our commitment to ecumenism, the Holy Father reminds us that at every age and in every generation, there have been those who have kept the vision of the unity to which Christ calls us. The context of the ecumenical effort today is the progress that has been made since the Second Vatican Council. It is true that ecumenism and the efforts at Church unity predate the Council. Nonetheless, the impetus that the ecumenical movement received in, through, and following the Council was a major factor in establishing the context of awareness, trust, fellowship, and respect for each other's faith tradition that is the foundation for any serious effort at Church unity.

The Importance of Dialogue

This bring us to the next section of *Ut Unum Sint,* in which the Holy Father stresses the importance of ecumenical dialogue, whether this is on the international, national, or local levels. He tells us, "If prayer is the 'soul' of ecumenical renewal and of the yearning for unity, it is the basis and support for everything the Council defines as 'dialogue'" (28.1).

We have seen in these past decades on a variety of levels—international, national, statewide, and local—advances in fellowship, trust, and an awareness of each other's convictions, as well as increasing mutual respect. These have all had a strong impact on the sad tradition of division, mistrust, bigotry, and exclusion, which were hallmarks of an earlier time—but one many of us can remember. The pope reminds us that dialogue is "a natural instrument for comparing different points of view and, above all, for examining those disagreements which hinder full communion between Christians" (36.1).

The promotion of ecumenical and interfaith understanding involves two distinct but related moments: the appropriation of commonly held truth and the recognition that differences in faith and moral teaching still exist. If we have benefited from more than a quarter century of ecumenical and interfaith dialogue to the point where we can calmly, serenely, respectfully, and even affectionately relate to each other in our commonality of faith, then it is time in that same spirit to address the issues that divide us with renewed conviction that this is Christ's will—even if we do not know at the present moment where such dialogue leads.

In the second chapter, entitled "The Fruits of Dialogue," the pope reminds us, "It happens more and more often that the leaders of Christian Communities join together in taking a stand in the name of Christ on important problems concerning man's calling and on freedom, justice, peace, and the future of the world." One of the benefits that we see with increasing satisfaction as the ecumenical movement works its way through prayerful settings and ongoing dialogues is what the pope describes as "solidarity in the service of humanity" (43.1).

When we begin to address social issues and modern secular thinking, it often becomes apparent that the various Christian communities and the Catholic Church have much more in common than what divides them from each other. It is this understanding that urges us to stand together in the proclamation of justice, the dignity of the human person, and the value of life. A host of other concerns also comes under the umbrella of "solidarity in the service of humanity."

As he lists the fruits of the ecumenical effort over the past decades, the Holy Father expresses appreciation for the gifts present among all Christians. He also points to a sense of growth of communion on a spiritual level. In reference to this last point, John Paul describes the ongoing dialogue with the churches of the East. Perhaps nothing so clearly manifested the sense of urgency in the pope's desire for the unity of the Church as did his continuous and constant outreach to the Orthodox churches, as he invited the full communion that surely is possible and that obviously reflects the will of Christ.

"How Much Further Must We Travel?"

In the third chapter, the pope asks the demanding question *"Quanta est nobis via?"* ("How much further must we travel?"). His response is a balance of encouragement and realism. We are reminded that substantial results have already been achieved but that there is still a long way to go. John Paul pledges his personal commitment to continue the ecumenical efforts that have brought us to a point of fruitful development that would have been unimaginable half a century ago.

In concluding this encyclical, the Holy Father reminds us of the gift of the Holy Spirit. "The power of God's Spirit gives growth and builds up the Church down the centuries. . . . [The Church] asks the Spirit for the grace to strengthen her own unity and to make it grow toward full communion with other Christians" (102.1).

From the encyclical *Ut Unum Sint,* we should be convicted that what is being required of us is an extension of what has already been required over the past decades. This includes knowing each other, understanding each other, and praying for each other. We need to be faithful to Christ and to one another. Perseverance, patience, understanding, and above all love are the qualities that are necessary for such faithfulness. Though less tangible than programs to which we can subscribe jointly and more difficult to articulate than mutually acceptable legislation, these qualities will bear the true fruit, the enduring fruit, the good fruit in the years ahead.

Chapter 19

A PRICELESS GIFT

Vita Consecrata

ENGLISH TITLE: **The Consecrated Life**
DATE ISSUED: **March 25, 1996**
TYPE OF DOCUMENT: **Post-Synodal Apostolic Exhortation**

In his introduction to the post-synodal apostolic exhortation *Vita Consecrata* (The Consecrated Life), Pope John Paul II clearly outlines the focus of this document. The consecrated life is a gift to the Church, and it is intended not only for the sanctification of the individual who receives it but also for the good of the Church. In the introduction to the exhortation, issued on March 25, 1996, the Solemnity of the Annunciation of the Lord, the Holy Father writes:

> The consecrated life, deeply rooted in the example and teaching of Christ the Lord, is a gift of God the Father to his Church through the Holy Spirit. By the profession of the evangelical counsels, the characteristic features of Jesus—the chaste, poor, and obedient one—are made constantly "visible" in the midst of the world, and the eyes of the faithful are directed toward the mystery of the kingdom of God already at work in history, even as it awaits its full realization in heaven. (1.1)

Describing the various models of consecrated life, all of which are expressions of the Spirit in various forms, the pope observes, "The Synod recalled this unceasing work of the Holy Spirit, who in every age shows forth the richness of the practice of the evangelical counsels through a multiplicity of charisms" (5.2).

The Many Expressions of Consecrated Life

The Holy Father points out that both in the Eastern Catholic churches and in the Latin church, there has been "a great variety of expressions" of consecrated life. Among these is the ancient Order of Virgins; members, who are consecrated by the diocesan bishop, are committed to serving the Church while remaining in the world. Men and women hermits belong to other ancient orders, which are also directly dependent on the local bishop. Known since apostolic times and again being practiced today is the consecration of widows and widowers. "These women and men, through a vow of perpetual chastity as a sign of the kingdom of God, consecrate their state of life in order to devote themselves to prayer and the service of the Church" (7.3).

The expression of consecrated life that most of us are familiar with is found primarily in the institutes or communities of religious. Some, composed of either men or women, are devoted to contemplation. These, the Holy Father points out, "are for the Church a reason for pride and a source of heavenly graces" (8.1).

There are also the communities of apostolic religious life. "Countless persons, renouncing the world, have consecrated themselves to God through the public profession of the evangelical counsels in accordance with a specific charism and in a stable form of common life, for the sake of carrying out different forms of apostolic service to the people of God" (9.1). The exhortation goes on to describe the various families of apostolic communities, and then turns our attention to secular institutes, whose members seek "to live out their consecration to God in the world through the profession of the evangelical counsels in the midst of temporal realities; they wish in this way to be a leaven in wisdom and a witness of grace within cultural, economic, and political life" (10.2).

There are also clerical secular institutes. In these cases, priests who belong to the diocesan clergy "consecrate themselves to Christ through the practice of the evangelical counsels in accordance with a specific charism" (10.3). We are also reminded of societies of apostolic life or of common life composed of men or women. "These pursue, each in its own particular way, a specific apostolic or missionary end" (11.1).

A Special Call from God

Chapter one, which speaks of the origins of the consecrated life in the mystery of Christ and the Trinity, proclaims that all vocations—to the lay life, to the ordained ministry, and to the consecrated life—are "at the service of one another, for the growth of the Body of Christ in history and for its mission in the world" (31.2).

Christ is the head of his body (Colossians 1:18). To live as Christians is to grow in Christ, to be more closely identified with him, and to have his rich life penetrate us more and more and be our very life. When we understand that the Church is the body of Christ, we learn to love the Church more earnestly and see in it more clearly the reflection of Christ. On all the members of the Church Christ pours out gifts and talents, but some of these charisms make special demands on the believer and are meant to be carried out in a family that we call a religious community.

In the gospels, Christ taught the rich young man that everyone is obliged to love God and his neighbor in the faithful observance of the commandments (cf. Luke 18:18-25). But God's grace stirs a hunger for a more demanding life in some men and women, who are called to share with Christ a willingness to give up much that the world offers so that they might cling to God in a richer freedom. Christ's invitation to follow him closely endures in the Church in a special way in the religious life. Those who enter religious life bind themselves, as the

Second Vatican Council teaches, "either by vows or by other sacred bonds which are like vows in their purpose" (*Lumen Gentium*, 44), to an observance of the evangelical counsels of perfection, that is, the gospel counsels of chastity, poverty, and obedience.

This decision to imitate Christ through the observance of his evangelical counsels involves cutting away many perfectly laudable objectives that one might otherwise pursue: sexual and domestic fulfillment in marriage, ownership of property, or the development of other abilities. Yet the giving up of these things is counted as nothing by those who long to share in that same emptying of self as Christ (Philippians 2:7), since such a disposition allows them cling to Jesus with a full and freer heart (cf. 1 Corinthians 7:32-35). The pope writes:

> It is the duty of the consecrated life to show that the Incarnate Son of God is the eschatological goal toward which all things tend, the splendor before which every other light pales, and the infinite beauty which alone can fully satisfy the human heart. In the consecrated life, then, it is not only a matter of following Christ with one's whole heart, of loving him "more than father or mother, more than son or daughter" (cf. Matthew 10:37)—for this is required of every disciple—but of living and expressing this by conforming one's whole existence to Christ in an all-encompassing commitment which foreshadows the eschatological perfection, to the extent that this is possible in time and in accordance with the different charisms. (16.2)

For examples of such commitments, we can turn to the founder of monastic life, St. Anthony, and his desire to pursue perfect communion with the Lord. Both St. Benedict and his sister, St. Scholastica, offer us examples of religious life lived according to a rule of holiness. Two equally engaging founders of religious communities are St. Francis and St. Clare, whose lives expressed their total self-giving to God and their dedication to the poor. St. Dominic offers us another example of religious commitment. In our own land, we have the extraordinary examples of St. Elizabeth Ann Seton and St. John Neumann. All of these ways of living a consecrated life represent a response to God's call.

Poverty, Chastity, Obedience

The Holy Father highlights the role of the evangelical counsels of poverty, chastity, and obedience and their direct relationship to the proclamation of the kingdom of God among us (22). As we struggle to make that kingdom come, God always blesses his Church with gifts—the gifts of the Holy Spirit. The fruits of the Holy Spirit are the result of living those gifts. But God also chooses to call some to bear witness publicly in a unique and special way—in the Church, for the Church, in the world, and for the world—to the reality of the kingdom and the coming of the kingdom. Religious life involves a decision to accept the evangelical counsels and live them for the sake of the kingdom, to choose to come together as a religious community, and to live a consecrated life so that all the world can see the coming of the kingdom.

Why are the evangelical counsels so important? Because all three of them speak clearly against elements of this world that continually overwhelm us. Poverty—a simplicity of life—says that no matter how much one can accumulate in this world, it can never substitute for the glory that awaits all of us in the kingdom. Thus one puts aside the accumulation of possessions. The renunciation of the goods to which one would be entitled is a sign to everyone—the Church and the whole world—that the gift of glory is the ultimate good.

Chastity for the kingdom is the counsel that urges one to set aside legitimate hopes of family and children so that what remains is a single-minded focus on Christ, his kingdom, and his work. We set aside all personal aspirations for the sake of the kingdom.

The hardest counsel, so we are told by some spiritual writers, is obedience because it touches the very core of our being. When Christ comes in glory, there will be no possessions except his glory. There will be no marrying because we will be one in Christ. And through the exercise of the gift of obedience, there will be no struggle against the will of Christ because we will be one with him. In this world, obedience is the effort to mirror the free choice of Christ in glory by allowing one's own will to genuflect to the will of Christ as manifested in his Church and in a religious community.

The evangelical counsels are the gifts that Christ has given to his Church to those who have chosen and been chosen to be religious and to live the consecrated life. As they live the counsels, all can anticipate the coming of the kingdom breaking into this world—a kingdom of peace, love, truth, faith, and the ultimate reality, heaven, where Christ will have dominion over our decisions, our will, and over all creation and the goods of creation.

The evangelical counsels are lived in what the Church has designated as canonical religious life. It's not that the counsels themselves cannot be lived individually, but they will never be lived individually in the same way that the Church recognizes them canonically in a community as a witness to the world—a collective witness to the world of the coming of the kingdom.

A Sign of Unity and Generosity

In chapter two, "Consecrated Life as a Sign of Communion in the Church," the Holy Father returns to the image of the Trinity and the idea of the apostolic community being a reflection of the life-giving unity of the Trinity. Here the pope highlights the significant role played by consecrated persons within the particular or local churches. He notes that on the basis of the Second Vatican Council's teachings, "this aspect of the consecrated life has been systematically explored and codified in various postconciliar documents" (48.1).

Vita Consecrata holds up for us the image of religious life as a communion of faith, lived out in such a way that it strengthens the larger community of the faithful, helping them in their fidelity to the Church's teaching and in their sense of participating in the very inner life of God. Chapter three, entitled "Consecrated Life: Manifestation of God's Love in the World," highlights again the significance of the evangelical counsels, their role in fostering consecrated life, and their significance in manifesting God's kingdom among us.

In concluding his reflections, Pope John Paul stresses that at its heart, the consecrated life is a sign of generosity:

Those who have been given the priceless gift of following the Lord Jesus more closely consider it obvious that he can and must be loved with an undivided heart, that one can devote to him one's whole life, and not merely certain actions or occasional moments or activities. The precious ointment poured out as a pure act of love, and thus transcending all "utilitarian" considerations, is a sign of unbounded generosity, as expressed in a life spent in loving and serving the Lord, in order to devote oneself to his person and his Mystical Body. (104.3)

This apostolic exhortation gives us the chance to reflect on the wondrous witness and extraordinary service provided to the Church by men and women in consecrated life. Over the years, women and men in consecrated life have enriched the Church in a whole range of ministries, including education, health care, and social service, as well as in individual expressions that have varied with the demands of the age. At the same time, the Church has been enriched by the prayer, spiritual energy, and testimony of those religious devoted to contemplation. One of the sentiments we feel immediately when reading this exhortation is our immense gratitude to those who have given themselves to Christ in and through the consecrated life.

Chapter 20

FAITH, REASON, AND THE TRUTH

Fides et Ratio

ENGLISH TITLE: **On the Relationship between Faith and Reason**

DATE ISSUED: **September 14, 1998**

TYPE OF DOCUMENT: **Encyclical Letter**

Is there a contradiction between faith and reason? Can one be both committed to scientific research and at the same time a faithful believer? Are philosophical reasoning and theological investigation antithetical? The encyclical letter *Fides et Ratio* (On the Relationship between Faith and Reason) offers a clear and compelling response to such questions. On September 14, 1998, the Feast of the Exaltation of the Holy Cross, Pope John Paul II issued *Fides et Ratio,* his thirteenth encyclical letter.

At the heart of this encyclical is the perennial affirmation of the Church that reason and faith are not only compatible but also are complementary gifts from God. As he opens the letter, the pope writes, "Faith and reason are like two wings on which the human spirit rises to the contemplation of truth; and God has placed in the human heart a desire to know the truth—in a word, to know himself—so that by knowing and loving God, men and women may also come to the fullness of truth about themselves."

One of the great journeys of the human spirit has been the effort to come to know more and more about ourselves by encountering the truth about reality and therefore the human enterprise. In the introduction to the encyclical, the pope tells us that this longing for knowledge finds expression in the admonition "Know yourself." Even a cursory glance at ancient history shows clearly that these fundamental questions arise: "Who am I? Where have I come from and where am I going? Why is there evil? What is there after this life?" (1.2). Ultimately, each one of us at some point in life asks the question "How shall I live?" This question and all of those similar to it have their common source in the search for meaning that has always driven the human heart.

As we undertake the study of the relationship of reason and faith, the pope observes, "The Church is no stranger to this journey of discovery, nor could she ever be. . . . It is her duty to serve humanity in different ways, but one way in particular imposes a responsibility of a quite special kind: the *diakonia* [service] of the truth" (2.1). Here the Holy Father refers to his first encyclical letter, *Redemptor Hominis,* and the reminder that "being responsible for that truth also means loving it and seeking the most exact understanding of it" (RH, 19).

Driven by the desire to discover the ultimate truth of existence, "human beings seek to acquire those universal elements of knowledge which enable them to understand themselves better and to advance in their own self-realization" (4.1). As we try to learn more about ourselves and the world in which we live, we find several sources of information or fonts of truth. For example, as we contemplate creation, we are filled with wonder at its overpowering beauty and overwhelming order. At the same time, we become aware that we are part of the world, that we live in relationship with others, and that we share a common destiny. The recognition of the relationships that we have with each other, with the wider community, and ultimately with creation and the Author of creation provides us with fertile ground for our intellectual investigation.

Fides et Ratio affirms the power of human reason and its capacity to arrive at truth. This is the starting point for the assertion that not only are faith and reason compatible but that they work together to deepen the human understanding of truth. The pope, an accomplished philosopher, points out that even though times have changed and knowledge has increased, it is still possible to discern a core of philosophical insights within the whole of history. "Consider, for example, the principles of non-contradiction, finality, and causality as well as the concept of the person as a free and intelligent subject, with a capacity to know God, truth, and goodness. Consider as well certain fundamental moral norms which are shared by all" (4.3).

Reaffirming the Truth of Faith

The unique gift that the Church brings to the human enterprise of discernment of the truth is the revelation of Jesus Christ. This gift of particular knowledge and insight into the very nature of God and God's plan for us is not meant to supplant human reason but rather to enhance and enrich its quest for the truth. "Sure of her competence as the bearer of the revelation of Jesus Christ, the Church reaffirms the need to reflect upon truth" (6.1), the pope writes, adding:

> I feel impelled to undertake this task above all because of the Second Vatican Council's insistence that the Bishops are "witnesses of divine and catholic truth" (*Lumen Gentium*, 25). To bear witness to the truth is therefore a task entrusted to us Bishops; we cannot renounce this task without failing in the ministry which we have received. In reaffirming the truth of faith, we can both restore to our contemporaries a genuine trust in their capacity to know and challenge philosophy to recover and develop its own full dignity. (6.2)

Over the centuries, beginning in the early sixteenth century, there arose among some thinkers the idea that human reason arrived at one truth while religious faith represented a completely different category of experience. This division of truth into different categories or realms implied that since only human reason used a method that allowed scientific proof, any other claim to truth must be subjective and reductively of no consequence. We hear something of that attitude today reflected in conversations about religious truth, values, and a moral order. While many people are prepared to accept that anything that science can demonstrate must be true, they are less prepared to accept that the revelation of Jesus would be binding upon people in the same way. Thus, when it comes to religious conviction, we hear, "It is your opinion versus my opinion."

Religious experience is personal and free; people can adhere to different religious convictions with equal tenacity. But not all religious conviction is equally true. It may be equally firm, but it is not therefore equally true.

God Is the Font of Truth

The font of truth—the unique font of truth—is God. The God of creation is the God of revelation. What we come to know through scientific method and intellectual endeavor, if it is true, should lead us to God who is truth. The same must be said of revelation. What Christ reveals to us is God and therefore the truth. Centuries ago, St. Thomas Aquinas spoke of all truth being one since God is one. Therefore, reason and revelation both have the same object. Reason uses the power of the intellect to attain truth. Faith uses the gift of revelation to secure truth.

In *Fides et Ratio*, the pope begins chapter one with the recognition that Jesus is the revealer of the Father—the revelation of God's wisdom. Here he reminds us that the Second Vatican Council stressed the salvific character of God's revelation in history: "The truth about himself and his life which God has entrusted to humanity is immersed therefore in time and history; and it was declared once and for all in the mystery of Jesus of Nazareth" (11.2). While human reason and faith both open us to the truth, revelation will always remain "charged with mystery" (13.1). In our human knowledge, we come to know with a certain level of assurance because of the evidence that is presented to us. The human intellect grasps the truth and is persuaded by it. While the object of faith is truth as well, revelation relies on our taking God's word for what he presents rather than proofs amenable to human reason. Thus, when it encounters faith, our reason always stands before a mystery.

In the human endeavor, to know more about ourselves, our world, and our relationship to the transcendent—to God—human reason is a powerful but limited tool. It can penetrate something of the mystery of human life, but it is guided solely by its own light. On the other hand, revelation breaks into this world and offers us the light of faith by which we interpret the realities of this world. "Revelation has set within history a point of reference which cannot be ignored if the mystery of human life is to be known" (14.1). Christian revelation, the pope says, "is the true lodestar of men and women as they strive to make their way amid the pressures of an immanentist habit of mind and the constrictions of a technocratic logic" (15.2).

What has clouded the compatibility of faith and reason today and what has raised questions about the complementarity of the two is the assertion in the scientific and philosophical community of the absolute priority and predominance of reason. It is assumed by some that the intellect alone can grasp truth and that faith merely grasps opinion. On the other hand, the Church has constantly taught—and *Fides et Ratio* affirms—that the truth of reason and the truth of revelation are the same. They are simply arrived at by different paths—human reason and faith in God's word.

The Relationship between Truth and Reason

In chapter two, the pope strongly reaffirms that there is "no reason for competition of any kind between faith and reason: each contains the other, and each has its own scope for action" (17.1). Here the pope stresses that faith, and therefore the light of faith that we bring to any investigation of the human condition, illumines our past and our understanding in a way that human reason simply cannot. What often brings a sense of antagonism to the mutual efforts of faith and reason is an exaggerated sense of autonomy that finds its roots in the pride that led to the first fall. "Because of the disobedience by which man and woman chose to set themselves in full and absolute autonomy in relation to the One who had created them, this ready access to God the Creator diminished. . . . This is the human condition vividly described by the Book of Genesis" (22.2, 3).

In chapter three, the pope asserts that it is not just the light of faith that illumines our search for truth but that the human intellect itself seeks to penetrate more deeply into an awareness of the human condition and thus eventually comes to God. "In the far reaches of the human heart, there is a seed of desire and nostalgia for God" (24.2). Thus any philosophical investigation will come to question the meaning and goal of life. "No one can avoid this questioning, neither the philosopher nor the ordinary person. The answer we give will determine whether or not we think it possible to attain universal and absolute truth" (27.1).

To know the difference between the truth arrived at by human reason and the truth arrived at by faith, one must turn "to the different modes of truth" (30.1). The mode of truth proper to everyday life and to scientific research depends upon immediate evidence or confirmation by experimentation. "In believing, we entrust ourselves to the knowledge acquired by other people" (32.1).

This gets at the heart of the issue. For the Catholic, truth is one, and we arrive at it either by scientific method (human reason) or by faith in accepting God's word (faith). In any case the object of both reason and faith is the same—the truth. Thus the pope affirms for us that there is a direct relationship between revealed truth and philosophy or human reason (cf. 35).

In chapter four, John Paul traces the history of philosophical development in the Western world and its relationship to the revelation of Jesus Christ presented in the Church. The encyclical praises the enduring originality of the thought of St. Thomas Aquinas:

> Thomas recognized that nature, philosophy's proper concern, could contribute to the understanding of divine Revelation. Faith therefore has no fear of reason, but seeks it out and has trust in it. Just as grace builds on nature and brings it to fulfillment, so faith builds upon and perfects reason. Illumined by faith, reason is set free from the fragility of limitations deriving from the disobedience of sin and finds the strength required to rise to the knowledge of the Triune God. (43.2)

The pope notes that Thomas Aquinas also perceived the role of the Holy Spirit in the process by which knowledge matures into wisdom, and he quotes this passage from Aquinas' *Summa Theologica*: "The wisdom named among the gifts of the Holy Spirit is distinct from the wisdom found among the intellectual virtues. This second wisdom is acquired through study, but the first 'comes from on high,' as St. James puts it. This also distinguishes it from faith, since faith accepts divine truth as it is. But the gift of wisdom enables judgment according to divine truth (II–II, 45, 1 ad 2)" (44.1).

In chapter five, the encyclical deals with the Church's exercise of the *diakonia* (service) of the truth. Increasingly it falls to the Church to speak to issues relating to the natural moral order since a growing number of secular philosophers and scientists simply ignore or reject this aspect of God's creation. The pope warns against both the rejection of the role of the Church in the realm of philosophical investigation and also the equally disturbing position of some that faith alone provides an answer and understanding to the human condition. "The censures were delivered evenhandedly: on the one hand, fideism and radical traditionalism for their distrust of reason's natural capacities, and, on the other, rationalism and ontologism because they attributed to natural reason a knowledge which only the light of faith could confer" (52.2).

The Power of the Intellect and the Mystery of Faith

The interaction between philosophy and theology is the subject of chapter six. Divine truth, as revealed in sacred Scripture and interpreted by the Church, "enjoys an innate intelligibility, so logically consistent that it stands as an authentic body of knowledge" (66.1). While there will always be differing schools of philosophy and conclusions derived from the examination of scientific data, there is radically common ground for both philosophical investigation and faith in God's revelation. Religious faith accepts the power of the intellect to further penetrate the mystery of revelation, while scientific knowledge should recognize the validity of God's revelation in setting direction and focus for scientific development.

The final chapter calls for mutual respect among philosophers and theologians and their disciplines:

> Philosophical enquiry can help greatly to clarify the relationship between truth and life, between event and doctrinal truth, and above all between transcendent truth and humanly comprehensible language. This involves a reciprocity between the theological disciplines and the insights drawn from the various strands of philosophy; and such a reciprocity can prove genuinely fruitful for the communication and deeper understanding of the faith. (99.3)

In concluding this stimulating and challenging encyclical letter, the Holy Father highlights the role of faith in the Church in the current contemporary search for truth. "Insisting on the importance and true range of philosophical thought, the Church promotes both the defense of human dignity and the proclamation of the Gospel message" (102).

Human reason and the gift of faith are both freely bestowed on us by God, who is Lord of creation and Father of revelation in Christ Jesus. As we make our journey along the path of human experience that leads us to God who is all truth, our task is to respect both the gift of human reason and the revelation of God's word. As we work to truly integrate them into our lives, we can be assured that the role of the magisterium is precisely to ensure that neither gift is overlooked.

Chapter 21

ENCOUNTERING CHRIST IN AMERICA

Ecclesia in America

ENGLISH TITLE: **The Church in America**
DATE ISSUED: **January 22, 1999**
TYPE OF DOCUMENT: **Post-Synodal Apostolic Exhortation**

As a sign of the significance of the Church in our hemisphere, bishops from North, Central, and South America met in a synod in late 1997 to discuss the needs of the Church in the Americas. On January 22, 1999, Pope John Paul II traveled to Mexico City and the Shrine of Our Lady of Guadalupe, patroness of the Church in America, to sign the post-synodal exhortation *Ecclesia in America* (The Church in America). The document is both a call to reflect on our faith and its meaning and an outline of important elements of the life of the Church and issues that are of particular concern.

Even the name of the bishops' gathering, "The Synod for America," and the exhortation, *Ecclesia in America*, speak of a particular vision that the bishops, together with the pope, have for the future. The use of the singular "America" is an attempt to express the unity that in some ways already exists. But, as the pope observes, it also points to that closer bond "which the peoples of the continent seek and which the Church wishes to foster as part of her own mission, as she works to promote the communion of all in the Lord" (5).

The New Evangelization

The entire document is set within the context of the "new evangelization." We are part of a faith community that has already received the gospel, and yet there are many who follow it only halfheartedly or who have drifted away completely from its practice. This exhortation calls our attention to the basic mission of the Church and, therefore, of every believer today: invigorating our own faith and inviting back to its full practice anyone who is less than zealous in living the gospel way.

"With the command to evangelize which the Risen Lord left to his Church, there goes the certitude, founded on his promise, that he continues to live and work among us: 'I am with you always, to the close of the age' (Matthew 28:20)" (7.1). We need not be afraid to undertake the work of the new evangelization because it is Christ who calls all of us to spread the gospel, and it is the same Christ who walks with us as we attempt to do so.

Within our own experience in the United States, we are fully aware that there are many who are baptized Catholic and who claim the name but who live out reluctantly the challenge of faith in Christ. Each of us individually and as Christ's faith community—the Church—must renew our commitment to reach out to those who once found their faith a source of strength and guidance, and invite them to return to it.

Years before he called together the bishops of America for a synod, the pope visited them to engage the Church in the Western hemisphere more fully in the task of stirring into flame the ember of faith that was carried there half a millennium ago. In *Ecclesia in America*, the pope says he had personally outlined "an initial program for a new evangelization on American soil" (6.1). As the Church throughout America was preparing to commemorate the five-hundredth anniversary of the first evangelization of the continent, he spoke to the Council of

Latin American Bishops gathered in Haiti and said, "The commemoration of the five hundred years of evangelization will achieve its full meaning if it becomes a commitment by you the Bishops, together with your priests and people, a commitment not to a reevangelization but to a new evangelization—new in ardor, method, and expression" (March 9, 1983).

Long before the term the "new evangelization" was as widely used and understood as it is today, the pope explained its meaning by noting that it was not an effort to reevangelize those who had already heard the gospel but rather, an effort to find new ways to enliven their faith. In what would later become a hallmark of his pontificate, John Paul challenged the Church in America, personally and on the ecclesial level, first to renew their own faith and then to invite and encourage others to renew their commitment to Christ.

This is no easy task. In America, as in other parts of the world, there is an increasing tendency to live for the here and now. The result is that concepts such as transcendence, spirituality, grace, and God's kingdom become increasingly alien to our society. It is not that they are denied outright; they are simply marginalized to the point that they have no impact on the way many people think or act. Even good Christians today are increasingly subjected to the suggestion that religious ideals and moral norms and guidance are totally private affairs that have no impact on our societal life.

Perhaps nowhere is this more evident than in our own country, where we regularly hear that moral principles and faith-based convictions should not have an impact on public policy. Under the mantra of "separation of church and state," we are told that there should be a separation or exclusion of moral principles from public policy. It is within this state of affairs that many good Christians experience a hesitancy to speak up for their faith and the moral values so essential to their lives. They may also be hesitant to expect that these most cherished values should be an integral part of the society in which we all live.

The challenge of the new evangelization is one that each believer needs to accept. We begin by personally renewing our commitment to Christ, to his gospel, and to the Church that proclaims both, and then we recommit ourselves to invite others—particularly those who at some point have made an initial commitment to Christ—to renew and enliven their faith. The new evangelization can be accomplished on the global and hemispheric levels when it begins first in the hearts of individuals.

Encounter with the Living Christ

Chapter one begins with the announcement that who we are and what we do are rooted in our encounter with the living Christ. "The Gospels relate many meetings between Jesus and the men and women of his day. A common feature of all these narratives is the transforming power present and manifest in these encounters with Jesus" (8.1). At the heart of our personal identification as a Catholic is our meeting with Christ in a way that we come to know him, love him, and invite him to be the focus and center of our lives.

Yet we do not encounter Christ alone, isolated from others. It is in and through his Church that the grace of Jesus is brought to us and made present among us. The Sacraments of Baptism and Confirmation as well as the Eucharist—where we encounter Christ in a dramatic and tangible way—introduce us to the person of Christ and sustain our friendship with him. These experiences allow us to authenticate the truth of our personal conviction.

A section in this exhortation is devoted to identifying the places of encounter with Christ, among them sacred Scripture read in the light of Tradition, the Fathers of the Church, the magisterium, and meditation and prayer. We also encounter Jesus in the sacred liturgy. "The Scriptures and the Eucharist, places of encounter with Christ, are evoked in the story of the apparition of the Risen Jesus to the disciples of Emmaus" (12.5). Here we see how deeply linked are the reading of the Scriptures and the living tradition of the Church, which reaches its sacramental fullness in the Eucharist—the real presence of Christ.

Encountering Jesus in America

To remind us that this exhortation is not just theory, even though it remains for the most part on the level of general observation, declaration, and exhortation, a whole chapter is devoted to encountering Jesus Christ in America today. Here we find an articulation of some of the concerns and problems on our continent in which the new evangelization must take place. The pope praises the strength of popular piety and its value, the presence of the Eastern Church and its rich heritage, and the extraordinary contribution of the Church in the fields of education and social action. In this chapter we are reminded of the need for a profound respect for human rights, which must be rooted in the truth. It is clearly understood that there can be no rule of law unless citizens, and especially leaders, are convinced that there can be no freedom without truth.

At this point in the exhortation, the pope turns his attention to the Christian identity of America. He points out that "the greatest gift which America has received from Christ is the faith which has forged its Christian identity." For more than five hundred years, America has benefited from the introduction of the Christian faith. However, "America's Christian identity is not synonymous with Catholic identity," the pope observes. "The presence of other Christian Communities, to a greater or lesser degree in the different parts of America, means that the ecumenical commitment to seek unity among all those who believe in Christ is especially urgent" (14.1).

Even though the introduction to the Christian faith occurred in different parts of America through the activities of various Christian groups, nonetheless, it is the gospel of Jesus Christ and faith in him that have formed so much of the way in which America envisions itself, recognizes its values, and relates to the rest of the world. It is not an exaggeration to say that America is a land with Christian roots and Christian values.

As if to highlight this point, the next section of the exhortation is devoted to the fruits of holiness in America. "The saints are the true expression and the finest fruits of America's Christian identity" (15.1). These "fruits of holiness" have flourished from the first days of the evangelization of America. As early as 1670, Pope Clement X proclaimed St. Rose of Lima, who died in 1617, as the principal patroness of America. Since then, the list of American saints has grown continuously. Among them we could list Jean de Brébeuf and his seven companions, Elizabeth Ann Seton, Peter Claver, Rose Philippine Duchesne, Turibius of Mongrovejo, Juan Diego, Katharine Drexel, Miguel Pro, Junipero Serra, Kateri Tekakwitha, and many others.

But the document is also aware of some of the darker sides of development in our part of the world. The phenomenon of globalization is addressed from the perspective of its ethical implications. Other problems are growing urbanization, the burdens of the external debt on many nations in Central and South America, and government corruption, as well as the illegal drug trade, ecological concerns, and a growing disregard for the dignity and value of human life.

Within our own nation, one of the darker sides continues to be the glaring moral failure of abortion. With a callous disregard for all the evidence of medical science today that what is conceived in the womb is the beginning of human life, those responsible for the law of the land continue to legalize the death of well over one million unborn children every year. In the United States, the onus for this intolerable situation falls on the courts of the land, particularly the Supreme Court.

In reviewing the many issues that call forth some response from the Christian faithful, the Holy Father makes it clear that that there is much that is praiseworthy about life in America and the Church in America. However, there is still much more to be done—within the Church to more clearly proclaim the gospel of Christ, and within the community to more justly address the great human issues of our day.

Ecclesia in America is divided into three major sections that are the direct result of our encounter with Christ: conversion, communion, and solidarity. Let us look briefly at each one.

Conversion

The chapter on conversion begins with a familiar theme taken from the Acts of the Apostles: "Repent, therefore, and be converted" (3:19). All conversion is a turning from ourselves and whatever leads us away from Christ and a turning back to him. The New Testament uses the word "*metanoia,*" which means "a change in mentality." Today we would probably be more comfortable speaking of a change in attitude or vision. In either case, the intention is the same—to change our way of thinking and acting.

Conversion is a lifelong task. It is ongoing, and we are all caught up in it at every stage of our lives. It is also totally dependent on the gifts of the Holy Spirit. It is for this reason that prayer plays such an important part in personal conversion. Prayer brings with it a change of lifestyle and a commitment to Christ that overflows into all of our daily actions.

Conversion, however, is not simply individual reconciliation with God; that would imply that we have no relationship with our neighbor. The great commandment from Jesus is to love the Lord our God; the second, to love our neighbor as ourselves (Matthew 22:37-39). In this exhortation the pope reminds us of the social dimension of conversion: "Conversion is incomplete if we are not aware of the demands of the Christian life and if we do not strive to meet them" (27.1). It is here that the pope chooses to quote from the First Letter of John: "He who does not love his brother whom he has seen, cannot love God whom he has not seen" (4:20; 27.1).

Aware of the complexity of issues when the gospel is applied to social and political conditions, the Holy Father teaches that "it will be especially necessary to nurture the growing awareness in society of the dignity of every person and therefore to promote in the community a sense of the duty to participate in political life in harmony with the Gospel" (27.2).

Gospel values should permeate the political, social, and cultural orders. But the Church, the pope reminds us, "can in no way be confused with the political community nor be tied to any political system" (27.3). The Church, in fact, is to be a sign and safeguard of the transcendent character of the human person. *Ecclesia in America* puts forth a vision of conversion that radically affects every Christian and, therefore, radically affects all of society. The exhortation calls for personal spiritual renewal rooted in prayer that is both private and liturgical. It also calls for an awareness that the universal call to holiness extended by God to every person involves us joined together, as a body, as we make our pilgrim way through this life.

The Need for Penance and Reconciliation

Another striking aspect of this portion of the document is the call to penance and reconciliation. "The present crisis of the Sacrament of Penance, from which the Church in America is not exempt and about which I have voiced my concern from the beginning of my Pontificate, will be overcome by resolute and patient pastoral efforts" (32.2).

The conversion that John Paul speaks about so forcefully "leads to an acceptance and appropriation of the new vision which the Gospel proposes" (32.1). Thus we are called in our journey to make a place in our own life for the ascetical practices that have always been a part of the Church's life and that culminate in the sacrament of forgiveness.

"Only those reconciled with God can be prime agents of true reconciliation with and among their brothers and sisters" (32.1). In a climate of renewal and new evangelization, the place of the Sacrament of Reconciliation must receive due recognition. If there is clearly a spiritual casualty in the struggle of Catholic pastoral practice in recent decades, it is this sacrament. While we have witnessed the many people who come forward to receive the Eucharist Sunday after Sunday, we have also recognized a proportionate decrease in the lines waiting for confession on weekdays and weekends. Renewal of our society and renewal of the Church itself must include the recognition of the need for sacramental reconciliation as an integral part of the spiritual life of all of the faithful—priests, religious, and laity.

Communion

The second major heading of the exhortation is "The Call to Communion." "As you, Father, are in me and I in you, that they also may be in us" (John 17:21). The Holy Father sees communion in the widest and deepest theological terms. It is the life of the Holy Trinity shared with us through an outpouring of God's grace in the sacraments of initiation and renewed each day in the Eucharist. To emphasize his point, John Paul quotes from the Second Vatican Council document *Lumen Gentium*:

> Faced with a divided world which is in search of unity, we must proclaim with joy and firm faith that God is communion, Father, Son and Holy Spirit, unity in distinction, and that he calls all people to share in the same Trinitarian communion. . . . We must proclaim that the Church is the sign and instrument of the communion willed by God, begun in time and destined for completion in the fullness of the kingdom. (2)

The pope's vision of our communion—our being together in Christ—that follows on our conversion is one that is made visible in concrete signs, such as communal prayer and the close ties among Catholics in their parishes in union with their bishops and through them, with the pope.

At the heart of this concept of communion is our faith, along with our commitment to know it and accept it as God's great gift. "Communion requires that the deposit of faith be preserved in its purity and integrity" (33.2). On this level we find the spiritual force that holds us together as God's people. We are not a social, political, cultural, or economic community; we are a faith community. We have been anointed by the Holy Spirit in baptism and confirmation and renewed in the gift of the Eucharist. "The Eucharist is the living and lasting center around which the entire community of the Church gathers" (35.1).

Bishops are to be the builders of communion as they exercise their role as successors to the apostles. "It is up to the Bishop with the help of the priests, deacons, religious, and lay people to implement a coordinated pastoral plan, which is systematic and participatory, involving all of the members of the Church and awakening in them a missionary consciousness" (36.1).

The Ministerial Priesthood

In view of the important role that priests have as leaders of God's flock, the Holy Father highlights the need to foster vocations to the priesthood. The Sacrament of Holy Orders allows one to participate in Christ's mission in a unique way. It makes the recipient an authentic, authoritative, and special representative of Christ, the head of the Church. Because one is called to minister in the person of Christ, head of the whole body, the *Catechism of the Catholic Church* identifies holy orders as a sacrament of service on behalf of the unity of the Church (1551).

It is in his treatment of the priesthood that the pope highlights the particular role of the priest as a sign of unity. "Each priest must be a sign of communion with the Bishop, since he is his immediate collaborator, in union with his brothers in the priesthood" (39.1). Today, as we experience a diminished number of priests in the United States, the need for a solid bond of unity among and between priests and bishops is all the more pronounced. While the fact of fewer priests does not necessarily mean less ministry in the Church, it does mean more coordination and oversight of all types of pastoral ministry. Bishops have the ultimate responsibility for the oversight of all pastoral and sacramental ministry in the diocesan Church. Yet this is carried out primarily through the pastors and other priests who are the principal co-workers with the bishop. Together bishops and priests in their own solidarity can provide a more effective vehicle for the coordination of all ministry done in the name of the Church, particularly at the parish level.

This section of *Ecclesia in America* goes on to assert that parish renewal is a significant part of building up the communion of the Church. "The parish is a privileged place where the faithful concretely experience the Church. . . . The parish needs to be constantly renewed on the basis of the principle that the parish must continue to be above all a Eucharistic community" (41.1). At every level in the Church, the bonds of communion are strengthened by the active participation of all of the faithful. It is for this reason that the exhortation devotes a section to the permanent diaconate, to the consecrated life, and, above all, to the role of the lay faithful in the renewal of the Church. In a particular way, the Holy Father singles out the dignity of women. "Unfortunately, in many parts of America, women still meet forms of discrimination. It can be said that the face of the poor in America is also the face of many women" (45.2).

Returning to a theme that has marked many of his papal documents, Pope John Paul reminds us of the challenges facing Christian families and of the serious need to prepare young people so that they understand the sublime mystery of Christian marriage. It is in this section that the synodal fathers and the pope turn their attention to young people, the hope of the future. Here we read of the need to provide proper and strong catechesis for our young people. "The particular churches throughout the continent are clearly making real efforts to catechize young people before Confirmation and to offer them other kinds of support in developing their relationship with Christ and their knowledge of the Gospel" (47.1). As we struggle to build up a sense of Christian community, the proper education of our young people in the faith, especially as they prepare to receive the sacraments, is a clear focus of the document and one that I expect finds an echo in the hearts of many religious educators in our parishes.

Solidarity

The third major section of the exhortation is devoted to the concept of solidarity. This virtue is described as the fruit of communion. There is a sense in which solidarity can be defined as a practical expression of the unity in love that is the Church. It is in this section that the document speaks of the Church's social teaching and reminds us that the Church's doctrine is "an answer which serves as a starting point in the search for practical solutions" (54.1). It is here, more than in any other part of the document, that we find some of the practical concerns that were so much a part of the discussion of the synod when it came to economic and social issues.

In *Ecclesia in America*, we are reminded that the ultimate foundation of all human rights rests on the dignity of each person created in the image and likeness of God. "The human being's dignity as a child of God is the source of human rights and of corresponding duties" (57.1). In this part of the apostolic exhortation, we find a call once again for the preferential love of the poor and the outcast, as well as a challenge to fight against corruption in government and an awareness of the depth of the drug problem across all borders and national boundaries. A special section is devoted to pointing out the damage done to the body of Christ and the human family from discrimination against certain groups of people.

In concluding this post-synodal apostolic exhortation, Pope John Paul II returns to the theme of the new evangelization. Chapter six challenges us to reflect on the mandate given to the apostles: "As the Father has sent me, so I send you" (John 20:21). Jesus Christ is the good news and prime evangelizer, yet he turns this task over to his Church, and we in turn are to assume the responsibility of proclaiming the good news to all those we meet.

Evangelization is not just a personal encounter with Christ but an effort to permeate the culture with the very essence of our Christian beliefs. It seems appropriate that at this point, as the exhortation draws to a conclusion, the Holy Father would highlight the extraordinary role of Catholic schools and Catholic education in passing on the faith and, in doing so, transforming our culture into a civilization of love. "It is essential that every possible effort be made to ensure that Catholic schools, despite financial difficulties, continue to provide a Catholic education to the poor and marginalized in society. It will never be possible to free the needy from their poverty unless they are first freed from the impoverishment arising from the lack of adequate education" (71.2).

This beautiful exhortation concludes with an invitation to all the Catholics of America "to take an active part in the evangelizing initiatives which the Holy Spirit is stirring in every part of this immense continent, so full of resources and hope for the future" (76.1).

Ecclesia in America is a document full of hope, expectation, challenge, and joy. It holds out to you and to me the promise of a wonderful world of truth, love, compassion, and faith. It also reminds us that this will happen only to the extent that we are faithful to our Christian obligation, personally and as a Church, to renew our encounter with the living Jesus Christ: the way to conversion, communion, and solidarity in America.

Chapter 22

UNITED TO MARY

Rosarium Virginis Mariae

ENGLISH TITLE: **On the Most Holy Rosary**

DATE ISSUED: **October 16, 2002**

TYPE OF DOCUMENT: **Apostolic Letter**

O ne of the most ancient and widespread realities in the life of the Church is popular devotion to Mary, the Mother of God, the Mother of Jesus, and the Mother of the Church. Almost anywhere you go, whether in our own land or in countries around the world, you will find expression of the Church's devotion and the devotion of God's people to the Blessed Virgin Mary. We find a living, permanent witness to Mary in the liturgical form of solemnities, feasts, and memorials; in the prayer form of popular devotions; and in the physical form of churches and shrines.

On October 16, 2002, Pope John Paul II issued the apostolic letter *Rosarium Virginis Mariae* (On the Most Holy Rosary). He begins his reflection with these words:

The Rosary of the Virgin Mary, which gradually took form in the second millennium under the guidance of the Spirit of God, is a prayer loved by countless Saints and encouraged by the magisterium. Simple yet profound, it still remains, at the dawn of this third millennium, a prayer of great significance, destined to bring forth a harvest of holiness. (1.1)

Our attention to and love for Mary are based on her relationship to Jesus Christ. Her son is God's eternal Word, coming from the very unity and inner life of God to dwell among us. Jesus, Mary's son, came to reveal to us who God is, to teach us the meaning of life, and to help us live. This could not have happened without Mary and her yes to God.

The Word became flesh because of Mary's cooperation. Mary's role in God's plan was to be the instrument by which the eternal Word entered our world, our history, and our time and became one of us, a human being with flesh and blood. Through her, the Savior learned to speak to us in our language, to use our symbols and signs, and to love us with a human heart. This is the basis for our devotion to Mary: She helped bring God among us; she was the virgin mother through whom the Word became flesh and dwelt among us.

A Christocentric Prayer

The pope teaches us that "the Rosary, though clearly Marian in character, is at heart a Christocentric prayer" (1.2). We cannot properly speak of Mary's identity, gifts, or prerogatives with any great insight or meaning if we lose sight of the fact that she was, and is, intimately related to Jesus Christ. In fact, the formal declaration of Mary as the Mother of God grew out of the Church's effort to articulate more fully who Jesus Christ is. The Church's answer to Christ's question "Who do you say that I am?" (Matthew 16:15) was specified and exactly formulated in those turbulent first five centuries of the Church when it grappled with these questions: Is Jesus truly God? If he is truly God, is he one of us? Is he truly human?

Everything we say about Mary—our love for her and our understanding of her role in the life of Jesus and therefore in our lives—is rooted in the mystery of her being chosen to be the Mother of God. All other teachings about Mary, such as her immaculate conception, her perpetual virginity, and her assumption into heaven, flow from this mystery.

The Scriptures depict Mary as a woman of great faith. Through her enormous devotion and openness to the word of God, she was able to accept that her child was to be the Christ, the Messiah. The opening chapter of the Gospel of Luke tells us something of that mystery and how it unfolded. "Then the angel said to her, 'Do not be afraid, Mary, for you have found favor with God. Behold, you will conceive in your womb and bear a son, and you shall name him Jesus. . . . The holy Spirit will come upon you, and the power of the Most High will overshadow you. Therefore the child to be born will be called holy, the Son of God'" (Luke 1:30-31, 35).

The Second Vatican Council's Dogmatic Constitution on the Church, *Lumen Gentium*, reminds us that "through the gift and role of divine maternity, Mary is united with her son, the Redeemer, and with his singular graces and offices. By these, the Blessed Virgin is also intimately united with the Church. As St. Ambrose taught, the Mother of God is a model of the Church in the order of faith, charity, and perfect union with Christ" (LG, 63).

In highlighting the importance of the Rosary, the pope writes:

In the sobriety of its elements, it has all the depth of the Gospel message in its entirety, of which it can be said to be a compendium. It is an echo of the prayer of Mary, her perennial Magnificat for the work of the redemptive Incarnation which began in her virginal womb. With the Rosary, the Christian people sits at the school of Mary and is led to contemplate the beauty on the face of Christ and to experience the depths of his love. Through the Rosary the faithful receive abundant grace, as though from the very hands of the Mother of the Redeemer. (1.2)

Mary is the model of contemplation. Highlighting her unique relationship to Jesus, Pope John Paul II holds up Mary as "an incomparable model" of contemplation of Christ. "The eyes of her heart already turned to him at the Annunciation, when she conceived him by the power of the Holy Spirit. . . . Thereafter Mary's gaze, ever filled with adoration and wonder, would never leave him" (10.2). Because the Rosary starts with Mary's own experience, it is an "exquisitely contemplative prayer" (12.1), and it is precisely through the eyes of Mary and remembering Christ with Mary that we are drawn into the mystery of Christ. "Mary's contemplation is above all a remembering" (13.1).

Mary is not just the Mother of Jesus and the Mother of God; she is also our mother. She offers us a role model of faith and gives us an example of what it means to be a true believer, a follower of her son, Jesus. This quiet woman of the New Testament continues to do for us what all mothers should do for their children. She helps us to understand how to live responsibly, how to grow to full Christian maturity, and how to assume our place in the world as men and women of faith. Mary is the role model of what it means to be totally committed to the Word of God. She is a witness that it is possible, in our life, in what we say and do, to make the Word of God present and visible in our world. This is the real and enduring reason why there is such enormous devotion and love for Mary.

"The Rosary is also a path of proclamation and increasing knowledge, in which the mystery of Christ is presented again and again at different levels of the Christian experience" (17.1). In our meditation on the mysteries of the Rosary with Mary, we experience the saving events of salvation in a way that touches our hearts and illumines our minds. Thus it is that as we pray, we are united to Mary in a bond of faith that nurtures our own spiritual efforts to draw more deeply into the mystery of Christ.

Mary put a human face on God. By cooperating with God through her faith, she allowed the eternal Word to become one of us and to come among us. The realization of this truth explains why we have such great devotion to her. Her belief is an example of how we can and should accept the challenge of the gospel. We should always approach the joys and sorrows of life in faith. No wonder we want to be with her in prayer and veneration!

Mary's role was to believe God's word to her and in her great faith make God visible among us. Our devotion to Mary is rooted in our desire to know Christ and live as Christ more fully—to make him visible. Mary's last recorded words in Scripture give us special insight into how she invites us to draw close to her son: "Do whatever he tells you" (John 2:5).

After highlighting the unique role of Mary as the spiritual guide of the faithful in making their spiritual journey to Christ, the pope goes on to speak of the mysteries of the Rosary. In chapter two, entitled "Mysteries of Christ—Mysteries of His Mother," he cites Pope Paul VI, who described the Rosary in these words: "As a gospel prayer, centered on the mystery of the redemptive incarnation, the Rosary is a prayer with a clearly Christological orientation. . . . The Jesus that each Hail Mary recalls is the same Jesus whom the succession of mysteries proposes to us now as the Son of God, now as the Son of the Virgin" (*Marialis Cultus*, 155; 18.2).

A New Set of Mysteries

It is at this point in his apostolic letter that the Holy Father introduces a new set of mysteries. "To bring out fully the Christological depth of the Rosary, it would be suitable to make an addition to the traditional pattern which, while left to the freedom of individuals and communities, could broaden it to include the mysteries of Christ's public ministry between his baptism and his passion" (19.2). Thus, as we continue our way through *Rosarium Virginis Mariae*, we now encounter the five mysteries of light that are joined to the joyful, sorrowful, and glorious mysteries of the Rosary.

In the new ordering of the mysteries, the Holy Father proposes a revision of the traditional pattern of the mysteries. The Rosary continues to begin with the reflection on the incarnation and the hidden life of Christ in the joyful mysteries. However, before focusing on the sufferings of Christ's passion in the sorrowful mysteries and the triumph of his resurrection in the glorious mysteries, the Holy Father introduces "a meditation on certain particularly significant moments in his public ministry" in the mysteries of light (19.3). These significant moments are (1) Jesus' baptism in the Jordan; (2) his self-manifestation at the wedding of Cana; (3) his proclamation of the kingdom of God; (4) the transfiguration; and (5) the institution of the Eucharist. These mysteries would have as their focus the manifestation of Jesus as Lord and the illumination he brings into our lives. As the Holy Father points out, "It is during the years of his public ministry that the mystery of Christ is most evidently a mystery of light: 'While I am in the world, I am the light of the world' (John 9:5)" (19.2).

The addition of these new mysteries is intended to give the Rosary "fresh life and to enkindle renewed interest in the Rosary's place within Christian spirituality as a true doorway to the depths of the heart of Christ, ocean of joy and of light, of suffering and of glory" (19.3).

The Joyful Mysteries

As we reflect on the Rosary, we necessarily encounter the mysteries that are at the heart of our faith. Saying the individual Hail Marys provides us with a rhythm of prayer that allows the mind to be free to reflect and the heart to meditate on the mystery unfolding—the mystery of God with us. Thus we begin with the joyful mysteries because it is in the first of these mysteries, the annunciation, that we encounter the extraordinary action of God coming among us to take on our human nature. It seems fitting that these mysteries be called joyful because this is the beginning, the announcement of our salvation.

In the annunciation the angel appears to Mary and tells her she is to be the Mother of God. In the visitation, in response to the angel's declaration that her cousin has conceived a child—John the Baptist—Mary hastens to visit Elizabeth. In the third joyful mystery, we celebrate the nativity, the birth of the Messiah. This is the completion of the incarnation begun at the annunciation. God is with us in this child, who is son of Mary and also Son of God. The remaining two joyful mysteries continue to have an overtone of joy as they fulfill the prophecies proclaiming the coming of a redeemer. It is in the presentation of the child Jesus in the temple that we learn that the long-awaited time of salvation is at hand. In the fifth and final joyful mystery, we rejoice in the finding of the child Jesus in the temple.

John Paul writes, "To mediate upon the 'joyful' mysteries, then, is to enter into the ultimate causes and the deepest meaning of Christian joy. It is to focus on the realism of the mystery of the Incarnation and on the obscure foreshadowing of the mystery of the saving Passion" (20.4).

The Luminous Mysteries

As we move from the infancy and the hidden life in Nazareth to the public life of Jesus, we encounter "those mysteries which may be called in a special way 'mysteries of light.'" The pope writes, "Certainly the whole mystery of Christ is a mystery of light. He is the 'light of the world' (John 8:12). Yet this truth emerges in a special way during the years of his public life, when he proclaims the Gospel of the Kingdom" (21). These luminous mysteries speak to "a showing" of the beginnings of the kingdom and its realization among us.

"Each of these mysteries is a revelation of the kingdom now present in the very person of Jesus" (21.2).

The first of the mysteries of light is Jesus' baptism in the Jordan. The New Testament describes the Spirit descending upon Jesus "to invest him with the mission which he is to carry out" (21.2). The emphasis of this mystery is Jesus as we visualize him coming forward to be baptized by John the Baptist. As he steps into the water and in the ritual of that moment, John protests that he should not be the one doing the baptizing. Then the heavens open and the Holy Spirit descends on Jesus, while the voice from heaven calls him "my beloved Son" (Matthew 3:13-17). The baptism of Jesus is essentially an epiphany event. In this epiphany, those present are helped to understand that this is no ordinary man; this is truly God-with-us.

At a certain point, Jesus begins his public ministry; now there is no turning back. The second luminous mystery tells us of the first of Jesus' miracles (John 2:1-11), of which there would be many more to come. He is invited to a wedding feast at Cana, and in the midst of the celebration, at the prompting of his mother, he changes water into wine. We can almost sense reluctance on his part to begin his public ministry because he knows where it will end. But now is the time to step out into the public arena; this was the reason he was sent. The first miracle is also an epiphany as Jesus manifests himself as the wonder-worker, the One empowered by God to verify with mighty works and signs the truth of his message.

The third luminous mystery focuses on something that Jesus keeps repeating over and over again throughout his ministry: The kingdom of God is at hand. He begins his public ministry with this announcement. In his sermons and teachings, he tries to help his followers—the people who are now flocking to him—come to an understanding about what it means to say that the kingdom of God is at hand.

It is in this mystery that we must reflect on the spiritual nature of the kingdom that Jesus proclaims. Perhaps in the crowd that heard him during his three years of public ministry, there were those that thought of a temporal kingdom—a throwing off of the Roman yoke and the reestablishment of a political kingdom. But Jesus reminds them over and over again that his is a kingdom of the Spirit. In the Sermon on the Mount in Matthew's gospel, beginning with the fifth chapter, we see an unfolding of the message of Jesus that calls us to understand the kingdom as rooted in the truth of his word. The kingdom means justice among all people, peace as the fruit of truth and justice, and a love that we are called to share with one another.

The fourth luminous mystery is another epiphany event. The transfiguration presents Jesus as he stands with Peter, James, and John and is changed before them so that they can see his glory—a glory hidden in his human nature. In this mystery, we are given a glimpse of Jesus' divinity. He is on his way to die for us. In order to strengthen the apostles in their faith, he lets them see a confirmation of his message, an epiphany of his glory.

In the fifth and final luminous mystery, we encounter the institution of the Eucharist. This is really the culmination of Jesus' public life. The night before he dies and right before the sorrowful events that lead to our redemption, Jesus gathers his apostles and celebrates the Passover with them. It is in this context that Jesus takes the bread and wine and establishes the mystery of his body and his blood in the Eucharist. As the pope reminds us in his encyclical letter *Ecclesia de Eucharistia*:

> When the Church celebrates the Eucharist, the memorial of her Lord's death and resurrection, this central event of salvation becomes really present and "the work of our redemption is carried out" (*Lumen Gentium*, 3). This sacrifice is so decisive for the salvation of the human race that Jesus Christ offered it and returned to the Father only after he had left us a means of sharing in it as if we had been present there. (11.3)

As often as the Eucharist is celebrated, Christ is present. The purpose of the Eucharist is to make available, generation after generation, what was going to happen in the next three days of Jesus' life—his death and his resurrection, and thus our salvation. We, then, receive the Eucharist, not only as a memorial of what Christ endured, but also as a pledge of our own share in his death and his resurrection. It is with this extraordinary proclamation of faith before us that we conclude the luminous mysteries.

The Sorrowful Mysteries

From the luminous mysteries we move to the sorrowful ones, rightfully named because they are the narration of the painful and sorrowful moment for which Jesus came into the world—his passion and death. The mysteries begin with the agony in the garden as Jesus prays, and then, in loving obedience to the will of his Father, accepts whatever must happen. The second sorrowful mystery is the scourging at the pillar. Jesus is arrested. He is taken into custody, and among the humiliations inflicted upon him is the terrible and brutal scourging. The third sorrowful mystery is the crowning with thorns. To ridicule him and his claim to fulfill the prophecies as the king of God's new spiritual kingdom, those maltreating him crown him with thorns.

In the next mystery, Jesus takes up his cross and carries it along the *Via Dolorosa*—the "Way of Sorrows"—and arrives at Golgotha. Thus we come to the fifth sorrowful mystery, the death of Jesus. Here we see him hanging on the cross, the victim for our redemption, the One whose blood will wipe away our sins.

The Glorious Mysteries

But the story of Jesus does not end with his death on the cross. Thus we turn to the glorious mysteries of the Rosary, which proclaim the triumph of the cross. This is the victory: Jesus, God's Son, the eternal Word come among us and filled with God's Spirit, is raised from the dead. Scripture speaks of this first glorious mystery, the resurrection, when it relates to us how the disciples came and found the tomb empty and Jesus no longer there among the dead. He has truly risen!

The second glorious mystery is the ascension. Now that Jesus' work has been completed and he has restored us to friendship with God, he returns in glory to his Father. We visualize the scene of Jesus bidding farewell to his apostles as he is taken up into heaven.

The next mystery, the third, evokes for us the outpouring of the Holy Spirit at Pentecost. Jesus turns over to us the work of continuing and completing all that he came to do. To make this possible, the Father and Son pour out the Spirit that Jesus promised upon his apostles.

In the final two mysteries, we reflect on Mary at the completion of her earthly life. In the fourth mystery, we celebrate her assumption into heaven. Mary is taken up as the most wonderful of all God's creatures. There in heaven she now reigns with her son. In the final and fifth glorious mystery, we celebrate the coronation of Mary as Queen of Heaven. She is the queen of all God's creation because of her fidelity and her faith. We are reminded that in faith, we, too, can go beyond meditating these mysteries and actually enter into them in grace—now in the kingdom at hand, and someday in fullness and glory.

As he concludes his reflection on these mysteries, the pope observes, "The cycles of meditation proposed by the holy Rosary are by no means exhaustive, but they do bring to mind what is essential, and they awaken in the soul a thirst for a knowledge of Christ continually nourished by the pure source of the Gospel" (24.1).

In chapter three of *Rosarium Virginis Mariae*, the pope notes that meditation on the mysteries of Christ "is proposed in the Rosary by means of a method designed to assist in their assimilation. It is a method based on repetition" (26.1). Not only is this a valid method that has withstood the test of time, but it is also, in effect, "simply a method of contemplation" (28.2). In announcing each mystery, we listen to the word of God. Then as we repeat the ten Hail Marys, we open ourselves to being renewed in the events of salvation as they are brought to both our minds and hearts.

We should not be surprised that this effective vehicle of prayer and devotion, developed "under the guidance of the Spirit of God" (1.1), should enjoy such widespread use throughout the Church and throughout the ages. In our constant effort to grow ever more close to Christ, the Rosary, as Pope John Paul II points out, is an invaluable instrument of prayer that works.

Chapter 23

A REAL PRESENCE

Ecclesia de Eucharistia

ENGLISH TITLE:	**On the Eucharist in Its Relationship to the Church**
DATE ISSUED:	**April 17, 2003**
TYPE OF DOCUMENT:	**Encyclical Letter**

T he Church draws her life from the Eucharist." This is the opening sentence of Pope John Paul II's encyclical letter *Ecclesia de Eucharistia* (On the Eucharist in Its Relationship to the Church), issued on Holy Thursday, April 17, 2003. John Paul is speaking here, not just about the regular experience of faith that we know from our own participation in the daily and Sunday Eucharistic liturgy, but about the very heart of the mystery of the Church. This is the theme he will develop throughout the entire encyclical letter.

In the introduction, the pope tells us why he chose this particular moment to issue the letter and how it is part of a much larger tradition, going back to the very beginning of his pontificate. He had always marked Holy Thursday by sending a letter to all the priests of the world. Since 2003 was the twenty-fifth year of his pontificate, he wanted to include "the whole Church more fully in this Eucharistic reflection also in a way of thanking the Lord for the gift of the Eucharist and the priesthood: 'gift and mystery'" (7.1).

It is Christ who is at the very core of the sacraments and particularly the Eucharist. In chapter one, "The Mystery of Faith," the pope reminds us that it was Jesus who instituted the Eucharist, which is the memorial of the Lord's death and resurrection, and that each time the Church celebrates the Eucharistic liturgy, the central event of our salvation becomes sacramentally but really present (cf. 11, 15). Jesus continues to act through the sacraments. It is the Lord who is present in every one of the seven sacraments, thus producing the spiritual effect that the outward sign demonstrates.

> The sacramental re-presentation of Christ's sacrifice, crowned by the resurrection, in the Mass involves a most special presence which—in the words of Paul VI—"is called real not as a way of excluding all other types of presence as if they were 'not real,' but because it is a presence in the fullest sense: a substantial presence whereby Christ, the God-man, is wholly and entirely present." (*Mysterium Fidei*, 39; 15.1)

The origins of the Eucharist are found in the Last Supper. In order to give us a pledge of his love and to be with us always, Jesus made us sharers in his Passover and instituted the Eucharist as the memorial of his death and resurrection. He also commanded the apostles to celebrate it until he returned. At the Last Supper, Jesus instituted the new memorial sacrifice. The true Lamb of God (John 1:29) was about to be slain. By his cross and resurrection, he was to free not just one nation from the bondage of human slavery but all of humanity from the more bitter slavery of sin.

The faith of the Church in the real presence of Jesus in the Eucharist goes back to the words of Jesus himself as recorded in the Gospel of St. John. In the Eucharistic discourse after the multiplication of the loaves, our Lord contrasted ordinary bread with a bread that is not of this world but that contains eternal life for those who eat it. He said, "I am the bread of life. . . . I am the living bread that came down from heaven; whoever eats this bread will live forever; and the bread that I will give is my flesh for the life of the world" (John 6:48, 51).

There is only one sacrifice—the self-giving of Christ on the cross at Calvary. Again, the Holy Father highlights this reality. Once and for all, Jesus, who was the victim for our sins, offered himself up for our salvation. As the Letter to the Hebrews affirms, "For this reason he is mediator of a new covenant: since a death has taken place for deliverance from transgressions under the first covenant, those who are called may receive the promised eternal inheritance" (9:15).

The one great sacrifice was accomplished by Jesus, the priest and victim, who offered himself on the altar of the cross for our redemption. This sacrifice not only need not be repeated but cannot be repeated. However, it can be re-presented so that today, in our moment in history, we are able sacramentally and spiritually to enter the paschal mystery and draw spiritual nourishment from it. John Paul returns over and over again to this theme throughout each chapter of *Ecclesia de Eucharistia*.

The Church Grows through the Eucharist

In the second chapter, entitled "The Eucharist Builds the Church," John Paul recalls that the Church's life and development are rooted in the sacrifice of the cross, which is re-presented on the altar (cf. 21). To begin this section, the pope turns to the Second Vatican Council's teaching in *Lumen Gentium* (The Dogmatic Constitution on the Church). The pope notes that the Council's response to the question "How does the Church grow?" is this one: "The Church, as the kingdom of God already present in mystery, grows visibly in the world through the power of God as often as the sacrifice of the cross . . . is celebrated on the altar" (LG, 3; 21.1).

The Holy Father reminds us that in the earliest chapters of the Acts of the Apostles, which describe the life of the ancient and fledgling Church, we find the description of the faithful coming together in order that they might devote themselves "to the teaching of the apostles and to the communal life, to the breaking of the bread and to the prayers" (2:42). The "breaking of the bread" refers to the Eucharist. Two thousand years later, we continue to relive that primordial image of the Church.

The Church shares in the very life of the risen Lord. Its members, through baptism into the Church, form a body with Christ as its head. By way of pastoral application, the Holy Father stresses that Eucharistic communion "confirms the Church in her unity as the body of Christ" (23.1). It is through this Church that men and women are saved by coming to know Jesus Christ, and through him they are united in grace to the Father through the outpouring of the Holy Spirit. As the pope makes clear, the mystery of the faith involves the mystery of the Eucharist and the Church.

Speaking of Eucharistic adoration, the pope writes, "The worship of the Eucharist outside of the Mass is of inestimable value for the life of the Church. . . . It is the responsibility of pastors to encourage, also by their personal witness, the practice of Eucharistic adoration, and exposition of the Blessed Sacrament in particular" (25.1).

The Church and the Eucharist Are Apostolic

The theological logic of the encyclical unfolds in chapter three, "The Apostolicity of the Eucharist in the Church." Here the Holy Father develops the Church's teaching on the relationship between priestly ministry and the Eucharist (cf. 27, 29), and we are encouraged to reflect on how the priest, acting in the person of Christ, brings about the Eucharistic sacrifice.

The pope addresses what it means to say that the Church is apostolic and how the Eucharist participates in this apostolic dimension. At the core of this teaching is the recognition that the Church rests on the foundation of the apostles. "The Eucharist, too, has its foundation in the apostles, not in the sense that it did not originate in Christ himself, but because it was entrusted by Christ to the apostles and has been handed down to us by them and by their successors" (27.1). Another sense in which the Church is apostolic is that with the help of the Holy Spirit, the Church hands on the deposit of faith that she received from the apostles. Here too the Eucharist is apostolic, "for it is celebrated in conformity with the faith of the apostles" (27.2).

Finally, the Church is apostolic in the sense that she continues to be taught, sanctified, and guided by the apostles until Christ's return. The Eucharist "also expresses this sense of apostolicity" since it is the ordained priest who, acting in the person of Christ, brings about the Eucharistic sacrifice and offers it to God in the name of all the people. "For this reason, the Roman Missal prescribes that only the priest should recite the Eucharistic Prayer, while the people participate in faith and in silence" (28.2).

A pastoral implication for this chapter is the "pastoral promotion of priestly vocations" (31.3). We are all obliged to pray and work for an increase in priestly vocations. "When a community lacks a priest, attempts are rightly made somehow to remedy the situation so that it can continue its Sunday celebrations, and those religious and laity who lead their brothers and sisters in prayer exercise in a praiseworthy way the common priesthood of all the faithful based on the grace of baptism," the pope notes. "But such solutions must be considered merely temporary, while the community awaits a priest" (32.1).

The Bond of Communion

Chapter four, entitled "The Eucharist and Ecclesial Communion," provides us insight into what it means to profess our faith in the Church as a "communion" of believers professing the same faith, celebrating the same sacraments, and recognizing the same hierarchical structure. The Eucharist is the supreme sacramental manifestation of communion in the Church, and therefore, those who receive Holy

Communion bear public witness that the outward bonds of communion are intact (cf. 34, 38, 40). John Paul teaches:

> The celebration of the Eucharist, however, cannot be the starting point for communion; it presupposes that communion already exists, a communion which it seeks to consolidate and bring to perfection. The sacrament is an expression of this bond of communion both in its invisible dimension . . . and in its visible dimension, which entails communion in the teaching of the apostles, in the sacraments, and in the Church's hierarchical order. (35.1)

In this section, the encyclical reminds us that we must be spiritually disposed to receive the Eucharist. "Anyone conscious of a grave sin must receive the Sacrament of Reconciliation before coming to communion" (36.3). The pope also explains why there can be no intercommunion among those who do not share the Catholic faith. Quoting from *Lumen Gentium*, he notes that Communion is the public statement that those who receive it are "incorporated into the society of the Church who, possessing the Spirit of Christ, accept her whole structure and all the means of salvation established within her, and within her visible framework" (LG 14; 38.1).

The fifth chapter, entitled "The Dignity of the Eucharistic Celebration," challenges us to recognize that the celebration of the Eucharist must be done with fitting simplicity and solemnity and thus always in accord with the ritual of the Church. The Eucharist is the patrimony of the Church and not the private property of the celebrant (cf. 47, 49, 52). The way the Eucharist is celebrated should reflect the faith and practice of the Church:

> With this heightened sense of mystery, we understand how the faith of the Church in the mystery of the Eucharist has found

historical expression not only in the demand for an interior disposition of devotion, but also in outward forms meant to evoke and emphasize the grandeur of the event being celebrated. This led progressively to the development of a particular form of regulating the Eucharistic liturgy with due respect for the various legitimately constructed ecclesial traditions. (49.1)

Pope Benedict XVI, in his apostolic exhortation *Sacramentum Caritatis* (The Sacrament of Charity), which followed the Synod on the Eucharist, continued this theme.

In the final chapter, "At the School of Mary, 'Woman of the Eucharist,'" Pope John Paul II leads us through a beautiful reflection on Mary's faith and her spirit of praise for God, which is a model for our own attitude as we approach the Eucharist (cf. 54, 58). As in all of his encyclicals, St. John Paul brings forth from his own deep and beautiful devotion to Mary a meditation on her place in the Church and in the life of each believer. "In the Eucharist the Church is completely united to Christ and his sacrifice, and makes her own the spirit of Mary. . . . The Eucharist, like the Canticle of Mary, is first and foremost praise and thanksgiving" (58.1).

In his encyclical letter *Ecclesia de Eucharistia*, Pope John Paul II celebrates the mystery of our faith so beautifully proclaimed at every Eucharistic liturgy. Jesus continues to be with us. His Eucharistic presence is the foundation of the Church and our pledge of life everlasting. How blessed we are with the gift of faith, and in that faith, the gift of the Eucharist!

Chapter 24
·····················

GOOD SHEPHERDS

Pastores Gregis

ENGLISH TITLE:	**The Bishop, Servant of the Gospel of Jesus Christ for the Hope of the World**
DATE ISSUED:	**October 16, 2003**
TYPE OF DOCUMENT:	**Post-Synodal Apostolic Exhortation**

O n October 16, 2003, the twenty-fifth anniversary of his election as bishop of Rome, Pope John Paul II issued an apostolic exhortation on the ministry and mission of bishops—*Pastores Gregis* (The Bishop, Servant of the Gospel of Jesus Christ for the Hope of the World). Later that day, more than four hundred cardinals and bishops from around the world joined the pope in concelebrating the Eucharist at St. Peter's Basilica before a crowd estimated at well over one hundred thousand. For many, the pope's life, as well as his twenty-six years of ministry as vicar of Christ and bishop of Rome, was a living example of the teaching contained in this exhortation on what it means to be a bishop. A bishop is first and foremost a pastor, or shepherd, of his flock

The exhortation followed the General Assembly of the Synod of Bishops, which had met in the fall of 2001 and which the pope attended. In the opening paragraph, John Paul writes:

> We were all agreed that the figure of Jesus the Good Shepherd represents the primary image to which we must constantly refer.
> . . . This is the fundamental reason why the ideal figure of the

Bishop, on which the Church continues to count, is that of the pastor who, configured to Christ by his holiness of life, expends himself generously for the Church entrusted to him, while at the same time bearing in his heart a concern for all the Churches throughout the world (cf. 2 Corinthians 11:28). (1.2)

As he did throughout his pontificate, the pope continually refers to the documents of the Second Vatican Council as the foundation for his teaching and to demonstrate the continuity of his proclamation with the living tradition of the Church. In a world that is increasingly skeptical of religious faith and influenced by secular and materialistic values, John Paul says that the task of the bishop is to be a beacon of hope, one that calls people to experience the truth of Jesus' message. This is a hope "based on the proclamation of the Gospel of Jesus Christ," a hope that awaits the riches of heaven (3.1).

Since the 2001 synod took place so soon after the terrible events of September 11, mention is made of that tragedy in the context of the synod's condemnation of all forms of violence. The reason for the perennial hope of the Church in the face of even the most horrible examples of human violence is our confidence in the power of God's grace to overcome the effects of sin and to touch human hearts in a way that brings them to Christ, his healing grace, his love, and his peace.

The framework for the core message of *Pastores Gregis* is the threefold *munus* ("function" or "ministry") that is the task of the successors of the apostles. The bishop as witness or servant of hope does so in the exercise of his tasks of teaching, sanctifying, and leading the Church. As an apostolic teacher, the pope says, the bishop is to "preach the word, be urgent in season and out of season, convince, rebuke and exhort—be unfailing in patience and in teaching (2 Timothy 4:2)" (5.2).

In the work of sanctification, the bishop is to oversee the administration of the sacraments, "of which we are the principal dispensers, moderators, guardians, and promoters. They form a sort of saving 'net,' which sets free from evil and leads to the fullness of life." Finally, in exercising the ministry of leading the Church "as pastors and true fathers, assisted by the priest and other helpers, we have the task of gathering together the family of the faithful and in it fostering charity and brotherly communion" (5.2).

Collegiality and the Ministry of the Bishop

In chapter one, the pope addresses "The Mystery and Ministry of the Bishop," highlighting for us that it was Christ who chose the Twelve, and it is the College of Bishops that continues the mission entrusted by Jesus to the apostles—a mission that is to last until the end of time.

Before moving into the unfolding of the three functions of the bishop, *Pastores Gregis* reminds us that all episcopal ministry is by its nature collegial in that it is exercised as part of the College of Bishops, the successor to the College of Apostles. "Through the personal succession of the Bishop of Rome to St. Peter and the succession of all the Bishops as a group to the Apostles, the Roman Pontiff and the Bishops are united among themselves as a College" (8.1). Here the pope teaches that this collegial union between the bishops is based on episcopal ordination and hierarchical communion. Thus the innermost being of each bishop is affected by the relationship he has with every other bishop and with the pope. This relationship is the will of Christ, who established the Church in a visible, structured, and hierarchical manner to continue his work in the world.

A bishop never stands alone or apart from either the College of Bishops or the Roman pontiff. Intrinsic to the very identity of the bishop is his participation in the College of Bishops, which acts always with and never without the bishop of Rome. It is precisely because of this relationship, intrinsic to the office of bishop, that the bishop is not only responsible for the governance of the diocesan church entrusted to his care but also for the good of the whole Church universal. At the same time, the bishop's relationship to the pope guarantees that the diocesan church shares in the catholicity, or universality, of the whole Church. "The collegial dimension gives the episcopate its character of universality" (8.6). Here the Holy Father refers to an earlier document, *Apostolos Suos* (On the Theological and Juridical Nature of Episcopal Conferences), which he issued on May 21, 1998, highlighting that "the unity of the episcopate is one of the constitutive elements of the unity of the Church" (AS, 8).

Today we are very much aware of the need for bishops to act in solidarity. Given the immediacy of communications and the tendency of the media to contrast and even place in opposition elements of the Church, the bishops must find ways in which to express their doctrinal unity and strive, wherever possible, to demonstrate pastoral communion.

Apostolos Suos tells us that while the conference of bishops does not possess "teaching authority" in its own right, it can provide a significant vehicle for communicating and disseminating the Church's teaching (AS, 21). *Christus Dominus* (The Decree on the Pastoral Office of Bishops in the Church), issued by the Second Vatican Council in 1965, reminds us that "it is often impossible, nowadays especially, for bishops to exercise their office suitably and fruitfully unless they establish closer understanding and cooperation with other bishops" (CD, 37).

Just as the bishop does not function apart from the College of Bishops and the pope, so too he does not function apart from the flock entrusted to his care. By Christ's will and through the Sacrament of Baptism, God's Church comes to be and is found in men and women throughout the world. It is out of this body of Christ, alive in the outpouring of the Holy Spirit and anointed in the gifts of the Spirit, that Christ calls some to be ordained ministers of that body. Just as the Sacrament of Baptism makes one a member of the Church, so too does the Sacrament of Holy Orders make some servants of that body. John Paul writes:

> As a gift of the Holy Spirit to the Church, the Bishop is above all else, like every other Christian, a son and member of the Church. From this holy Mother he has received the gift of divine life in the Sacrament of Baptism and his first instruction in the faith. . . . On the other hand, by virtue of the fullness of the Sacrament of Holy Orders, the bishop is also the one who, before the faithful, is teacher, sanctifier, and shepherd, charged with acting in the name and in the person of Christ. (10.2)

The pastoral ministry that he receives in his episcopal ordination places the bishop in the midst of the baptized faithful as teacher, sanctifier, and leader, but at the same time, it does not diminish his "being with" them in his journey toward personal sanctification and redemption.

The Spiritual Life of the Bishop

Having begun this exhortation by clearly identifying the bishop as the member of the whole body of Christ who is charged with all the other bishops throughout the Church to teach, to lead, and to sanctify the faithful entrusted to his care, the Holy Father speaks in chapter two about the spiritual life of the bishop. He calls our attention to the fact that Jesus called the Twelve as apostles to share his own life. "This sharing, which is a communion of mind and heart with him, also appears as an inner demand of their participation in Jesus' own mission. The functions of the Bishop must not be reduced to those of administration alone" (11.1). In order that the bishop might carry out his many responsibilities, including a substantial amount of Church administration, he must develop his own spiritual life focused on "an attitude of service" (11.4). It should be marked by personal strength, apostolic courage, and a trust in the work of the Holy Spirit.

It is precisely in the exercise of his ministry—no small part of which is sacramental—that the bishop finds the focus of his own spirituality. First of all, it will be a spirituality of communion, that is, spirituality lived in harmony with the baptized faithful so that the bishop avails himself of the spiritual goods of the Church, particularly the Eucharist and the Sacrament of Penance. Together with the priests who work with him, the bishop must advance his own growth in holiness through his ministry of the Lord's word and of the sanctification and spiritual advancement of the people of God.

There is a specific spirituality for the diocesan bishop and therefore the diocesan priest. This spirituality is rooted in the identification of the priest and bishop with Christ as head of his Church and is strengthened each day by the exercise of that priestly ministry reserved to those in holy orders—the anointing of the sick, the forgiveness of sins, and above all, the celebration of the paschal mystery in the Eucharist.

At each moment of their sacramental ministry, not only do the bishop and priest make present the healing and saving power of Christ to those for whom the sacrament is administered, but they also make Christ present for themselves. Precisely in this sacramental encounter, repeated day in and day out by the bishop or priest, does the unique spirituality of priestly ministry develop and flower. "Just as the Paschal Mystery stands at the center of the life and mission of the Good Shepherd, so too the Eucharist stands at the center of the life and mission of the Bishop, as of every priest" (16.1).

In his reflection on the spirituality of the bishop, the Holy Father also reminds us of the role of the evangelical counsels and the beatitudes. Just as the apostolic, communitarian, and pastoral character of priestly obedience is a part of the life of the priest, so too these same hallmarks "appear even more markedly in the obedience of the Bishop." The bishop must feel "committed to living intensely this relationship with the Pope and his brother Bishops in a close bond of unity and cooperation, and thus conforming to the divine plan which willed to unite the Apostles inseparably around Peter" (19.2). The bishop is also called to a spirit and practice of poverty and the recognition that he is "committed to mirroring the virginal love of Christ for all of his faithful ones" (21.1).

In concluding the reflection on the spiritual life of the bishop, John Paul highlights that prayer is itself a particular duty for a bishop and for all those who have received the gift of a vocation to the consecrated life. Every bishop is also called upon to pray with his people and for his people. "He himself is supported and assisted by the prayer of his faithful: priests, deacons, consecrated persons, and the lay people of all ages" (17.5).

We are all reminded that just as the bishop prays for the flock, so too must the flock pray for its shepherd. We are bound together in a spiritual communion that is strengthened by our prayers for each other. Let us never forget the importance of asking God's blessing upon those called to shepherd the flock so that together, both the pastor and those whom he guides might truly rejoice each day in the blessings of God's grace.

Having explained the collegial nature of the episcopate and the unique spirituality of the bishop, the pope now turns to those duties that form the frame of reference for all episcopal activity: teaching, leading, and sanctifying.

The Ministry of Teacher

In chapter three, "Teacher of the Faith and Herald of the Word," the pope directs our attention to the "teaching ministry" of the bishop ("*munus docendi*"). "The risen Jesus entrusted to his Apostles the mission of 'making disciples' of all nations, teaching them to observe all that he himself had commanded" (26.1). The living continuity between the apostolic Church and our day is verified in the office and ministry of the bishop. While the duty of proclaiming the gospel is incumbent upon the whole Church and each of its members, this is particularly so for bishops because on the day of their sacred ordination, which places them in apostolic succession, they assume as "one of their principal responsibilities the proclamation of the Gospel" (26.2).

There are two aspects to the bishop's mission of teaching: proclaiming the faith and safeguarding its integrity. In the episcopal ordination in the Roman ritual, the open Book of the Gospels is placed over the head of the bishop-elect just prior to his consecration. "This gesture indicates, on the one hand, that the word embraces and watches over the Bishop's ministry and, on the other, that the Bishop's life is to be completely submitted to the word of God in his daily commitment of preaching the Gospel in all patience and sound doctrine (cf. 2 Timothy 4)" (28.2).

As the Church makes its way through this world, she does so guided by God's word—divine revelation. This deposit of divine revelation is handed down generation to generation through the living apostolic Tradition. "This Tradition, which comes from the apostles, makes progress in the life of the Church. . . . There is likewise growth and development in the understanding of the realities and the words handed down" (28.4).

It is the task of the bishop to see that the integrity of the faith is maintained and that what is passed on from generation to generation is what has been received from the apostles. Thus the bishop has the fundamental mission of authoritatively proclaiming the word of God. "Indeed, every Bishop, by virtue of sacred ordination, is an authentic teacher who preaches to the people entrusted to his care the faith to be believed and to be put into practice in the moral life" (29.1).

The Holy Father is addressing the phenomenon of how Christ's revelation comes to us from the earliest days of God's intervention in human history. God made himself known through the prophets. God did not, however, communicate through them all that he wanted us to know. Finally, God spoke to us "through a son, whom he made heir of all things and through whom he created the universe, who is the refulgence of his glory, the very imprint of his being" (Hebrews 1:2-3).

Thus the teaching of Jesus is different from that of any other person. Christ in his being, his deeds, and his words is the perfect revelation of the Father. Jesus is God, who has come into our midst to reveal to us the inner life and the very word of God. Through him we have learned how we should live.

The question that arises for many is this: "How does the revelation of God in Christ Jesus continue to come to us?" This is what the pope addresses in great detail in *Pastores Gregis*. The revelation continues to reach us through the Church. God sent Jesus, and Jesus sent the apostles. Just as the word of God spread through the twelve apostles, so it must continue to be taught through today's apostles—the bishops. The Church continues to pass on the revelation of truth through the bishops today as it did in apostolic times through the apostles.

From the first days of the Church, bishops appointed by or succeeding the apostles were recognized as shepherds who rightly ruled and guarded the Church in the name of Christ. Loyalty to Christ was visibly expressed by loyalty to the bishops. St. Ignatius of Antioch, in a letter written in or about A.D. 106, praises the Church at Philadelphia in Asia as "a source of everlasting joy, especially when the members are at one with the bishop and his assistants, the presbyters, and deacons" (*Letter to the Philadelphians*, 1).

It falls to each bishop personally to proclaim the faith. It is the task of the bishops or the magisterium to define the teaching of the Church, to nurture acceptance of the faith, and to increase understanding of the faith through contemplation, study, and prayerful reflection on what has been handed on to us.

Interpreting the word of God is a task of the magisterium or teaching office in the Church. This does not mean that the authentic teachers of the Church are above the word of God. They are servants of God's word. The bishops help the faithful to understand each element of God's word in the light of the whole message of salvation. They must be faithful to God's word as taught and lived under the inspiration of the Holy Spirit and guarded by the assurance of truth that the Holy Spirit gives to the continuing apostolic office.

The proclamation of the faith takes many forms. Bishops regularly give homilies in the context of the liturgy, as well as talks and discourses at events both ecclesiastical and civil, and very often they publish pastoral letters. Bishops also enhance their teaching office by participating in the work of provincial, regional, or national conferences of bishops, which regularly issue statements meant to be instructive to the faithful.

While the bishop is a teacher of the faith directly and personally, at the same time, he exercises his office by overseeing the teaching of the faith by all those who participate in this essential mission of the Church. The supervisory, or oversight, role of the bishop is every bit as important as his own personal proclamation of the faith. John Paul writes:

Conscious, then, of his responsibility in the area of transmitting and teaching the faith, every Bishop must ensure that a corresponding concern is shown by all those who by their vocation and mission are called to hand down the faith. This means priests and deacons, the faithful who have embraced the consecrated life, fathers and mothers of families, pastoral workers and in a special way catechists, as well as teachers of theology and teachers of ecclesiastical sciences and religious education.

The Bishop will thus take care to provide them with both initial and ongoing training. (29.5)

The development of diocesan policy to coordinate the teaching of the faith and to ensure through doctrinal guidelines that the content of the faith remains secure is another way by which the bishop exercises his teaching office. All who claim to teach the Catholic faith within the diocese, whether in a school, a religious education program, or from the pulpit, do so with the understanding that they are in communion with the bishop and, through him, with the teaching of the universal Church. Many times diocesan policies are meant to reassure that continuity and to guarantee the authenticity of individual religious education programs.

As the bishop carries out his *munus docendi*, he is responsible not only for what he proclaims but also for what is proclaimed in the name of the Church by all those who seek to pass on the gospel and its implications for life today. This is no small task, yet it is rooted in the very office of bishop.

While we identify the bishop with his teaching chair in the cathedral, we most often think of the bishop as he celebrates the Eucharistic liturgy. More often than not, when a bishop visits a parish or some other institution, his pastoral stay culminates in the celebration of Mass. It is here that we see one expression of the bishop's responsibility for the holiness of his flock.

The Ministry of Sanctification

In chapter four, the pope turns our attention to the "ministry of sanctification" ("*munus sanctificandi*"). Here he reminds us, "The Bishop carries out his ministry of sanctification by celebrating the Eucharist and the other sacraments, by praising God in the Liturgy of the Hours, by presiding over the other sacred rites, and by promoting liturgical life and authentic popular piety" (33.1). Throughout the entire diocesan Church entrusted to his care, the bishop is to ensure that the sacraments are celebrated and most particularly that the Eucharist is made available to the faithful. Since it is impossible for the bishop to provide direct sacramental ministry to all of those entrusted to his care, he appoints pastors in parishes and priests to special ministry throughout the diocese to carry out this activity in communion with himself. Nonetheless, the bishop's role as the one charged to share in the sanctifying ministry of Christ should be a visible one within the diocesan church.

The pope highlights the importance of the cathedral church:

The bishop, while carrying out his ministry of sanctification in the whole Diocese, has as his focal point the Cathedral Church, which is as it were the Mother Church and the center of convergence for the particular Church. The Cathedral is the place where the Bishop has his Chair, from which he teaches his people . . . and from which he presides at the principal celebrations of the liturgical year and in the celebration of the sacraments. Precisely when he occupies his Chair, the Bishop is seen by the assembly of the faithful as the one who presides *in loco Dei Patris*. . . . It is the presence of this Chair which in fact makes the Cathedral Church the physical and spiritual center of unity and communion for the diocesan presbyterate and for all the holy People of God. (34.2)

Pastores Gregis point out that the bishop has the ultimate responsibility of oversight of the administration of all the sacraments within the diocese. In this way he carries out a part of his ministry of sanctification.

Shepherd of the Flock

In the fifth chapter, the pope calls our attention to the exercise of the bishop's "governing function" ("*munus regendi*"). The bishop's authority rests in his ordination as shepherd of a portion of God's flock. "The Bishop is sent in Christ's name as a pastor for the care of a particular portion of the People of God" (43.1). The image for the exercise of this power is Christ the Good Shepherd and Christ who washes the feet of his apostles the night before he dies. All pastoral authority is meant for the good of the flock and their salvation. Thus it should be exercised with that love and care that marks the life and ministry of the Good Shepherd.

The pope writes, "The power of the bishop is true power, but a power which radiates the light of the Good Shepherd and is modeled after him. . . . In virtue of this power, Bishops have the sacred right and the duty before the Lord to make laws for their subjects, to pass judgment on them, and to moderate everything pertaining to the ordering of worship and the apostolate" (43.3).

As he nears the end of this exhortation, the pope calls our attention to the challenges of the day. There is always the temptation to be overwhelmed by the currents of our secular culture and the pressures of life that militate against the Church's proclamation of the word of God. Here the pope tells us that we must not give in to fear. "Does not Jesus himself call his disciples a *pusillus grex* ["little flock"] and exhort them not to fear but to have hope (cf. Luke 12:32)? Jesus also said, "In the world you will have fear; but be of good cheer, I have overcome the world' (John 16:33)" (66.1).

Part of the bishop's task is to be a promoter of justice and peace and to condemn violence and all those acts that attack the dignity of human life. He is also to engage in interreligious dialogue, especially on behalf of world peace. The voice of the bishop should be heard in the civil, social, and economic spheres of life. "The pastoral activity of the bishop cannot fail to manifest particular concern for the demands of love and justice arising from the social and economic situation of the poor, the abandoned, and the mistreated" (69.1). In this seventh and final chapter of his exhortation, the pope calls upon bishops to translate the demands of the gospel into every aspect of life so that, permeated by the word of God, our culture might truly reflect the beginnings of God's kingdom here on earth.

As he concludes this exhortation, John Paul reminds all of us that the bishop cannot carry out his ministry to proclaim the gospel for the salvation of the world by himself:

> The Bishop needs to be able to count on the members of his diocesan presbyterate and on his deacons, the ministers of the Blood of Christ and of charity; he needs to be able to count on his consecrated sisters and brothers, called to be for the Church and for the world eloquent witnesses of the primacy of God in the Christian life and the power of his love amid the frailty of the human condition; and he needs to be able to count on the lay faithful, whose greater scope for the apostolate represents for their pastors a source of particular support and a reason for special comfort. (74.1)

Pastores Gregis offers a clear blueprint for the work of the Church as we make our way through the twenty-first century. The Holy Father paints a beautiful image of God's family as his flock gathered around its pastors, who are the shepherds, and united among themselves and with the Holy Father in the proclamation of the gospel and the living out of its challenge. It now falls to us—bishops, priests, religious, and faithful—to take this exhortation and keep it before us as our guideline and encouragement as we work together to proclaim and manifest the kingdom of God among us.

CONCLUDING THOUGHTS

The news from the Vatican Information Service that Pope Francis had approved the miracle to advance the process for the canonization of Blessed John Paul II led me to the chapel of our new archdiocesan college pre-theology seminary, then called "Blessed John Paul II Seminary." Here I was able to pray quietly before the Blessed Sacrament and then move to the side of the chapel and visit the relic of John Paul II.

The relic is a piece of the cassock that Pope John Paul II was wearing on the day he was shot in St. Peter's Square. It is drenched in his blood. He survived that assassination attempt. His life, by the grace of God and the Blessed Virgin Mary's intercession, was spared because his work had not yet been completed.

Every time I sit before that relic in reflection, I am reminded that there is a providential plan for each one of us. Human events may intervene, but in the end it is God's will that wins out. There was still much more ahead for Pope John Paul II.

Memories of this extraordinary priest, bishop, pope, and genuinely holy man fill this seminary that bears his name and is part of the enduring legacy of the 264th Bishop of Rome. On display in the entranceway to the chapel of now Saint John Paul II Seminary is an amice worn by our newly canonized saint at the celebration of Mass. Cardinal Stanislaw Dziwisz, now Archbishop of Krakow and for decades the personal secretary to Pope John Paul II, kindly sent it so that we could be constantly reminded of the example St. John Paul gives to every disciple of the Lord Jesus.

We are truly blessed to have witnessed Pope John Paul's single-hearted and unwavering love and commitment to God's plan and to the Church. One reason why our seminary is named after him, and why we invoke his intercession before God, is precisely because of this witness, not only to all Christians, but particularly to priests and those discerning a call to the priesthood. St. John Paul II manifested a total dedication to the call to serve the Lord configured to him as a priest.

The holiness of this pope gradually unfolded for the whole world to see. Now it is part of the public proclamation of the Church he served so well and so lovingly. Over the more than twenty-six years of his reign as pope, it became clear to the whole world that he was truly a man of God. In an interview I had not that long ago on national television, I was asked if I thought the process leading to the canonization of John Paul II moved too quickly. Was there enough time to carefully examine his life?

I responded that there are few other people in modern history whose lives have received as much scrutiny as that of Karol Wojtyla, certainly during his decades as Pope John Paul II. He underwent a microscopic examination by the media and others focusing on every moment, every hour, every day of his life. This one human being, we are told, was seen in person by more people than any other figure in all of history. Every move he made, every word he said, every action he took, was scrutinized, analyzed, and dissected. In the end, what we saw was the equivalent today of "canonization by consensus."

While the formal and official canonization of St. John Paul II awaited the declaration and action of Pope Francis, as soon as Pope John Paul II died, the faithful by acclamation began to call for the public recognition of his sanctity. On Friday, April 8, 2005, as the simple wooden coffin of the pope was presented to the crowds at the door of St. Peter's Basilica at the end of his funeral, the people, many waving banners, spontaneously chanted, "Santo subito!" ("Sainthood now!").

On July 5, 2013, Pope Francis, successor to St. John Paul II and to St. Peter, in recognition of the sanctity of his predecessor, approved the last step that would lead to the title "Saint," simply confirming what the crowds had already proclaimed and what corresponds to the sentiments in the hearts of millions and millions of Catholics around the world: John Paul II was a holy man. He is a saint.

Now we not only rejoice in his enduring legacy as a wise, courageous pastor of souls, but we invoke his intercession as we say, "St. John Paul II, pray for us."

the WORD
among us ®
The *Spirit* of Catholic Living

This book was published by The Word Among Us. Since 1981, The Word Among Us has been answering the call of the Second Vatican Council to help Catholic laypeople encounter Christ in the Scriptures.

The name of our company comes from the prologue to the Gospel of John and reflects the vision and purpose of all of our publications: to be an instrument of the Spirit, whose desire is to manifest Jesus' presence in and to the children of God. In this way, we hope to contribute to the Church's ongoing mission of proclaiming the gospel to the world so that all people would know the love and mercy of our Lord and grow ever more deeply in love with him.

Our monthly devotional magazine, *The Word Among Us*, features meditations on the daily and Sunday Mass readings, and currently reaches more than one million Catholics in North America and another half million Catholics in one hundred countries around the world. Our book division, The Word Among Us Press, publishes numerous books, Bible studies, and pamphlets that help Catholics grow in their faith.

To learn more about who we are and what we publish, log on to our website at www.wau.org. There you will find a variety of Catholic resources that will help you grow in your faith.

Embrace His Word, Listen to God . . .

www.wau.org